ORIEL COLLEGE

AND

THE OXFORD MOVEMENT

VOL. I.

REMINISCENCES

CHIEFLY OF ORIEL COLLEGE AND

THE OXFORD MOVEMENT

BY THE

REV. T. MOZLEY, M.A.

FORMERLY FELLOW OF ORIEL

SUCCESSIVELY PERPETUAL CURATE OF MORETON PINCKNEY, NORTHANTS
RECTOR OF CHOLDERTON, WILTS ; RECTOR OF PLYMTREE, DEVON
AND RURAL DEAN OF PLYMTREE AND OF OTTERY

IN TWO VOLUMES — VOL. I.

LONDON

LONGMANS, GREEN, AND CO.

1882

Complete set - S. B. N. - 0: 576. 02189. X
This volume - S. B. N. - 0: 576. 02967. X

Republished in 1969 by Gregg International Publishers Limited
Westmead, Farnborough, Hants. , England

Printed in offset by Franz Wolf, Heppenheim/Bergstrasse
Western Germany

PREFACE.

———•◦•———

THE story of the Oxford Movement has yet to be told, and there is much reason to fear that it never will be told as it should be. The greater part of those at all concerned in it, whether as friends, or as foes, or as spectators, and likely or competent to contribute matter for the historian, have passed away—many of them, indeed, long ago. Of the survivors, nearly all have disqualified themselves, more or less, one way or another. They may make most praiseworthy, most interesting, and most valuable contributions, but those contributions will have to be carefully sifted and largely discounted, and a mean will have to be struck between their conflicting utterances. They that have gone over to Rome, as they must hold in the legitimate line of the Movement, will see everything, measure everything, accept or reject, remember or forget, from that point of view. Some of the survivors are scattered far away in places where all things are forgotten except parochial duties and the incidents of rural life. Some have been long absorbed in courses or enterprises of their own. Some are bound by political or official obligations. The rapid current of modern thought in the entirely negative direction has intensified some opinions and hardened some hearts from which candour or kindness might once have been hoped for. They cannot tell the story of faith who believe in nothing but matter and themselves

Now for a long time I have seen with more and more sadness that a period, which in my memory is as a golden age, has been vanishing from common mortal ken like a dream. The characters themselves, even to those of a less relation and a humbler degree, have to me an unearthly radiance, and I grieve to think that they should be forgotten : *carent quia vate sacro.* To do them justice would require much more history and much more biography than will be found in these volumes, which are but planks saved from a great wreck of time. Even now I should rejoice to hear that they had encouraged some one to fill the void which I do but point out ; but I see none to make the attempt. Scanty, imperfect, and trifling as these Reminiscences may be—reminiscences and no more—the generous reader will admit that I should have been deaf to a Divine call had I allowed them to sink with me into my not very distant grave. I began to put them together in March last year, and completed them, with the exception of a few pages and the Addenda, by November 30. As I wrote, death after death removed many whom I had introduced, or who might be specially interested—

twenty, at the least, in so short a time. Upon sending the first ninety-nine chapters to the publishers, I wrote to Cardinal Newman to acquaint him with the fact, lest he should hear it first from any other quarter. At the same time I enclosed the titles of the ninety-nine chapters, but with no account of the text. He acknowledged my letter with his invariable kindness, only reminding me that even where the persons named in my headings were no longer here, there were survivors and friends whose feelings had to be respected. He also observed on the fact that I had no personal acquaintance with him till he became my tutor in 1826. He added that he had a dread of controversy. I can only hope that he will find his warnings anticipated, though of course I cannot be sure of that from his own point of view.

I may be excused saying that this is my first publication, and will most probably be the last. Into the Addenda I have thrown some matter which I have at times hoped to treat separately, but at the pace of the world and of death it seemed to me presumptuous to reserve them for the bare chance of a future opportunity. One thing more I will add, for it is a matter on which people are very tender. With all the care I can take, I find myself misspelling names. The ' readers ' have saved me from a good many mistakes, but they might easily not know how Dr. Copleston spelt his name. Of course I ought to have remembered, but I have a triple

excuse. The Devonshire hamlet near Crediton is
spelt with a final *e*, as I have inadvertently spelt the
name. I always understood that the Provost's deri-
vation of the word referred to some remarkable
stone, either the finial of a building or a natural
object. To these excuses I must add what I have
lamented in the text, that this very remarkable
scholar and conversationalist has left no work of the
sort to stand before your eyes and keep his name in
daily remembrance.

7 LANSDOWN TERRACE, CHELTENHAM :
May 1882.

CONTENTS

OF

THE FIRST VOLUME.

——◦◦——

CHAPTER I.

INTRODUCTION.

CHAPTER II.

JOHN HENRY NEWMAN.

CHAPTER III.

THE OLD ORIEL SCHOOL.

CHAPTER XXI.

JOHN ROGERS.

CHAPTER XXII.

A COLLEGE FOR STUDY AND ACTION.

CHAPTER XXIII.

TWO CANDIDATES.

CHAPTER XXIV.

COLLEGE ELECTION OF 1829.

CHAPTER XXV.

THOMAS BENJAMIN HOBHOUSE.

CHAPTER XXXIX.

'THE THEOLOGICAL LIBRARY.'

CHAPTER XL.

THE REFORM BILL.

CHAPTER XLI.

WHATELY ARCHBISHOP OF DUBLIN.

CHAPTER XLII.

UNIVERSAL MOVEMENT OF 1831–1832.

CHAPTER LXI.

NEWMAN, 1836–1837.

CHAPTER LXII.

SOME INCIDENTS.

CHAPTER LXIII.

SPREAD OF THE MOVEMENT.

CHAPTER LXVIII.

DEAN HOOK, DEAN CHURCH, AND CHARLES MARRIOTT.

REMINISCENCES.

CHAPTER I.

INTRODUCTION.

As all the world knows, Reminiscences are very suspicious matter. They are a lower form of Recollections, which, at the best, must share the common infir-
mities of mortal memory. The mental picture of events
long passed by, and seen through an increasing breadth
of many-tinted haze, is liable to be warped and
coloured by more recent remembrances, and by impressions received from other quarters. When the
event itself is more striking or more important than
any particular mode of knowing it can possibly be,
memory deals very unscrupulously, so to speak, with
the inferior matter.

For example, I have read scores of Reminiscences
and biographies—the latter, of course, affecting to be
made up from journals and letters—about the incidents
and the sensations attending the receipt of the news
of the Battle of Waterloo ; and I grieve to say they
have greatly lowered my estimate of the historical
value of such records. They have told me little that I
was not familiar with from my childhood ; and what-

ever I was not familiar with was evidently fictitious.
My father used to read his newspaper to us, dwel-
ling with exultation on the passages most likely to
take our interest or our fancy. Going in and out, he
saw many people, and heard news, which he told us.
Now, in the Reminiscences I am referring to, some by
very distinguished persons, by ladies of quality, perhaps— supposed to have special access to headquarters
for information—I really may say I have never
found anything that was not public property by the
end of June 1815. Of course I am not speaking of
alleged particulars most improbable and almost in-
conceivable. I am not speaking of the story of the
company at the dinner-table where the despatches
were delivered being unable to decipher them, or too
impatient to open them ; of the officer sinking down
in a chair too exhausted to give a coherent answer,
and of some shrewd old military gentleman solving
the difficulty by asking the number of guns captured,
and being answered ' All,' or some very large number.
Such statements are reminiscences in their lower de-
pravation—that is, blending with fiction.

Nor is it a matter in which confidence is any
assurance ; for they who remember most confidently,
or most exactly, are often the most wrong. At
least they are not more likely to be right than others.
I once heard Lord Panmure exclaim at a Charterhouse Brooke Hall dinner, ' Fancy a man forgetting a
thing !' Not long after, he had personal experience
that it was not only possible but quite easy. Some
years since there was a discussion in the Lords as to
the antecedents of a man who had failed of his duty

in a responsible and well-paid office. It was a Whig appointment. Lord Granville said the man had excellent recommendations, including one by the late Lord Chelmsford. Thereupon Lord Chelmsford sprang from his seat and declared he had never recommended the man ; he knew nothing about him ; so it was quite impossible he could have recommended him. Lord Granville took a note out of his pocket and passed it to Lord Chelmsford, who recognised his own handwriting and surrendered at discretion.

It is true these are cases of bad memory, not of memory too good to be true ; of forgetfulness, not hallucination. But the truth is they go together, for when a man forgets what is necessary to the truth of events, he fancies something untrue ; and if he inserts unconsciously some illusion of his own, it unfairly occupies the ground to the exclusion of the truth. Even exaggeration compels diminution, if not entire suppression, in giving too much to some persons, and that much less, or nothing, to others.

To confess oneself fallible is to claim no more than mortal excellence, and I have learnt to think no more of infallible people than of fallible. I will say even more. Is not a very distinct and vivid memory of persons and things in continual change, itself a disease of memory ? As persons and human affairs are not the same always, and do not continue in exactly the same bearings and relations, the best memory of them must be a certain abstract or mean rather than a picture or a stereotype. Many years ago, sitting by Page Wood at a dinner-table, I asked him if he was not haunted by the long and anxious causes in which he had been engaged. He replied, ' No. They pass away from my thoughts. It's all logic.' The Irish have very exact and vivid memories, simply because their memory is subordinate to imagination and passion. They remember too easily, too quickly, and too much as they please. The reader, I trust, will not think the worse of me and my testimony because I have felt the truth to be a matter requiring much care and vigilance. But he may fairly ask what are my claims to publish reminiscences of such men as the chief personages in this volume.

I came into residence at Oriel College after Easter 1825. Coplestone was provost, and Tyler, Hawkins, Dornford, and Jelf tutors. Newman was then much in the College, holding the office of junior treasurer. Early in 1826 he took Jelf's place in the tuition, and his pupils, including myself. I took my B.A. degree in the Michaelmas term 1828. In those two years and a half I saw very much more of Newman than pupils usually saw of their tutors even in those days when tuition meant something. From Christmas to Easter I was private tutor to the present Lord Doneraile at Cheltenham, but was in correspondence with Newman. At his encouragement and urgency I stood for a Fellowship at the next Easter, and was elected. From that date—that is, from Easter 1829 to Christmas 1831 I resided, not only in term time, but also a good deal in the vacations, on intimate terms, with Newman's mother and sisters, and with his circle of friends.

At Christmas 1831 I was ordained deacon by Bagot, Bishop of Oxford. Through Newman and his friends I went to Colchester to take sole charge of James Round's two parishes. In less than three months I found it too much for me, and after some weeks in Devonshire, was back again at Oxford. Then I took charge of Buckland, an easy ride from Oxford, myself and Newman interchanging visits. At Michaelmas I went to reside at Moreton Pinckney, a small college living thirty miles from Oxford, to the perpetual curacy of which I was afterwards licensed by Marsh, Bishop of Peterborough. The place was well known to Oriel men. Newman and my other Oxford friends often came over to pay me visits, and I often rode or walked in to Oxford. It was at Moreton Pinckney that I had to put the 'Tracts for the Times' into circulation, and do some other little affairs, such as getting up a petition against the Marriage Bill. I frequently came across Litchfield, of Merton College, then himself engaged in worrying Arnold, but he did not take cheerfully to the new movement at Oxford. Church and Land was then the ruling idea.

At Easter 1835 I came up to Oxford, took college office, came into rooms, and asked to be relieved of Moreton Pinckney. I do not think I could say that Newman suggested to me this change of plan, but I knew he wanted all the help he could get. Possibly he did not think I was doing such a work in my parish as should excuse me from taking a share in the larger work he had then in hand. I found it not so easy to be relieved of my parish. The Provost went by rule, and offered the living to every unbeneficed clergyman down to the bottom of the list on the college books, where at last he found a worthy man, who took the

living, and had a hard fight to live on it, which he
did, I think, thirty-four years or more. Till my place
was supplied I had often to go up and down. From
Easter 1835 to Michaelmas 1836 was a period of
great excitement. There was much to be done, and
I had generally a hand in it ; always, so to speak, at
Newman's side.

By the end of September 1836 I had become
Newman's brother-in-law, I had accepted the rectory
of Cholderton, in Salisbury Plain, and I was on my
way to that place. It was a long way from Oxford,
but still I went backwards and forwards. Newman
came to see me more than once. We also corresponded
much. Most of my clerical neighbours warmly sym-
pathished with Newman, even if they did not all of
them altogether agree with him. It was a great thing
to hear of anybody standing up for Truth and for the
Church.

It must have been about the time of my going to
Cholderton that Newman asked me to translate Vin-
cent of Lerins. I was slow about it, and I found myself anticipated by some quicker hand (C. Marriott,
I believe). But I have my translation half done.

In 1838 I published 'A Dissection of the Queries'
on education circulated by Lord J. Russell, 'by a
Clergyman of South Wilts.' Newman told me it was
a great pity I had not sent it as an article to the
'British Critic,' of which he had become editor. So I
began to write for him, and contributed to most of
the numbers for two years. He then proposed to me
to take the editorship, which, I need scarcely say,
would in such a case be better described by sub-

editorship, though I am sure this was not Newman's intention. I consented, and did so act till October 1843, when I resigned, and the periodical ceased to exist.

At the same time there came to me, through my brother James and another member of our Oriel circle, the offer of employment in a quarter then supposed to be friendly, not only to Newman, but to the movement of which he was now held to be the real leader. After a good deal of conversation in Temple Gardens, in which I declared myself very strongly, for specified reasons, against the Corn Laws and Protection generally, I agreed. This act was necessarily a departure, as far as co-operation was concerned, and from that time there could not be confidential correspondence on the heart of affairs. But I had frequent letters from Newman, and occasional reminders that what I did must be for heaven as well as for earth, and would have to be so judged.

Three years before this, early in 1840, Newman consulted me about the conventual house to be constructed out of a range of stabling at Littlemore, and there ensued a correspondence. I sent some drawings and suggestions, which would have somewhat redeemed the ugliness of the building. I went several times to see Newman and the brothers, as I may call them, at Littlemore. I should add that though I was, I really believe, as much in Newman's secrets as anybody else—at the time, I believed, as much in his secrets as he himself was—I could not have said, till he actually went over to Rome, whether he was even likely to go over. I was repeatedly asked the question ; I was even told that the Court of Rome had certain grounds for being sure of his submission. But the Italian temperament is so entirely different from the English ; it is so sanguine, so ill content with imperfect development, so resolved that a man shall be either one thing or the other, and so habituated to make events, that I did not credit the most positive announcements from that quarter. Nevertheless the end was no surprise to me.

The reader will notice that in this summary of two lives I have said very little indeed of Newman's works. My present purpose is to show what basis I have for Reminiscences. If I have a memory at all—if I have even a particle of truthfulness, I ought to be able to tell something. Newman's publications are before the world ; they are before all time, as long as the English language is spoken, and as long as this is a people and an empire. If I said not a word about them they would suffer no wrong from me. But my personal recollections, whatever they are worth, would be lost if I did not collect and publish them. Newman appears here as the centre of a group. I may honestly say that, with the exception of Keble, I do not think one of them would be a living name a century hence but for his share in the light of Newman's genius and goodness. Yet even as the planets of such a system they are worthy of a better record than I am about to offer.

One thing more I must say. These are Reminiscences, and Reminiscences only. I possess a great mass of letters, journals, and other documents that might have helped me to make these volumes a little more interesting and more authentic. But I have now only a small remainder of my eyesight—one eye gone, and not much left of the other—while my prospects of life and strength are also a small and doubtful remainder. I should soon have lost myself had I attempted to penetrate into all this buried material.

Some years ago various incidents brought before me the possible fate of documents in that contingency which is certain and which may be any day. Cardinal Newman's letters and manuscripts I knew to be his property in the eye of the law, as far as publication is concerned. That question was brought before the Oxford world when Whately went to the publishers of Blanco White's Life and threatened legal proceedings in case his own letters were included in the publication. The result of that interference is that the most important part of Blanco White's Life—viz. the later period of his residence at Oxford—is left a blank. No reasonable person could blame Whately for that step, or found any surmise upon it, for the letters of intimate friends are always supposed to be interchanged in an inner council, quite apart from the open circle of the Church or the world. To Newman's own letters I added whatever was worth sending in the correspondence relating to the ' British Critic.' Some time after a kind and good Irish Roman Catholic gentleman, who, though in a dying state, had given himself much trouble for me, asked for Newman's autograph. The only one I could then find with considerable search was Newman's acknowledgment of the returned letters, which I sent to poor Mr. Frank Harris, since dead.

There cannot be much, then, in the nature of a biography here. Nor could I have attempted any account
of Newman's works, for I have always been a bad
reader, and have now less power than ever of mastering any work requiring close attention and continued
thought. Moreover, I very much distrust the impar-
tiality of the gentlemen who, past the middle age,
sit down, as they would fondly persuade themselves,
to form a right judgment upon a work written by
some one whom they utterly disagree with. They set
to work (they know it well) with a foregone conclusion.
As a member of the Anglican communion I am bound
to admit that my own foregone conclusion must be
to some extent against all Newman's later works, not
only those published since his submission to Rome,
but also those in which he has since maintained his
final course to have been involved. But that foregone
conclusion would in my case be good for nothing, and
I see no possible good to the world, or to myself, in
sitting down now to the task of analysing a series of
great works, which I have always felt to be above both
my working powers and my mental qualifications.

Even as regards the grand subject, these Reminiscences are superficial, sketchy, and often trivial. As
regards some other subjects they are even more so.
Perhaps I shall even be found to come under the old
description of those that remember the evil more
easily than the good. Be it so. I feel myself bound
to give a testimony, and it must be in my own kind.

But why have I not waited, anyhow, till the Cardinal is history, and fair prey to the biographer? I
hope I should have to wait long enough for that—nay,

that I shall not then be found waiting. I am not quite six years the Cardinal's junior. Since I put pen to this work, death has visited the names contained in it again and again ; yes, again and again since I wrote these very words, 'again and again.' Several times have I had to sit down to correct the tenses. There has also been a whole crop of Reminiscences. I much wished the Dean of Westminster to see what I had written ; but he has gone, after giving another contribution to the history of that period—a contribution which, in my humble opinion, showed that even his unique powers could have a decline.

The sum is, one cannot wait for ever. I shall be glad to reflect that the Cardinal will have the opportunity of correcting my errors, and will have some mementoes of interest. But, again I say, this is but a superficial work, for I am not much of a logician, or of a metaphysician, or of a philosopher. Least of all am I a theologian.

CHAPTER II.

JOHN HENRY NEWMAN.

CARDINAL NEWMAN was born in the City of London, and baptised a few yards from the Bank of England, early in 1801. His father was of a family of small landed proprietors in Cambridgeshire and had an hereditary taste for music, of which he had a practical and scientific knowledge, together with much general culture.

From being chief clerk to a bank he became a partner
in the firm, Ramsbottom, Newman, Ramsbottom & Co.,
72 Lombard Street, which appears in the lists of
London bankers from 1807 to 1816 inclusive. The
firm would seem to have had particular relations with
another firm styled first Fry & Sons, afterwards
Frys & Chapman, established at the same time. John
Newman was an enthusiast in his way, and he bestowed
some labours of calculation upon the various popular
schemes of the day, such as that for making England
independent of foreign timber, by planting all our
waste lands. He was a Freemason, and had a high
standing in the craft, into which, however, no one of
his three sons was initiated. He was also a member
of the Beef Steak Club. In 1800 he married Jemima
Fourdrinier, of a well-known Huguenot family, long
known in the City of London as engravers and paper
manufacturers. Two of Mrs. Newman's brothers introduced from Italy the machine for making endless
coils of paper, which up to that time had been only
made in sheets, by the slow work of the hand. The
mother was from first to last thoroughly loyal to her
family traditions, and all the early teaching of her
children was that modified Calvinism which retained
the Assembly's Catechism as a text, but put into
young hands Watts, Baxter, Scott, Romaine, Newton,
Milner—indeed, any writer who seemed to believe
and feel what he wrote about.

Throughout the whole of what may be called his
youth, John Henry Newman happily had no suspicion
that theology would be to him more than the saving
of his soul, for his parents intended him for the law,

and he actually kept some terms at Lincoln's Inn. He expected to be 'converted ;' in due time he was converted ; and the day and hour of his conversion he has ever remembered, and no doubt observed. Without a thought of converting the world—which, indeed, he formerly held to be the impossible ambition of fanatics and worldlings—and thinking of nothing but the openings he saw here and there through the drift into the glory beyond, he accepted from early years every text, every expression, every figure, every emblem, and every thought thereby suggested, as a solemn and abiding reality which it was good to live in. It would hardly be too much to say that he knew the Bible by heart. In his later years he has described in very touching language the impossibility of shaking off or even modifying this sweetest of his early possessions. He might study the Fathers, and many a weary volume of annals or of controversy ; he has had to master the Vulgate, but his first and last love has been the Authorised Version. His recollections of his early spiritual life, published in the 'Apologia pro Vita Sua,' contained some novelties, not to say surprises, to his longest friends, and it is quite possible that a new search into first memories, under a strong suggestion, may have varied their order and prominence.

In that most interesting record, however, he omits some important particulars. At a very early age indeed he was sent to Dr. Nicholas's, at Ealing, said to be the best preparatory school in the country. There were 300 boys there, and many of them became distinguished in various ways. John H. Newman rose,

almost at a bound, to the head of the school, where
before long he was followed by his no less remarkable
and even more precocious brother, Frank Newman.
From boyhood the two brothers had taken the opposite
sides on every possible question, and perhaps the fact
that one of the born disputants was more than four
years younger than the other accounts somewhat for
their respective lines of divergence. If they argued
at all on an equality, the younger must be the cleverer,
the elder more mature. There was also another brother,
still living, not without his share in the heritage of
natural gifts. John H. Newman used to be sensible
of having lost something by not being a public-school
man. He regarded with admiration and a generous
kind of envy the facile and elegant construing which
a man of very ordinary talents would bring with him
from the sixth form of any public school. 'You don't
know how much you owe to Russell,' he would say to
me, though I was never one of those facile construers.

In the biography referred to, John H. Newman has
not done justice to his early adventures and sallies
into the domains of thought, politics, fancy, and taste.
He very early mastered music as a science, and attained such a proficiency on the violin that, had he
not become a Doctor of the Church, he would have
been a Paganini. At the age of twelve he composed
an opera. He wrote in albums, improvised masques
and idyls, and only they who see no poetry in 'Lead,
kindly light,' or in the 'Dream of Gerontius,' will
deny that this divine gift entered into his birthright.

From Dr. Nicholas's he went straight to Trinity

College, Oxford. Not long afterwards his brother
Frank, too old for Ealing, but too young for a college
even in those days, came to Oxford and pursued his
studies, as far as compatible with an amiable but
universal and persistent antagonism, under John
Henry Newman's direction, in lodgings. When the
latter had been at Trinity a term or two, a great
blow fell on him and changed his destiny. The bank
in Lombard Street was one of many London banks
which, with as many as a hundred country banks,
succumbed under the pressure caused by the con-
traction of the currency and the rapid fall of prices
upon the return of peace. Henceforth Newman
could have little or no aid from his friends. The
father took the Alton Brewery, which for two or
three years became the head-quarters of the family,
making the place ever after very dear in their memories.
The three Eclogues forming the first three pieces in
the 'Memorials of the Past'—printed 1832, and dated
Alton, July 1818; September 1818; April 1819—
show how intensely the writer appreciated the well-
known features of Hampshire scenery. Gilbert
White's 'Natural History of Selborne' (a few miles
from Alton) was a great book with Oriel men of those
days, and when Newman became a Fellow of Oriel
he was often proud to name him as one of the college
worthies, and to recommend a careful reading of his
book. The father could not make the brewery
answer, though he seems to have studied the business
thoroughly and to have applied himself to it with
much diligence. There finally remained nothing but
the mother's jointure, which was soon sadly diminished

by the successive reduction of the interest from 5
per cent. to 4, and then to 3. John Henry Newman
could now help others as well as maintain himself.
In the declining fortunes of his family he read the
call to a higher and more congenial profession than
that for which he had been actually preparing.

His academic sympathies and associations ex-
panded all the more because his prospects were closed
in other quarters. For his college and what could recall
it to his memory he acquired a passion which has never
died. But there was one unlucky consequence of this
change in his expectations. He passed his examination
for his degree at the earliest possible time, Michaelmas
1820, when he had not quite completed his nineteenth
year. Various explanations are given of what occurred. It is said that Newman was very ill ; that
he had had no sleep latterly, and had neglected even
to take food. It is also added that the examiners
were not the men to discover a genius under this
disguise. Newman always maintained that he had
been too discursive to make the proper preparation ;
that he had been properly examined ; and that he
alone was answerable for his failure. The result in
those days turned on the *vivâ voce* examination, not
on the paper work, as now. When the class lists
came out Newman was found 'under the line,' as
low as then he could be. The comparison with those
to whom higher honours were accorded, and with the
examiners themselves, is at least suggestive ; but it
really was a question of 'results,' as they are now
called, and the results were not forthcoming on this
occasion. Was it likely ? He was not yet nineteen,

the age when most men now enter a university. Five years and a half afterwards his brother Frank gained without any apparent effort one of the best double-firsts ever known.

For three years after taking his B.A. degree Newman resided at Oxford, enjoying the much-prized position of a scholar of Trinity, and some friendships that became ever stronger and stronger. In the year 1821, together with Henry Boden, he published first one canto, then a second, of 'St. Bartholomew's Eve,' which might now be supposed the first fiery outbreak of a spirit destined to wield the masses of Exeter Hall. In a note to the second instalment he explains that he had been much surprised to find by the remarks of his academic readers that the learned university knew nothing about St. Bartholomew's Eve. So he undertook to enlighten it with a brief narrative beginning :—'The year of our Lord 1572 will ever be branded with infamy and recollected with horror, as the date of this most barbarous and cold-blooded massacre. The Queen Mother, Catherine de' Medici, actuated by zeal or ambition, conceived this design, so pleasing to the Court of Rome,' &c., &c.

Notwithstanding this bold adventure into the realms of history, poetry, and polemics, it does not appear that Newman attempted to retrieve his examination disaster by writing for either the English or the Latin essay. He remained for years in the very distinct circle of his Trinity acquaintances. As that college was his home for the first six or seven years of his academic life, he retained for it, to the last, the tenderest affection. For Izaac Williams and W. J. Copeland he had the love which passes that of common relation. Many years afterwards he typified his life's aspirations in the snap-dragon fringing the wall opposite the rooms in which he spent his first three solitary weeks at college.

————————

CHAPTER III.

THE OLD ORIEL SCHOOL.

THUS in the most impressible period of his mental growth, Newman was external to the college most associated with his life, work, and name. Oriel College at that time contained some of the most distinguished personages, the most vigorous minds, and the most attractive characters in Oxford. From the Provost, Dr. Coplestone, to the youngest undergraduate they had been carefully selected, for to get a son into Oriel was a great thing in those days. Keble, Whately, Tyler, and Hawkins were tutors. Arnold, though not then residing, for he did not reside beyond his probationary year, was present in spirit. Much the same might be said of the softer and milder influence of Samuel Rickards. Richard Hurrell Froude, and a younger brother, who lived but to die, Robert Wilberforce and latterly Samuel, Sir George Prevost, Dallas, Proby J. Ferrers, William Falconer, John Colquhoun, Edward Denison, William Heathcote,

Charles Wood, and Charles Porcher, were among the undergraduates. Though the distinction was rather on the decline—for other colleges were joining the race— Oriel had more than its share of university honours.

What was more, its most prominent talkers, preachers, and writers seemed to be always under-mining, if not actually demolishing, received traditions and institutions ; and whether they were preaching from the University pulpit, or arguing in common room, or issuing pamphlets on passing occasions, even faith-ful and self-reliant men felt the ground shaking under them. The new Oriel sect was declared to be Noetic, whatever that may mean, and when a Fellow of the College presented himself in the social gatherings of another society, he was sure to be reminded of his pretence to intellectual superiority. Perhaps the topic was getting rather stale when I was elected Fellow in 1829, but even then, being in University common room, on Plumtree's invitation, I was most unmerci-fully baited upon it by Booth, a Magdalene Fellow, and one of the many victims of Routh's cruel longevity.

For Whately was claimed by his admirers a spiritual as well as mental pre-eminence, but it would not be possible to describe now the terror his presence was sure to infuse among all who wished things to remain much as they were in their own lifetime. In-stead of being comforted and built up in the good old fashion, they were told they were altogether wrong, and must first retrace all their steps and undo all they had been doing. What was worse, the efficacy of the cure which had become necessary consisted in the hearers thinking it out for themselves. Yet for many years after this date, and long after Newman was a member of the same college as Whately, it would not have been easy to state the difference between their respective views, unless it might be found in Newman's immense and almost minutely reverential knowledge of Scripture, and in a certain yearning to build as fast as men cast down, and to plant again the waste places. Something like a conspiracy there seemed to be—all the University thought that—but Newman had never liked a movement to destroy. He used to talk of the men who lash the waters to frighten the fish when they have made no preparation to catch them.

As a matter of fact, there was something more than a morbid intellectual restlessness in the so-called Oriel School of that day. It was not behind the most bigoted, or the most fanatical school of theologians in its readiness to impose certain opinions and expressions when the opportunity offered itself and the persons to be indoctrinated might not be on their guard. In the last century one Dr. Bosworth left a sum for a series of divinity lectures to be read every year in chapel. Every old Oriel man will remember the 'Bossies,' and his own sensations when, at the end of Morning Prayers, instead of his being dismissed to his breakfast, one of the Fellows rose and delivered a very cut-and-dried lecture. It came to every clerical Fellow in succession. As these were young men, it had been, not improperly, the custom to read the same lectures every year ; only the MS. was changed from time to time. The manuscript then in use was the production of the Old Oriel, that is, the Noetic school, and was by no means that neutral composition which would have been proper under the circumstances. Certainly it was an unfair use of authority to surprise either the young lecturer, or the boys that were supposed to listen to him, into new theological terms and definitions.

I must have heard the ' Bossies ' frequently, without being conscious of receiving either harm or good from them, but upon my return to residence in 1835 I was appointed the lecturer—I suppose, by the Provost—for the following year. This was after the new arrangement of the tuition, and during the issue of the ' Tracts for the Times.' Not having paid much attention to the lectures, I now found myself in a serious difficulty. The MS. explained the word ' Person,' in the Athanasian Creed, in the Litany and in the Communion Service, by the word Office, in the sense of representation. As far as I can remember, after so long an interval, what I really could not understand at the time, the new explanation—for it hardly disguised that it was new—amounted to saying that the Second Person in the Trinity was a representation of the Father's mercy, and the Third of His sanctifying power, or something to that effect. It certainly suggested to my mind a very misty, shadowy, and unreal idea of Him we read of in the Gospels, as if He were but a phantom form, or at best an archangel. I really should be glad to be corrected by the production of the MS.

This ran through all the lectures in an ascending scale of prominence and distinctness. I managed, however lamely, to qualify, or omit, the passages in the earlier lectures, the Provost making no sign. When the last, or the last but one came, I found my difficulties face to face, and insuperable. I worked all night in the vain attempt to find expressions compatible with the Creeds, and with the general drift of the MS., but an hour before chapel I found the task still unaccomplished and seemingly impossible. I therefore returned the MS., to the Provost, stating my sad case, and also pleading that I was not then in a fit state to read the remaining lectures. The note must have reached the Provost just as he was beginning to dress for chapel, for he was too hard worked and too late worked, to be a particularly early riser. However, he wrote the kindest possible reply ; and also another note, which he sent with the MS. to William J. Coplestone, requesting him to finish the series. This he did, and of course received the remuneration, such as it was. Not very long after there came to me from Coplestone a handsomely-bound copy of Britton's 'Cathedral Antiquities,' duly inscribed, a kind and welcome gift, which had the disastrous effect of making me an architectural enthusiast, and wrecking me on that rock.

But I have now to retrace my steps some twelve or fifteen years, to the period when Newman was not even yet a member of Oriel, and when Coplestone and Whately ruled the college, and threatened to dominate over the university. It is sixty years ago. Many who have since passed away, leaving loved and honoured names, were proud to be numbered among their friends, and justly proud. But, whatever the personal merits of these two remarkable men and the

sincerity of their convictions, it is necessary to consider these as elements in the condition of the college
and university when Newman came into public view
Whately—for Coplestone was now content to be represented, not to say personated, by his disciple—regarded
High Church and Low Church as equal bigotries.

In the Evangelical scheme he saw nothing but
a system of dogmas framed to create a groundless self-
confidence, and to foster spiritual pride. The man
inwardly sure of his own salvation and of his Christian
sufficiency, and equally sure of the damnation of
most people around him, particularly of those he did
not like, Whately used to compare to the self-sufficient
Stoic of the Roman satirist. Such a man was naturally indifferent to further knowledge and improvement, being, indeed, as good as he need be, and only
in danger of being so good as to rely on his own
merits. Even though the Evangelicals had their
favourable side in their affinities with the Noncon-
formist body, and, upon their own principles, had
little to say to formularies, and even to creeds, still
Whately had far less respect for them than for the old
High Church, for it was learned and cultivated, and
it could appeal to something more than those incom-
municable sensations which it is impossible to reason
upon. St. Edmund Hall was then the head-quarters
of the Evangelical system. It is difficult to convey an
idea of the very low position it had in the university;
and it is even painful to recall it, for it was religion
in the form of a degradation utterly undeserved.
There were in most of the other colleges one or two
men who inherited or imbibed sympathy with the

despised sect. But to Whately, in his lofty eminence
of free speculation, the Evangelical system as presented at Oxford was below contempt. If there were
differences between him and Newman when they came
to work together, it must have arisen from Newman's
deep convictions in favour of the Evangelicals, while
Whately could only feel the obligation of a common
Christianity.

Whately dealt more freely with the Ten Commandments than I had been accustomed to. He strongly
deprecated the prevalent idea of the Sunday taking
the exact place of the Jewish Sabbath, or being
properly called the Sabbath. But anyone coming
to Oxford from the country at that time would have
received a little shock to his provincial strictness. It
often occurred that on Sunday there was an unusual
muster at the High Table and in the common room,
of strangers as well as men of the college. In order
to escape this there were occasionally private dinners,
which some would think worse. Sunday was thus a
Feast Day. One of Whately's topics was that the
prohibition of idolatrous likenesses and emblems in
the second commandment pointed beforehand to the
true Image of God in his Son, the reception of which
would be impeded by such preoccupations.

Whately's personal habits are too well known
perhaps to be noticed. He used to take daily walks
round Christ Church meadow with a little company
of dogs, and provided with sticks and big round
missiles for their amusement. As soon as people heard
he was Archbishop of Dublin, the first question they
asked was how would he amuse his dogs. He used

to lecture his awkward squad of elderly under-graduates at St. Alban Hall, lying on a sofa, with one leg over the back or the end. Like Macaulay, he had a healthy appetite, possibly because he had not been playing with it during the day. To provide against the danger incident to those who talk and eat at the same time, when he was to dine at Oriel, a large dish of currie, or calf's head hash, or other soft and comminuted meat was provided. Repeatedly when I have been serving this dish at High Table a plate has been brought to me, and I have put on it what seemed to me a liberal help. 'It's for the Principal, sir,' the servant whispered, and then I began entirely *de novo*. I believe Whately rather astonished the Dublin waiters at the hotel where he had to put up on his arrival there. There is no point on which constitution and habits so much differ, but I suppose the brains will not do their best work without ample and generous diet: Dr. Johnson, to wit.

I am conscious that in these Reminiscences there are things which some will think had better not have been said, for one reason or another. But remi-niscences cease to be reminiscences when they are much weeded and pruned. I will also add this. While I confess, as I do, to the large place a man like Whately holds in my memory, in my regard, and in the course of my early thoughts, by that very confes-sion I assign to him a far higher place than I should to some with whom I could find no fault, and of whom, in fact, I have nothing to say. All this time there were men at Oxford, able and learned men too, as irreproachable in their opinions and manners as in

their lives; but who to me were nothing and are
nothing, for they were concerned only for themselves,
and perhaps for some other people in some subordinate degree.

CHAPTER IV.

NEWMAN, FELLOW OF ORIEL.

IT was in 1823 that Newman was elected to a fellowship at Oriel ; and it was always a comfort to him
that he had been able to give his father this good
news at a time of great sorrow and embarrassment.
The father died not long after, and the family may
be said then to have had no home.   They resided for
short periods at Brighton, at Strand-on-the-Green,
and other places ; and some members of the family
paid long and frequent visits to Samuel Rickards, a
quaint, patriarchal, and truly saintly man, at Ulcombe,
near the Earl of Winchelsea's place.   Lord Maid-
stone—rather eccentric then, in due time the very
eccentric earl—was Rickards' pupil.   He had considerable powers of caricature, as Etonians all remember, and he was glad to contribute to any lady's
album.   Though Rickards lived to be left far behind
in the race of development, he and his surroundings,
whether at Ulcombe, or at Stowlangtoft, near Bury
St. Edmund's, were always very dear to the Newman
family.   In October 1827 Newman and his sisters

paid a most interesting visit to Highwood, where Mr. Wilberforce then resided, and where the three younger sons were then assembled.

In the summer of 1829 the family took a furnished cottage in a very out-of-the-way spot at Horspath, of which Dr. Ellerton, a well-known Fellow and tutor of Magdalene College, had charge. This was pleasant enough in the summer, but when Dornford, a Fellow of Oriel, who was serving Nuneham Courtney, and had the use of a cottage there, offered it to the Newmans, they were glad to avail themselves of the opportunity, though the change did not bring them nearer Oxford. The cottage formed part of the new village built in uniform style by Simon Lord Harcourt, in place of the ancient village, cleared away because too near the magnificent new mansion, so conspicuous an object as seen from the river. It was said to have been intended for the parsonage, but was by no means a picturesque building. Indeed, in the Midlands it would have been set down as the habitation of a family of weavers or stockingers.

It was not, however, without associations. Jean Jacques Rousseau occupied it for some time under the patronage of the Harcourt family, and is said to have sown seeds of many foreign wild flowers in spots where they were likely to grow. The fact of such plants being found about Nuneham has been adduced to support the tradition that this is the true Auburn of Goldsmith's 'Deserted Village.'

Another not less interesting association is an incident not to be found in Canon Ashwell's account of the late Bishop of Winchester's early years. Among the many hands through which Samuel Wilberforce passed, was the Rev. E. G. Marsh, then occupying this cottage, and finding room in it for a family and some pupils. Samuel was then hardly twelve years old, but he had decided tastes. He conceived a great dislike of his tutor and the whole *ménage*, and one day, after a violent collision, demanded to be sent home immediately. The tutor demurred. Thereupon the lad ran into the road before the cottage, then traversed by a score or two of London coaches a day, threw himself flat on the ground, in the very track of the coaches, and announced his intention of remaining there till he was sent home. After he had remained there several hours the tutor struck his colours, and Samuel was sent home.

A special interest attaches to this cottage from its being the scene of a remarkable family group, including the whole surviving Newman family, in chalk, by Miss Maria R. Giberne, an early and ardent admirer of Newman, and his follower to Rome.

Upon Dornford leaving college, the family had to quit Nuncham, and then took a cottage in Iffley, well known for its massive Norman church, overlooking the Isis, a mile and a half out of Oxford. Here they took in hand the school and the poor at Littlemore. After a time they moved to 'Rose Bank' Cottage, then just completed, on the Oxford side of Iffley.

To no period of Newman's life do his younger friends turn with more curiosity than to his position in the Oriel common room for the first two or three years. The truth is, it was very easy for a man to have no position at all there, especially just at that time. Newman, a shy man, with heart and mind in a continual ferment of emotion and speculation, yearning for sympathy and truth, was not likely to feel entirely at home with some, whom it would be needless either to name or to describe. From the first he loved and admired the man with whom eventually he lived most in collision, Edward Hawkins.

He would also have been ready to love and admire Whately to the end, but for the inexorable condition of friendship imposed by Whately—absolute and implicit agreement in thought, word, and deed. This agreement, from the first, Newman could not accord. His divergence was in fact radical. He used to say that Whately's Logic was a most interesting book, but that there was one thing not to be found in it, and that was logic. The truth is, every man in these days is his own logician. However, they lived for some time in close intimacy, and it is painful to remember that a time came when they were in the same city for seven years, passing one another in the streets, without even recognition.

Newman was, however, unaffectedly deferential to his seniors, some of whom could little have suspected the future of their shy probationer. Dr. Coplestone, seeing him less frequently, and on less familiar terms, could never quite understand him, though he understood, and even too kindly appreciated, some men of much less originality, power and address. This was all the more remarkable as no man in Oxford ever so studied and admired Coplestone's famous Prælections as Newman did. He read

them with his favourite pupils, pointing out their
originality, and their felicity of expression. Coplestone
had more 'breadth of culture,' as it is now called,
than is commonly found united with exact and
elegant scholarship, and it is to be regretted that
the ephemeral form of his writings has thrown them
much out of date. The Latin of the Prælections,
Newman used to say, was very good, but Coplesto-
nian, not Ciceronian. All that Coplestone saw in him
was, as the Greek poet expressed it, a lion without
the spirit of a lion.

In 1824 Newman took orders and became Curate
of St. Clement's. This was then a quaint little church,
in a very small churchyard, adjoining the toll-taker's
shed, at the east end of the picturesque bridge over
the Cherwell, at the London approach to Oxford. At
this time Newman was Secretary to the local branch
of the Church Missionary Society, an occasional
frequenter of the religious soirées held at the Vice
Principal's of St. Edmund Hall, and on terms of more
or less familiarity with a considerable number of men
destined soon to part in many directions. His church
was soon filled, and although his sermons, from the
first, rather puzzled Mr. Hill and his weekly synod,
they passed the censorship and were pronounced, on
the whole, spiritual.

The parish of St. Clement's was increasing, and it
devolved on Newman to undertake the building of a
new church, on a more open site. This he had to
leave very much to others, and the result was the
singular edifice compared by irreverent undergraduates to a boiled rabbit, on some low ground, on the

bank of the Cherwell, opposite Magdalene Walks. There could hardly be imagined a building with less indications of the architectural reformation which has marked the last half-century. Part, if not the whole, of the old parish church was allowed to stand for some years, for use at the funerals still occasionally performed there. The chief university solicitor persisted that it would make no difference in the status of the new church, notwithstanding a resolute protest of Newman's that it would ; and the result was that some years afterwards an Act of Parliament had to be obtained to give validity to the marriage ceremonies performed at the new church while the old church was standing.

In 1825 Whately became Principal of St. Alban Hall, and Newman his Vice-Principal. Both took their parts in such tuition as could be given to a dozen young men, whose sole aim was to get a degree with the least possible trouble.

At Easter 1826, while Newman was still assisting Whately, two Oriel men were elected to fellowships— Robert Wilberforce and Froude. The former of these, second son of the great emancipationist, besides being a laborious and conscientious student, and a good writer, had recommendations which were then rare in Oxford. Even under his father's declining health and circumstances, he had seen a good deal of the political and 'religious' society of the metropolis, and of the great world. He had also travelled. At that time the Continent had not been opened more than ten years to the English tourist, who could scarcely be said to exist before 1815, for the few

people we sent to other parts of the world were
not tourists, but discoverers.   Even in 1825 a Continental tour had its difficulties, and consisted chiefly of
troublesome and costly incidents with vetturinos,
guides, and hotel-keepers ; road accidents, and brig-
ands, real or imaginary.

Robert Wilberforce had been much impressed
with Cologne Cathedral, and with the galleries of
early art at Munich.   It is an illustration of the turning of the tide, and of the many smaller causes contributing to the 'Movement,' that in 1829, German
agents, one of them with a special introduction to
Robert Wilberforce, filled Oxford with very beautiful
and interesting tinted lithographs of mediæval paintings, which have probably, long ere this, found their
way to a thousand parsonages—a good many to Bromp-
ton Oratory. ʿEven one such picture was a pleasant and
wholesome relief to the battle-scenes, the sporting pictures, and pretty female faces, which had been the chief
subjects of English art now for a whole generation.

About the same time—that is, in 1829—there came
an agent from Cologne with very large and beautiful
reproductions of the original design for the cathedral,
which it was proposed to set to work on, with a faint
hope of completing it before the end of the century.
Froude gave thirty guineas for a set of the drawings,
went wild over them, and infected not a few of his
friends with mediæval architecture.   As an instance
of the way in which religious sentiment was now beginning to be dissociated from practical bearings and
necessities, Froude would frequently mention the
exquisitely finished details at York Minster, and other

churches, in situations where no eye but the eye of
Heaven could possibly reach them.

Newman had attended the regular lectures of Dr.
Lloyd, Regius Professor, and also his private lectures,
or rather conversations, in which the origin of the
' Book of Common Prayer' had a prominent place.
Dr. Lloyd had received this task from others before
him, and he hoped to accomplish it or to pass it on.
It was a year after this that Froude was invited by
Lloyd to attend a course of lectures on the same
subject, viz. ' an historical account of the Liturgy,
tracing all the prayers, through the Roman missals
and breviaries, up to their original source.'

CHAPTER V.

NEWMAN, TUTOR. HIS PUPILS AND ORIEL FRIENDS.

ONE morning in 1826 Newman received a very short
note from Lloyd—' Dear Newman, step in, please, for
a moment.' Newman thought it might be a reference
or a memorandum, something lent, or lost, a date,
or what not, and ran to Christ Church. Upon
his opening Lloyd's door the Professor asked, ' Newman, how old are you ?' ' Five-and-twenty.' ' Get
away, you boy; I don't want you,' was all the explanation given, and Newman had almost forgotten it
when he heard next day that Jelf had, through

Lloyd, been selected for the tutorship of Prince George of Cumberland. The only restriction to Lloyd's choice was the limitation of age—twenty-seven.

Boundless is the vista of consequences with which this little difference of age may be credited in this instance. Historians have sometimes amused themselves with following up the probable consequences of events that impended, but did not come to pass. What if Alexander had turned his course westward instead of eastward ? What if Harold had been the survivor at Hastings ? What if Newman had become the adviser of the Court of Hanover, and of all the smaller German States? His politics occupy an earlier place in the memory of his pupils than his theology, for he had analysed the Constitution and history of every State in the world, ancient or still existing. A very good judge of men and things used to call Newman a Lord Chancellor thrown away, and there are plenty of examples to show that even though a man does not find his place in legislative assemblies, or in appeals to the people, he may still have the highest capacity for government and diplomacy.

The first consequence of Jelf's leaving Oxford was that Newman became tutor at Oriel in Jelf's place, receiving his pupils ; for it was then the custom of the college—indeed, the law of the university—that every undergraduate should be entered under a tutor, who should be, to a great extent, answerable for him. As Newman was resolved to understand the office of tutor by the law and spirit of the university, the change proved very important to the pupils transferred to his charge, and eventually to himself. As I write this, however, I feel bound to add that Jelf was a very good lecturer, and a kind and conscientious tutor. It is needless to say that he was a good scholar ; his explanations were simple and easy ; his utterance was soft and even musical. Perhaps he too readily assumed that his pupils were as well grounded and industrious as himself, and as capable of reading Herodotus without a frequent recurrence to the lexicon.

Personally I am under a great obligation to Jelf. At Christmas 1825, I was persuaded by a very hard-working but eccentric acquaintance to stay up the vacation and read with him. I had been latterly encroaching far on the night to make up for lost time. The result of that, and of strong coffee, was that the very first night of the vacation, a few days before Christmas, I was seized with violent pains. The scout called in a medical practitioner often seen in the college. He gave me a large bowl of Epsom salts, I lay in agony all night, worse and worse every hour. About seven the scout went to Jelf, who immediately came over. He sent at once for Dr. Bourne, then the leading physician in Oxford, of whom it used to be said that once, finding himself despised for his youth, his good looks, and gaiety of manner, he had disappeared for a month, and then reappeared with a wig, a graver tone, and a more measured utterance. He pronounced the illness peritonitis, told me I was at death's door, that the salts had nearly killed me, and I must be bled. This I was, the only time in my life. At every visit, he told me of young men thus attacked, who, from taking too much beef tea, or buttered toast, had died in twenty-four hours. Jelf had me moved from my close and dismal garret to the best rooms in college, those between the two Quads, then Welby's. He wrote to my parents who came up immediately, and were much relieved to find me alive and mending ; and were also much impressed with Jelf's kindness. He visited me every day while he remained up. Hawkins also called on me on his return to college, and seemed to detect in me more than usual wandering and incoherency.

This was at Christmas 1825. In the course of the next year, as stated above, Jelf was succeeded by Newman, who took over his pupils. A few months afterwards Tyler, a most energetic and genial man, then Dean and tutor, accepted the Rectory of St. Giles's-in-the-Fields ; and early in 1828 Dr. Coplestone resigned the Provostship on becoming Bishop of Llandaff and Dean of St. Paul's. About the same time Pusey, who had now been Fellow of Oriel four years, showing himself, however, very little latterly, returned to Christ Church as Regius Professor of Hebrew. Upon the vacancy in the Provostship three names presented themselves for what was then deemed one of the highest objects of academic ambition, so illustrious had Coplestone made it.

Keble was still Fellow, and had very recently given up the tutorship and taken to parish work. His 'Christian Year' had now been published a twelvemonth and had gone through several editions. But he was always a shy man, and on the rare occasions on which he revisited Oxford, he preferred some quiet domestic hearth to Oriel common room. The world

associates Keble very intimately with Oxford, and
with Oriel College, and the world is right in doing so ;
but there is something in the mode of this association
which has to be explained. The usages of Oxford are,
in some respects, different from those of Cambridge,
and still more so from the ideas naturally formed by
strangers. In most of the colleges, especially those
where the reputation of the tutors attracted undergraduates, the Fellows were politely requested to give up
the rooms to which they had a foundation right for the
use of the undergraduates. This reduced the resident
Fellows to those engaged in tuition, for though they
might go into lodgings if they were so minded, that
was not the same thing as being in college and having a gratuitous home, which they could leave or return to when it suited them. When John Keble gave
up the tuition to assist his father at Fairford, though
he would probably have retained his rooms in college
had that been the usage, he did not provide himself
with lodgings in their place. In 1835-36 he was glad
to have the use of my rooms for a week or two. But
the fact was that from his giving up the tuition to his
vacating his fellowship by marriage many years after,
he was very little indeed in Oxford, and then only at
a private house in the city. Yet everybody who
visited Oriel inquired after Keble, and expected to see
him. It must be added that he was present in everybody's thoughts, as a glory to the college, a comfort
and a stay, for the slightest word he dropped was all
the more remembered from there being so little of it,
and from it seeming to come from a different and
holier sphere. His manner of talking favoured this,

for there was not much continuity in it, only every word was a brilliant or a pearl.

The Rector of St. Giles's-in-the-Fields was still in his year of grace, and eligible.

Hawkins, who had long striven to keep an even course between all sides, had really won the love and esteem of all. In whatever he wrote or said, he laboured to concede to anyone what he asked, without sacrificing what was due to the truth, as he conceived it. He spoke incisively, and what he said remained in the memory and seemed to come from him. He was fond of business and wished to keep it in his own hands. Keble humorously proposed that the Fellows should divide the prize—give Tyler the red gown, Hawkins the work, and himself the money. The junior Fellows looked to Newman to see which way he was going. To the great surprise of some old members of the college who knew everybody there and everything, he gave all his weight for Hawkins. He liked the man and hoped much from him, but he could hardly have expected much unless he also thought that Hawkins was impressible and compliant, which he decidedly was not.

But what reason could Newman have for not welcoming back to college the author of the 'Christian Year'? Keble always understood that the reason was Newman's distrust of his power to manage young men, and said that it was a mistake, for he felt himself peculiarly fitted for it. It certainly was the fact that he had private pupils as well as college pupils, and that they respected him. A former Fellow of the college, a friend of Whately as well as Newman, a quaint, patriarchal man, with a century of wisdom on his still young shoulders, wrote to Newman, 'You don't know Hawkins as well as I do. He will be sure to disappoint you.' But then, it must be added, the dear good man did not quite know Newman himself, and lived to be disappointed in him.

Whatever thoughts Newman might have had about his own part in the election he kept them to himself, for his most intimate friends cannot remember a single word of self-accusation. It was his wont to accept his own acts as Providentially overruled to purposes beyond his own ken. He was, therefore, much surprised and concerned when he read in a sermon preached by Pusey at the consecration of the chapel at Keble College, that Newman had lived to regret the part he had taken in Hawkins' election to the Oriel Provostship.

Thus in 1828 Newman found himself in a college at that time held to be in the very front of academic progress, with some half-dozen very important, intractable personages just cleared away ; with a Provost who owed his election to him ; himself tutor, and with two other tutors, Robert Wilberforce and Richard Froude, entirely devoted to him. At what date he began to move in the direction which seems now plain enough, it would not be easy to say. It never was possible to be even a quarter of an hour in his company without a man feeling himself to be invited to take an onward step sufficient to tax his energy or his faith ; and Newman was sure to find out in due time whether that onward step had been taken. But though we may now construct a design, still we shall have to admit that it is only by being wise after the event, or with the event near in view.

Newman wrote about this time an elaborate article on Apollonius Tyanæus for an Encyclopædia, drawing the line strongly between true and fictitious miracles. He had early faced fairly the question of evidences, by the study of infidel writers. He was one of the few people who could be called thoroughly acquainted with Gibbon's great work. He could recite many long passages of it, particularly the famous one in which Gibbon describes the changelessness of agriculture and the simple arts in the midst of changing governments, religions and manners. He knew well Hume's Essays. He had Tom Paine's works under lock and key, and lent them with much caution to such as could bear the shock. Indeed, his carefulness to master the other side of the great question has suggested to some critics that his faith and his scepticism contended for the ascendancy on such equal conditions as to leave the issue sometimes doubtful.

CHAPTER VI.

FRANK EDGEWORTH.

WHAT has Frank Edgeworth to do with this story, for he was a Cambridge man, and only a visitor at Oxford? Well, he was part of my life, and part of the circumstances of the day. His name was public from his childhood, for his very much older half-sister had made Frank the hero of several then very popular but now forgotten tales. Her tales, indeed, are not so wholly forgotten as her sensational novels, hardly distinguishable from burlesque, written to damage the character of the statesmen, the aristocracy, and the Church of this country—indeed, of English society in general. Maria Edgeworth cared for the actual Frank as much as he cared for her, which was so little that it was better not to mention her. He showed an early and strong revolt against the hollowness, callousness, and deadness of utilitarianism. He affected, however, no saintliness, for his humour ran the other way.

He was a little fair-haired, blue-eyed, pale-faced fellow, ready and smooth of utterance, always with something in his head and on his tongue, and very much loved in a small circle at Charterhouse. With a fertile imagination and with infinite good-nature he would fall in with any idea for the time and help you on with it. He cast aside altogether his father, of whom he knew nothing, and the above-mentioned half-sister, with whom, when she was mentioned, he was careful to say that he had little in common. Among his friends at Charterhouse was David Reid, of the family of brewers, a man of many hobbies rapidly succeeding one another. At school he was on Perpetual Motion, so often the first round in the ladder that leads nowhere. The result was the usual story. The theory was sound, but the machine had a trick of stopping, and when it stopped would not go on again.

Edgeworth was second for the English Poem on Carthage in 1823, and I was third. As the Duke of Wellington is related to have said about his De- spatches, I may reasonably wonder how in the world I came in third for even a school prize-poem. The circumstances of the incubation were exceptionally favourable. I spent the St. Bartholomew's vacation— that is, August and half September—at Filey, going thither straight by sea from London. At Filey there was nothing to distract my attention, no society out of our own family, no amusements, no books. There were none there but fishermen, and not a house much better than a hut. I think I was rather inclined to shirk the poem altogether, pleading my total ignorance of the history of Carthage. But only three miles off, at the village of Hunmanby, Archdeacon Wrangham had one of the best libraries in the north of England. My father sent me off with a note to the Archdeacon, requesting that I might be allowed to consult some of his books. I was received most kindly into a house where the book-shelves began at the front door, and, I should think, ran up into the garret and down to the cellar. However, I was taken into the library proper, which I had to myself for a couple of hours. I made the most of this by reading the article on Carthage in the ' Encyclopædia Britannica' a good deal more carefully than it was my wont to read. I made notes. So I had nothing more to do with books. The composition was done on the spacious sands and stormy ' Brigg' or natural break- water of that then very lonely and primitive place.

It was some years after this that the Wilberforces

told me the Archdeacon had obtained an introduction
to their father. He was not of the same way of thinking,
or, indeed, of any particular way of thinking, but, as
he explained at once, it was that he might have a
copy of the first edition of every book printed at the
presses, which were being sent to the South Sea
Islands and other like countries.

The Carthage of history had no future, nor had
mine. The next year the subject was Saul, and
Edgeworth came in first. I have a sad story to tell.
I set to work diligently on the history of Saul and
David, and, by way of a solid foundation, attempted
a chronological order of events, with the proper
developments of character to suit each stage ; and I
made a mess of it. I floundered in a sea of enigmas,
which I laboured to solve, instead of leaving alone.
When a knight of romance does but flourish his
sword, the visionary obstructions vanish ; and it
ought to be the same with a flourish of the pen. It
was not so here. The result was a very laboured,
heavy, and, after all, a very imperfect composition, not
placed at all in the award. When I came to Oriel I
attempted to retrieve my disaster by availing myself
of the liberty to send in verses instead of essays, but
I soon received from Tyler a kind but impressive
warning to addict myself rather to prose.

About the time of this unhappy attempt on the
books of Samuel and Kings, I did the same with
the first book of Livy, then treated at Charterhouse
almost exclusively as an exercise of scholarship, even
in the First Form. I carefully wrote out some results,
illustrated by chronological diagrams, and showed

them to Russell, who glanced his eyes over the contents, made a humorous grimace, and returned the paper without a word.

Reid, named above as Edgeworth's friend, was in the same house with him, and a constant companion. Somehow—I never knew why—he had incurred very early Russell's extreme dislike. He always called him 'Veneer,' which was hardly deserved, though a man who takes up one thing after another is likely to be superficial. At least he cannot have much ballast or groundwork of knowledge and action, which is perhaps what Russell meant. Reid came to University College, took to books in extravagant bindings, then to boating, then to philosophy, then to freemasonry—in all an enthusiast.

Edgeworth soon came to him on a visit, full of Platonism, in which his old Carthusian friend, Eaton, was taking a lead at Cambridge as member of a Platonist club. Among the friends he met at my rooms one only did he much admire, and that was John F. Christie, destined to a humble and brief, but not the less noble, career in duty's straightest course. Edgeworth pinned me to my chair about eight o'clock one evening at University College, and demanded point-blank the grounds of my faith. It was not a matter to which I had ever given a serious consideration, for, as it was fatal to doubt, it was superfluous, and indeed very foolish, to inquire. However, I had studied, or rather had had to study, Paley's 'Evidences,' and of these I had to reproduce a floating plank or two from a fatal shipwreck. So I began as seriously and in as set form as I could.

Self.—This is a question of fact, and therefore a matter of testimony. Is it possible to doubt the authenticity or the truth of writings quoted substantially and often literally by well-known and good men living only two or three generations after ?

Edgeworth.—It is possible to doubt, for I doubt myself, and what I want is to have my doubts removed. I wish to believe, but I do not, and cannot. The statements themselves are incredible, unless supported by testimony, and we all acknowledge testimony to be a thing that requires much sifting. Our courts of law are sifting it continually, and often in vain, for they cannot get at the truth. Were the Fathers who quoted the gospels men to inquire, or only anxious to believe ? What do we know about them ?

Ah me ! This struck at the root of my defence, for I knew nothing about the Fathers. Even had I known more it would have been all book knowledge, nay, worse than that, mere 'cram.' I had never realised any of the persons cited as authorities for the sacred canon, or their position, or their work, or their lives, or anything about them. To me they were names. So what I said must have been all milk and water, or, to speak more german to the matter, pen, ink, and paper. But then, after I had been standing long on the defensive, came my turn for assault.

Self.—What have you to show instead ? Truth there must be somewhere. Where is it ? What is it ? Can we suppose the world left without it ? Can we suppose it undiscernible ? Is truth important or not ? Is there or is there not such a thing ?

My attack was desperate and revengeful, for I had been on the rack a couple of hours or so. It was met with perfect self-possession, and much alacrity, for it was the very thing desired.

Edgeworth.—Yes, undoubtedly, there is truth ; it is most desirable— indeed, necessary ; it is quite discoverable and ascertainable. But it is not confined to certain narrow limits of space and time. It is in all things and everywhere. The truth meets us in all sayings and all doings. There is nothing from which we may not extract truth. Granting all you say about the traditions of one remote corner of the world, and one race of no figure in history, only discovered to be conquered, enslaved, absorbed or scattered—granting all that, why is not truth human and divine to be found also in the traditions of Greece and Rome in which we have been educated, and which are part of our very being ?

Finding my antagonist well in position I pressed onwards.

Self.—Is there truth, then, in Jupiter, in Venus, and in Hercules ?

Edgeworth.—Yes. Truth mixed with error and extravagance, as in all religions, in all opinions—indeed, in all human affairs. We must go back very far ; into the very well of antiquity. All bow to antiquity. We must strike off additions, interpolations, variations, and all plainly foreign and inconsistent matter. All truth is charged with judicial functions.

Self.—But where are we to find the pure wisdom of antiquity ; the tradition of a golden age ?

Edgeworth.—Greek philosophy may not give it, but it shows the way. It leads back to a sacred source, and it retains the fragrancy of Eden.

I saw now, or seemed to see, that the question lay between the Bible and Lempriere, and I was, unhappily, more familiar with the latter than with the former. As I had not yet begun to write sermons, I had turned over the leaves of ' Gradus ad Parnassum ' oftener than those of Cruden's ' Concordance.' However, I had to fight on.

Self.—Does not Herodotus tell us that the Greek, and by consequence the Roman, divinities, all came from Egypt ?

Edgeworth.—True. Egypt has a good deal to say to all religions, and to all civilisation ; both to the matter and the form ; the truth and the error.

Fortunately for me, Sagas and Vedas, and Rig Vedas, were then only known to a few Oriental scholars, and the only Arians then ever heard of were the early heretics so named. In these days you have only to quote an eminent Sanscrit writer who flourished 5,000 years ago, and you are silenced, for even if you know half a dozen stages of Sanscrit, there is always an earlier one you know nothing of. The discussion lasted without the chance of a conclusion in which both could agree, till one of the disputants at least was glad to find it was midnight.

Reid must have sat by and heard all this, for it was in his rooms, but it was not the direction in which his mind wrecked itself. His final quarrel was with social and domestic traditions. He revolted against all usages and forms. He would not rise, take his meals, or go to bed, when other people did. He would not believe that night was night, day day, or that summer and winter were different things. One day when snow lay on the ground, he ran full speed from his friends, dashed through a river, and continued his flight for miles into space. In a very hot June day, he suddenly presented himself at my lodgings in Oxford, a wild, haggard figure, announcing that he had escaped from his keepers in St. John's Wood, and had just been engaged in a long argument with Plumtree and the other tutors of University. He had proved to them till they had not a word to say, first that he was not mad and never had been mad ; secondly, that man could live by water and the Spirit, entirely without other food. He had been long baffling all the tricks of his keepers ; he had drunk pitchers full of water, and had buried himself in blankets to perspire it off. Thus he raved for precious hours. But he had promised the tutors at University to return to them. He kept his appointment, and as they were better prepared this time, he was laid hold of, and conveyed back to his friends.

Some weeks after, Edgeworth wrote to me asking for information about Reid. This I gave. Then came a letter from him asking for a meeting. The only appointment that could be made was a very homely business house in the city. Edgeworth came and said he had seen Reid ; he was quite under control, and his friends were agreeable to Edgeworth taking him a tour abroad. I remonstrated against the plan, on the ground of its dangers, the inevitable excitement, the chance of paroxysms far from help, the little good a maniac would derive from new scenes and experiences. Edgeworth persisted. The plan actually answered for months and even years, and it was at a time of comparative rest, and after a not unsuitable marriage, that poor Reid threw himself from a window at Venice into the canal below.

I had a long summer's day ramble about London with Edgeworth. It was before the days of cabs or omnibuses, and we could stop often and look about. The General Post Office was just finished. Edgeworth strongly condemned the sacrifice to architectural effect ; and to an effect not suited to our climate. I could not but admire the portico. What was it for ? It shut out the light, which is the want of this country. He would have had centre and wings all alike. Edgeworth was no utilitarian, but light and sunshine are matters that come home to those who read and write. We went to the National Gallery, then in its embryo state, at a house in Pall Mall West. He gave a very long look at the ' Raising of Lazarus.' The picture, the conception, the grouping he much admired ; the principal figure, he said, was ' Jewish.' ' But our Lord was a Jew,' I observed, not very wisely. ' A Jew,' Edgeworth replied, ' but not Jewish.'

I met Edgeworth again. He was looking out for ' an Eve,' and pleasant it was to know that he was at least on the first step of Christian tradition. He settled near London, had to work for himself and his wife. He took pupils, and had appreciating friends. But he wanted physical stamina, and he died young.

In Carlyle's ' Life of John Sterling,' is a very in-

teresting, and indeed tender, notice of Frank Edgeworth, upon which, however, some comments have to
be made. 'Frank,' he says, 'was a short neat man,
of sleek, square, colourless face (resembling the portraits of his father), with small blue eyes in which
twinkled curiously a joyless smile; his voice was
croaky and shrill, with a tone of shrewish obstinacy
in it, and perhaps of sarcasm withal. A composed,
dogmatic, speculative, exact and not melodious man.
He was learned in Plato, and likewise in Kant; well
read in philosophies and literatures; entertained
not creeds, but the Platonic or Kantean ghosts of
creeds; coldly sneering away from him, in the joyless
twinkle of those eyes, in the inexorable jingle of that
shrill voice, all manner of Toryisms, superstitions; for
the rest, a man of perfect veracity, great diligence, and
other worth;—notable to see alongside of Sterling.'

Carlyle then gives a long passage about Edgeworth from one of John Sterling's letters, more interesting as indicative of the writer's state of mind, than
as illustrating Edgeworth's 'moral scheme.' This,
Sterling says, contained the fundamental unsoundness
of asserting the certainty of a heavenly futurity for
man, because the idea of duty involves that of merit
or reward, whereas duty, says Sterling, seems rather
to exclude merit. Edgeworth, in his opinion, had
advanced so far in speculation as to have the title
deeds to an estate from which the idea of futurity is
carefully excluded, but had not yet got possession.

'This good little Edgeworth,' resumes Carlyle,
'had roved extensively about the Continent, had
married a young Spanish wife'—I think a sister of

David Reid's widow—' whom by a romantic accident
he came upon in London ; having really good scholarship, and consciousness of faculty and fidelity, he now
hoped to find support in preparing young men for the
university, in taking pupils to board ; and with this
view was endeavouring to form an establishment
somewhere in the environs ;—ignorant that it is mainly
the clergy whom simple persons trust with that trade
at present ; that his want of a patent of orthodoxy,
not to say his inexorable secret heterodoxy of mind,
would far override all other qualifications in the
estimate of simple persons, who are afraid of many
things, and are *not* afraid of hypocrisy, which is the
worst and one irremediably bad thing. Poor Edgeworth tried this business for a while, but found no
success at all ; went across, after a year or two, to
native Edgeworthstown, in Longford, to take the
management of his brother's estate ; in which function
it was said he shone, and had quite given up philosophies and speculations, and become a taciturn grim
land manager and county magistrate, likely to do much
good in that department ; when we learned next that
he was dead, that we should see him no more. The
good little Frank ! '

Early in the spring of 1836, at Sterling's invitation, Carlyle walked with him to Eltham to see
Edgeworth and the big house he had taken for pupils.
The day proved very bad ; they came home wet,
weary, and bemudded. Sterling had been failing.
This fixed his disorder. He was confined to his
house a long time, and cannot be said to have ever
recovered.

Carlyle, it is evident more from casual words than from full-blown sentences, felt a singular, and even affectionate, interest in Edgeworth. Yet some of his expressions are so harsh and so unmerited, as must rouse the susceptibility of Frank Edgeworth's early friends. They jar on my memories very much. My ear still testifies that there was sweetness in Edgeworth's voice, and gentleness in his manner and tone. My eye still recalls his soft and steady gaze. I felt sure then, and I feel sure now, that he wished to be a Christian. What invincible impediments he found in the creed, in the world, or in himself, I know not. While he seems to have puzzled Sterling by the frank admission that his soul had not found rest in philosophy, he hardly seems to have done justice to himself with Carlyle, who could not help tyrannising over one so little his equal in physical or other energy. But after Edgeworth had probably sacrificed Toryism, superstition, and a good deal more with a readiness which even amused Carlyle, he seems to have fallen back on a standpoint from which he would not recede, and to which indeed he clung with an obstinacy which offended Carlyle's egotism, making himself the object of a compassionate rather than respectful interest.

Frank Edgeworth was torn by conflicting systems, and I may add conflicting sensibilities, from childhood. He was a most sympathetic, self-sacrificing being. If anyone thinks this too much to say of him, I believe I may confidently refer him to Canon Cook, the well-known editor of the 'Speaker's Commentary.'

CHAPTER VII.

BLANCO WHITE.

BLANCO WHITE was now residing at Oxford, a member of the university, and of Oriel College, and, by courtesy, of the common room, where he brought to the common stock of information, apt to be limited at a university, no small contribution of literary gossip, scholastic lore, and philosophy. He was always ready to talk about Spain, and the Church he had left, when asked about them, but he was generally content with an allusion, or an incident. He had in truth said pretty nearly all he had to say in his published works.

I asked him one day a question of simple curiosity about the smaller religious houses in Spain. The answer was that in Spain you knew that there were friars in a town, and you knew that there were pigs, and that was all you cared to know about either of them.

Seville Cathedral, with its numerous aisles, its forest of pillars, and its awful gloom, had made a deeper impression upon him than our English cathedrals could do. The latter were cold and dull, and were too long for their other dimensions. Their great length he ascribed to the severity of our climate, which compelled the processions to be done indoors instead of outside, and he stated that their length was exactly adjusted to the length of the processional hymns. One incident may or may not be found in his books.

There was a great preacher at Seville, who was engaged during Lent to preach as many as seventy sermons of what is now called a sensational character. Wherever he preached multitudes flocked to hear him, and hung on every word. An old woman of remarkably grotesque face and manner, one day got a place opposite the pulpit a few yards off. In her eagerness to catch every word she unconsciously rose from her seat, still keeping her eyes fixed on the preacher. The light fell upon her, and the preacher's eye was fascinated by the strange object before him. She riveted his gaze. He looked on and on, and utterly lost the thread of his discourse. He stood a minute in helpless embarrassment, descended from the pulpit, and never preached again.

Blanco White had a good deal to say about the 'Prince of the Peace,' the Court of Spain, and the French occupation, but no more than what books and newspapers could say. Holland House was not a favourite subject in my time at Oriel, not at least in the common room. It was taken for granted that people went there prepared to drop some of their prejudices and superstitions. The circle assembling there had the same relation to the universities as that afterwards taken up by the Pall Mall clubs in a larger and more dominant form. Blanco White's own stories of Allen, Lord Holland's 'tame Atheist,' were amusing, but far from pleasant. That uncanny personage, however, must have been a kind as well as a very clever man.

Blanco White had had occasion to give some thought to a new translation of the Bible into Spanish, of course the revision of an existing translation. On this subject he frequently made a remark which is more or less true of all vernacular languages, possibly more of Spanish than of any other. The language, he said, had been too vitiated by vulgarity, licentiousness, and slang, to be the vehicle of a sacred matter. Every word had its double meanings and coarse associations. Yet in this halo of many colours and changing forms that surrounded every word consisted the principal charm and the very life of the language. No Englishman, Blanco White said, could possibly enter into the drollery and the local allusions of ' Don Quixote.'

He had a literary rather than political quarrel with the ' Times.' How he had found himself in that quarrel I know not; but he gravely related one day in the common room that a certain well-known author had given the editor several hundred pounds not to be noticed at all, dreading alike his censure and his commendation. This sort of black mail he described as a considerable element in the revenue of that journal.

Soon after he had become a member of the university, he preached once at St. Mary's, and occasionally assisted in services, but it shortly became evident that he was neither physically nor mentally in a state to perform service in the Church of England. He still, however, attended the services at St. Mary's, whether those of the university or those of the parish, very often. One inducement was the exquisite performance of the young organist, who to the extreme grief of many friends and all lovers of music, was killed with some others, by the upsetting of a coach, on his way to one of the festivals of the Three Choirs. Music was Blanco White's chief solace, for he could almost forget himself when listening to Beethoven ; but it was with a smile of depreciation that he described the old ladies at a concert beginning to beat time when they heard their own familiar Handel.

He repeatedly said that if he were a man of fortune he would employ somebody to keep all the street barrel-organs in tune. He gave a lecture on musical sounds at the Ashmolean, illustrated with a great variety of instruments. It was very interesting. What, however, I most distinctly remember, is Tom Churton, in his Proctor's velvet sleeves, advancing to the table, taking up something like an organ pipe, putting it to his mouth, and blowing a blast which shook the building, and made him fall back quickly into the rank.

From the time I became Fellow I resided a good part of the Long Vacation at Oxford. Blanco White did the same. I did not venture to intrude much on an elderly gentleman engaged in study—indeed, in writing, too, as we understood. It was generally possible to make up a party to dine in the common room, and one of the servants, under-butler, or under-cook, had to go round every morning, as in term time, and ask the residents whether they intended to dine in common room. Of course they did not, unless at least a pair could be made up. So a little negotiation became necessary ; and this was just the point at which my courage failed. Whatever the reason, I was seeing very little of Blanco White. Mr. Joseph Parker asked me to dinner. Shortly after my arrival, Blanco White arrived, and chanced not to catch a sight of me in the room. Mr. Parker asked about the college. Was it not dull in Long Vacation time ? Who was up ? The answer was that Newman was up, very busy with his work and his parish, and one other young Fellow. ' But,' he added, in my hearing, ' I see very little of him. I suppose he thinks an old man dull company.' Thereupon Mr. Parker turned round to me, and, bringing me to the front, said, ' Here is Mr. Mozley to answer for himself.' Of course they were all amused. I said that I should very much like to call on Blanco White when I should not be in the way. The result was I did often call, and saw a good deal of him, though I had often to feel it was as much as his strength could well bear.

I think it probable that during the whole period of Blanco White's Oxford residence he was the victim of an inward struggle. With frequent impulses to religious acts, whether in public or in private, he never gave way to them without the immediate sense of a check that made it impossible to complete the act. As he painfully relates, he could not bless a child, or utter a short prayer, without the instant recurrence of the question, ' Is there a God, and does this mean anything ? '

He had a good deal to say of authors, for he had been among them now many years in the metropolis, and he had got to regard them generally as mere book-makers, writing for money. Southey he corresponded with, but he described him as a man with

many pigeon-holes, who spent his days in jotting
down ideas and particulars, on slips of paper, which
he filed for future use, each in its own pigeon-hole.
This might have been suggested by the mosaic formation and frequent incongruity of Southey's writings. Blanco White, however, was carried away, like
the rest of the world, by the Waverley novels, to
which he returned again and again.

About the year 1829, together with Whately,
Arnold, Senior, and others, he started the 'London
Review.' Newman wrote for it an article on Poetry,
evidently with an aim to make it the ladder of Faith ;
but the composition was an essay, not a review, like
some of the other contributions. The 'London
Review' soon came to an end, followed to the grave
with lamentations on the stupidity of the British
public. Newman did not take its decease much to
heart.

Every Oriel man of that day may look back with
regret at the little use made of what was really the
very interesting episode of Blanco White's connection
and residence. It might have recalled many similar
incidents in the past ages, when marvellous personages, specially endowed with a migratory instinct,
roamed about connecting the centres of knowledge.
Palmer's lodgings, opposite Merton, where he resided,
were those traditionally, but incorrectly, assigned to
Duns Scotus. For some time after Blanco White's
arrival at Oxford he much enjoyed its quiet, for he
hated noise, and the sound of a few voices, heard a
little way off, was to him the bellowing of 'the great
beast'—his notion of the British populace. He was

really incapable of rest and composure, for his head and heart alike were in a continual flutter and turmoil, and his memory was heavily charged with painful sores. He had probably never enjoyed a day's thorough rest, or a night's uninterrupted sleep in his life. A small bottle of cayenne pepper, of exceptional pungency, the gift of some City friend, was his inseparable companion at dinners, and without it his digestion was powerless even for the plainest food. It made him shudder to see the young Fellows slicing up big pears and despatching them. 'The least bit of that pear,' he said, one day, 'would keep me in agonies the whole night.'

He was the most sensitive of men, and, as is often the case with such men, he seemed doomed to small annoyances. He had one at the very outset of his Oxford career, though, even as he told it, he could have afforded to laugh at it. The royal diploma conferring his degree had to pass through Convocation. Hare, of New College, was much puzzled by the affair, and suspicious of something behind it; so he thought the best way to meet it was a general protest. But when the question was put to the vote, his voice, which was a weak one, quite broke, and he could only squeak out 'Veto' in a tone that moved some merriment as well as surprise. Some kind friend told Blanco White this as a good story, but the poor man was exceedingly exasperated, and often alluded to it, mimicking the false tone of the single, heart-failing dissentient.

He once dined at Magdalene College, and was in a sad state of mind the day after. There were some old Fellows there who had become fixed to the place. They desired no addition to their knowledge and ideas, for they were incapable of it, and they rudely resented all attempts to force it on them. Blanco White had been encouraged to talk a good deal, for he was the lion of the occasion. One of these—Old Grantham—in a very bluff way and very audibly expressed his dissent from almost everything the guest said, even to the simplest statement. Most Oxford men would have thought no more about it than about the barking of a lap-dog. Blanco White never forgot it.

Dining in Merton College Hall, he chanced to praise their home-made bread, in comparison with the white, insipid, and not very wholesome baker's bread at his lodgings. A most eccentric Fellow of Merton, proud of his college, told him he would send a loaf the next morning. There was nothing to be done but to thank him. The loaf came and was appreciated. But it came the next day, and the day after, and continually. Blanco White found himself a dolesman—a poor scholar allowed his commons from the buttery hatch—nay, publicly, for the loaf had to cross the street every day and be delivered at the front door. He resisted, gently at first; but it was not easy to check the flow of his benefactor's bounty. He became miserable, almost wild, and had at last to use a violence very alien to his nature, to the poor gentleman's consternation.

When his health at all permitted he attended the university sermons, but got little comfort from them. They never admitted a question, not at least in his own direction for he had been born and bred in a

controversy generally going one way. Edward
Churton preached one Sunday a sermon designed to
recall and settle the troubled spirits of Oxford, of all
schools, in what to him was the faith and practice of
his forefathers. ' That man must have brains of cast
iron,' was Blanco White's first ejaculation on meeting
his friends, and he was evidently more exasperated
by the singular quietness and confidence of the
preacher than he would have been by the most in-
flammatory tirade. It was pouring oil on the volcanic
heat of his own nature.

Nothing could exceed Blanco White's kindness
to those who would receive favours from him, seek
information, and show that they valued his opinion.
He might have been happy in a world of such cases
as long as the illusion lasted or the performances
could be kept up. But that is not the condition of
human existence, in our days at least.

As an instance of his excessive kindness : having
arranged to leave Oxford for some months, and
finding me unsettled in my lodgings, he offered the
use of his very comfortable apartments. I accepted
the offer gladly, but with an explanation that I must
take his place in the arrangements with Palmer, the
householder. Blanco White would not hear of it,
and was so indignant at the idea that I could not
press it again, and I actually enjoyed the use of his
lodgings for nothing for some time. It was a little
before this that Blanco White had done me two very
different acts of kindness. He had presented me
with Coleridge's ' Aids to Reflection,' urging me to
read it ; and had strongly impressed on me the im-

propriety of leaving money and other valuables lying about, and so putting temptation into the servant's way.

Blanco White found individualities at the university as strong as his own—in a moral sense, much stronger. He had passed years of his life in continual dissolution. At Holland House everything was questioned, though with one foregone conclusion. At Oxford his best and most congenial friends found that they must take a stand, and from that time there was a widening chasm between them and Blanco White. Oxford was no longer the same place to him when Whately had gone. After a restless interval, Blanco White followed him to Dublin, and soon found that it was impossible, with the convictions he had come to, and was now freely expressing, that he could be a member of an archbishop's private society. He returned to England, but not to Oxford.

In 1838 his son Ferdinand, in the Indian military service, came home on leave a Christian, and returned to India an unbeliever. This I had from Newman at the time, and he spoke of it with great sorrow. Among Blanco White's familiar topics was one to which he often returned with much bitterness. I do not think I have mentioned it. This was the ' fantastic notion ' of Marriage being a type of the mystical union between Christ and his Church.

CHAPTER VIII.

EDWARD CHURTON.

ABOVE is mentioned the sad effect produced on Blanco White by Edward Churton's quiet and grave advocacy of the old Church of England. I cannot pass him without a memorial. He was one of our masters at Charterhouse. All I had to do with him was that he assisted Russell in looking over the themes, verses, and translations of the upper school. Occasionally he did the whole work. We were summoned one after another to an anteroom, where we found Churton already prepared with neatly-written criticisms and corrections. He did not say much, but he said it gently and in a way to reach the understanding and remain there. It was the only teaching addressed to oneself individually that I had at that school, and I felt it invaluable.

Nor was I alone in this. Thackeray had the benefit of this personal instruction, and he acknowledged the debt. Meeting him one day in the Strand, I told him I had just had a talk with Churton. He exclaimed, ' O tell me where he is, that I may fall down and kiss his toe. I do love that man.' I told him I was afraid he would not be able to do that, for it was at the exhibition of the Royal Academy I had just met Churton.

Russell was rough with Thackeray, not more so

perhaps than with many others, but when he saw Thackeray's spirit and humour rising with him, that made matters worse. Hence a life-long resentment much to be lamented. One of the very few times when I felt really angry with Russell was when he was guilty of great rudeness to Churton. Yet there was a coldness in Churton's manner and expression sometimes almost chilling. Becoming an archdeacon, living in Yorkshire, and having to deliver charges studiously within the lines—a Providential survivor, too, as he felt, of Norris, Sykes, and Watson —he early felt himself bound to give notes of warning, and even of remonstrance, at the development of the Oxford school.

On one occasion, some bad quarter of an hour on the eve of publication, I penned for the 'British Critic' a very saucy reply to one of these attacks, for so I counted it. Churton was indeed cold the next time I met him. He was too serious to smile ; indeed, I cannot remember him ever smiling except sadly. But when you have once thoroughly liked a man, it is hardly in his power to make you like him much less. In after years we went very different ways, but my memory of him has never changed.

CHAPTER IX.

JOSEPH PICKFORD.

THERE are men who are interesting from their associations, but whom no associations can redeem. Such
was Joseph Pickford. I first became acquainted with
his figure and circumstances at Derby, in 1815. His
father had been architect and builder; and the intimate
friend of Wright, the painter, remarkable for his illustrations of the varieties of light and their effects ; and also
of Whitehurst, a mechanician and author of a 'Theory
of the Earth.' It was a coterie contemporaneous and
on friendly terms with the Philosophical Society
founded by Erasmus Darwin, but with a difference of
caste, for philosophers are, socially, as exclusive as
other people. The father had built in the Friargate
a house of some architectural pretensions, his *chef
d'œuvre*, people said. The son had divided it. He
occupied the smaller portion, entered by a side door,
much as it had come from the builder's hands. The
only pretty thing in his sitting-room was a charming
picture, by Wright, of Pickford and his brother, playing with a spaniel, of the date of 1785, I should think,
and in the gay costume of that period. It passed
into the hands of a branch of the Curzon family.
When I called on Pickford it was a 'caution' to see
what a beautiful child might come to.

The larger part of the house and the front door
he let. It adjoined the school to which I went for
three years. My young eyes used to watch for the

sight of a pretty little girl, who, with her lady in charge, paid daily visits to Mrs. Knightly, Pickford's tenant. This was the Baroness Grey de Ruthyn, then residing at Castle Fields, adjacent to the site of the present Midland station. She became Marchioness of Hastings, and grandmother of the present Duchess of Norfolk.

Pickford, even then, was insulated and disagreeable. The old ladies used to mention it as an extraordinary thing that he had once been very pleasant company. He now visited the News Room every morning and afternoon, wrangled politics, of course on the Tory side, lost his own temper and several other tempers too, and was voted a nuisance. He had a living three miles out of Derby, and also a Rectory on Salisbury Plain. It was said that he was a good Greek scholar. In those days it was generally assumed that if a man was very disagreeable, and good for nothing else, he must be a Greek scholar. It was added that he had very nearly been Professor of Greek. This is not easy to understand, for Jackson was Professor from 1783 to 1811. Was some hope of this sort part of the system of cajolery of which Pickford described himself the unfortunate dupe?

It was not till my name was down in 1822 for future admission into Oriel College that I was aware he had been a Fellow there; but after my matriculation, and still more after my election, I compared notes with him about our college, and he readily disburdened himself of his grievances. He often reverted to them, and they are much as follows.

About the year 1780 an ancestor of the Leighs
of Stoneleigh left a very large and valuable collection
of books to Oriel College. In my time the undergraduates generally believed that once a year Lord
Leigh walked into the college Quad, and with a loud
voice demanded recovery of the library as a family
heirloom which could not be alienated. That performance I never witnessed. The books had to be
stored in cases in a set of rooms between the Quads,
and, of course, were inaccessible. The college slowly
saved the money for building a new library. This
was done at last. Oriel library is handsome, but not
convenient, and it has some considerable faults : one
of them is that there is no light or ventilation on the
gallery level. Though lofty and spacious, it is apt to
be hot and close. What now remained was to arrange
and place the whole collection, 30,000 volumes at
least, I should estimate from memory. Several sets
of steps were provided, one of them very tall, as, indeed, was necessary.

All the Fellows shied the work, and particularly
these steps. They remembered the old saying about
the pitcher that often goes to the well. Then it was
not quite the pleasantest way of spending a Long
Vacation. Beeke, afterwards Dean of Bristol, had
undertaken the work, but he must have somebody to
render the manual aid. Here was head work, hand
work and foot work, very monotonous, unrelieved,
and even dangerous. It was the treadwheel, but
without its security, its easy rhythm and its mental
repose, said by some unfortunate actors to be a grand
opportunity for recollecting forgotten parts.

So the Provost and Fellows looked about them, and fixed their eyes on the active, tidy, and clever little builder's son, from Derby. He seemed to have no special calling, and he had no friends. They elected him probationer, and immediately set him his probationary exercise, which was to help Beeke in the library. Much pleased with his election, he consented at once. From that time he ceased to be his own master, and found Beeke a very hard one. He had to be in the library from sunrise to sunset. The Leigh collection had now been twenty years in their cases, while the original Oriel collection, most of it very antiquated, had been stowed away in close quarters for a much longer period and very little handled. When the books were spread out, and shaken, and dusted, the atmosphere became charged with an acrid dust, the result of long fermentation, germination, secretion, humectation, and exsiccation, and all kinds of natural processes. The summer proved very hot. The dust penetrated everywhere. Pickford could not mount the steps, or take up a book, without raising a cloud. Brushes and dusters only diffused it more thoroughly through the atmosphere. Pickford found himself stifled and choked. He became really alarmed for himself. Beeke sitting quietly below, in the cooler stratum of the atmosphere, and taking the writing part of the work, would allow no pause. He must have been a Prospero to gain such a dominion over his Caliban. Whether he coaxed, or cajoled, or bullied him to do his bidding I know not, but he certainly impressed well on Pickford's mind that he was on trial, and liable to dismissal.

As long as I remember Pickford had an angry eye, and a carbunculous complexion, and I have often thought of him toiling up and down those weary steps, full of rage and dust, aching all over, and cherishing an implacable grudge with all mankind. From that time he hated books. I cannot remember to have seen one in his only sitting-room. He found it necessary to wash down the dust, at least to try to do so, for the necessity increased—nay, it never ended. Long past fifty, he assured me that he had not washed it quite down yet. It was his honest conviction that it was there still, a disagreeable, pungent dust, that had established itself in the tissues of his throat.

As his memory went back to the last century, and he was contemporary, more or less, with Mant, Beeke, Coplestone, and other remarkable men, I asked him one day for some account of the Oriel life of those days—that is, before and after 1800. He began, 'We lived loosely—I may say, luxuriously.' Of course, by the former word he only meant a rather free-and-easy life, without formality or strict rules. Such were his habits at this time that an ordinary High Table dinner would seem to him a wasteful luxury. However, he went on. They dressed for dinner at three o'clock. After dinner they went to the common room, so he declared, and had pipes and ale. Then they walked up and down High Street till five, when they read and wrote in their rooms till seven or eight. They then returned to the common room to play at cards, and drink brandy and water to a very late hour. There must have been supper in this programme, but I forget it. He declared he had seen some of them the worse for drink. If he could be made worse by anything himself, no doubt he was so too. He also declared there was no carpet in the common room, and that it was furnished with Windsor chairs. As the whole building was only just completed, it is possible the Fellows may have occupied their new quarters in this simple fashion for a short time. But most probably his recollections were a sad jumble, and he had misplaced persons and scenes.

As soon as his task was finished and he was full Fellow, he perceived that the college was watching for the earliest opportunity to get rid of him. The rectory of Cholderton, on Salisbury Plain, fell vacant the first year of the century, and it was intimated to him that he must take it and be off. He left me to understand that he had been the victim of trickery, insult, and something like violence, which of course was most ungrateful. Happily there was no parsonage at the living, so he was not bound to reside, and he was equally fortunate in finding another living, near Derby, without a parsonage, in which he need not reside. So he betook himself to a corner of his paternal mansion, as I have related.

I never remember his doing more than one act that could possibly be interpreted into an act of virtue, and that he immediately repented of. My father, being churchwarden, had made the discovery that all the galleries of the parish church, amounting to several hundred sittings, and occupied mostly by the genteel folks, had lapsed to the parish for failure of the conditions expressed in the Faculties. So he resumed them all and made a scheme for their re-appropriation on proper principles. Summoning a vestry, he laid it before them, with the intimation that a day would be named for carrying the change into effect. There was a large attendance of rate-payers. Pickford came with the rest. They were all rather taken aback, but did not know what else could be done. The minutes of the meeting were handed round, and all, including Pickford, subscribed their names. In a few days an eminent Evangelical minister, who chanced to be the reputed owner of one of the pews, rallied the pew-owners, roused their Vicar, and appealed to the Bishop. Imme-diately Pickford sent to withdraw his signature, lest it should seem to countenance a proposal which met with his unqualified disapprobation. This was in 1830, and he expressed to me his belief that this was part of the great revolutionary movement.

As to the matter itself, after much controversy, the Bishop appointed a Commission, which drew up an award substantially and almost entirely confirming my father's scheme and fully recognising the re-version of the seats to the churchwardens. He con-firmed it. The Bishop of Exeter, to whom I recently showed the Award, after giving it careful perusal, observed that it was probably the first general Epi-scopal act in the matter of pews in modern times.

When I became Fellow I soon heard enough of Pickford. He had left a deep impression. More than once at college meetings, Copplestone had solemnly declared, ' I say it deliberately, Mr. Pickford is the most ungentlemanly person I ever met in the whole of my life.' I am not sure it was not 'the most disagreeable ;' perhaps 'the least like a gentleman.' Possibly it was all three at different times, and more, and stronger too.

The college had now to build a parsonage at Pickford's living, and every step of this process he regarded with horror, as leading to expense, and possibly involving residence. The first question was the site. Keble and Froude undertook this. They found a small, very narrow slip of glebe land nearly opposite the Manor House, and with a hovel upon it near the road. Turning up this narrow slip they came half-way on two handsome sycomine trees. Here must be the parsonage, with the two trees just opposite the front door. Three leaps from the windows on either side would take you out of your domain. Finding chalk cob the common material of the country, they thought nothing better, though the Manor House and the farm-houses were of brick. The cob walls would have to be an immense thickness, and the extra thickness would have to be taken out of the rooms, unless you would have a much larger roof. There was not only a total absence of modern accommodations, but an utter impossibility of making them anywhere, unless you pulled half the house down.

I found that the Lord of the Manor and his friends had been earnestly desirous to give the college a much better site in exchange for this. It was a larger and higher piece of ground, on which still stood a great number of elms and other trees that had surrounded a mansion of historic name and interest.

Mr. Foyle sent his carefully-written proposal to the college, and never had an answer. I am afraid it must be said that colleges used to suspect everybody, whereas it is my own experience that when a gentleman makes an offer it is probably generally to his own advantage, but he takes care to offer an ample equivalent. The Long Vacation, too, is a terrible gulph. A gentleman writes to a college very early in June, and expects an answer in a week or two at the latest. He is pretty sure to receive no answer till the end of October, if even then ; but the odds are his letter is forgotten, or not to be found.

But for the parsonage. It was settled at last that Pickford must do the tenant's fixtures. He battled every point. There was an interchange of letters on the question of one or two bell ropes and wires for each sitting-room. Two he thought preposterous. Changing his tone he begged for mercy, and besought the college not to press too hard on ' the sear and yellow leaf.'

After this he paid a visit to his parish—-whether from a wholesome interest in his new parsonage I know not. He passed through Oxford and called on me. I had either the kindness or the malice to press him to dine in hall, and he came to the common room. In his breeches and top boots—mahoganies, as they were then called—he somewhat astonished the undergraduates. He was not at ease in the common room, nor did he contribute to its cheerfulness. Once of it was more than enough. Some years after he had a bad accident. He went up into his hayloft in the dusk of the evening to see what stock of hay was

there, when somebody laid hold of him and threw
him down to the ground.   So he said.   He was very
much shaken and bruised.

Soon he began to fail.   When he mounted his
pulpit at his small Derbyshire living, he took out his
account-book instead of his sermon, and was a long
time fumbling at it without finding his mistake.   He
was shortly laid up.   Good people came and urged him
to make a will, but he could not be persuaded to make
that parting with the seven or eight thousand he had
scraped together.   When I succeeded him at Cholderton I found that for many years he had used
phrases to leave the impression of a wife and large
family to be provided for.   'How are Mrs. Pickford
and the children?' I was immediately asked.   If he
could be supposed to care to save his conscience his
words might refer to two respectable young women
who came from Nottingham at intervals to keep up
their interest with him.   They were regarded as
nieces, but not being blood relations they took no
benefit out of the property, which all went to the
keeper of an apple-stall at Warwick that Pickford had
never heard of.   Such was a Fellow of Oriel, a contemporary of Mant and Coplestone.   Yet better
men have not done more work than was got out of
him, one way or another, in Oriel library.

CHAPTER X.

HENRY THOMAS ELLACOMBE.

WHOEVER has read the last chapter faithfully will think himself entitled to some relief. The material is at hand, however I may present it. Very early did I hear of Henry Thomas Ellacombe. Happy were they that knew him, or had talked with, or even seen him. Yet I am ashamed to say I did meet him once in Oriel common room and failed to retain an image which was not eclipsed by the name. Ellacombe survives, and is of about the Provost's standing, ninety-three, or thereabouts. He is of that fortunate race—'sons of the gods' they may be truly called—that care for everybody and everything. There is no wealth like sympathy, for it is inexhaustible. I had heard of Ellacombe's addiction to church bells, to plants and flowers, to armorial bearings and genealogies, but when I went into Devonshire, I might say that not half had been reported to me.

His magnificent quarto on the bells of Devonshire gives the size, tone, quality, date, and legend of every church bell in the county, with full particulars of their condition and surroundings. The first thing that strikes the reader is the evidently strong attachment of the people to their bells, and the lead bells have taken in church restoration. Long before Simeon was skeletonising our sermons, churchwardens were recasting our bells, and doing it very well too. They made mistakes sometimes, and they dealt rather recklessly with the church towers. When they had not room for a larger peal, or even one more bell, they thought nothing of scooping out a waggon-load of solid masonry. What was worse, when the 'cage' would oscillate so much as to disturb the ringing, they drove in big wedges between it and the wall, thereby communicating the oscillation to the walls, and in many instances cracking them from top to bottom.

Ellacombe went about suitably apparelled and with proper tools and materials, running up every tower in Devonshire. He did not think it always necessary to ask the parson's leave, but when the parson heard his bells tinkling, clanging, and jangling, he knew somebody must be at them, and rushed out to see who or what it was. He found an extraordinary figure that might have stepped out of a scene of German *diablerie*, ascertaining the key-note of the bells, or taking a tracing of the legend, or a cast of the devices. One clergyman exorcised Ellacombe at once, and his church is conspicuous by its absence from the book.

After a very kind invitation, and some unsuccessful attempts, at last an appointment was made, and we drove to spend a day at Clyst St. George. There had now for ten years been an interesting link between us. The Clyst, which gives its name to a dozen villages or hamlets, rises in my parish and reaches salt water in Ellacombe's. The tide there works its way up the watercourses to within a few hundred yards of the parsonage. There are ships and shipbuilding at Topsham, a mile off. Within a mile, in another direction, is a splendid mansion, surrounded by gardens, terraces, balustrades, statues and vases, strange to the eyes of those who have lived long among dairies and cow-sheds. This is the residence of Joshua Dixon, brother of the late member for Birmingham, a kind neighbour, and forward to help the Church in material things.

Clyst St. George is the ancient birthplace of the Gibbs family, so renowned for its munificent doings at Keble College, and elsewhere. The church is handsome, and has been as much restored and decorated as it is possible for a church to be, by Ellacombe's taste, and chiefly by his means. The painted windows, the heraldic ornaments, the mosaics on the font and on the walls, are beyond me altogether. I will freely confess that, earth-worm as I am, I should appreciate better the contents of the parsonage. Every wall of room or passage, upstairs as well as downstairs, we found covered with engravings, portraits, and caricatures of the great turning-point of history at which Ellacombe was born. But you might pass to and fro between church and parsonage, for they were close together, hardly a fence between them ; and the church, I think, was very likely open from sunrise to sunset. Heraldry, I may observe, is no trifle in Devonshire, where a single name and coat may ramify into some dozen differences. At least a dozen of my labourers could have shown good coats of arms.

Ellacombe's garden was, or rather had been, one of the wonders of the county. He was his own gardener, employing only labourers. But his staff was now low, and there had been a long drought. He had a record of 5,000 different plants and flowers

grown with success. They had come from all parts
of the world, and here had been the first introduction
of many to English society. The old gentleman
talked to me more of people than of flowers, or church
ornaments, or church bells ; for he was as full of men
as of anything.

After we had done our duty to the church and the
grounds, he proposed to take me to a grand point of
view. So we passed out of the churchyard by a wicket
into a pathway, four or five feet above the carriage
road. I immediately saw what I at least had never
seen before, or expected to see, in England. Six men
in clerical vestments were marching at a rapid pace in
the middle of the road, three before and three behind.
The middle one of the three first was somewhat older
than the rest, and held before him a book, from which
he was reading aloud. Ellacombe, standing at his
own church gate, said, with great promptitude and in
a very distinct voice, ' Gentlemen, you are strange to
me.' The reader, without the least abatement of his
pace, answered, ' We are strange, indeed,' and resumed
his reading as he passed by. These six men had at
that moment an object before them to move the curiosity and reverence of every common mortal. Ellacombe is a very short man, very much bowed by age,
with a white beard reaching half way to the ground,
a beaming countenance, a pair of bright eyes, and a
good, clear, ringing voice. He was in his own sacred
ground. Of course he was surprised, as I was, at their
repelling so rudely an aged man's courtesy, but we
had no occasion to be hurt, for if they had met a
company of angels, they would have done just the

same. I cannot even guess whether they were Roman Catholics or Anglican imitators.

Ellacombe had had a great sorrow, for which his own generous aspirations and high standard of duty might be held accountable. He had had to learn that counsels of perfection, and the sense of a Divine call, may clash with common routine, and even with engagements, and may do that with sad results. Yet, after the lapse of many years, he still regarded with unabated affection and respect the preacher to whose exaggerated tone, as he felt it, he owed what had befallen him.

One could not be in Ellacombe's company five minutes without learning something worth knowing, and in a distinct and positive form. What a loss it is that there are not the men to rescue these accumulations of knowledge before they sink into the grave where all things are forgotten. But the aged only speak as one memory raises another, and you may not catch the fish you have baited your hook for.

Ellacombe was undergraduate for some time, if not all his time, under Provost Eveleigh. A certain vague college tradition ascribed to the joint efforts of Eveleigh and Coplestone the elevation of the college from a state of mediocrity, in which it lay till the end of last century. A long time ago there chanced to be a majority of Welshmen in the college, and the clan feeling was so strong as to make Oriel the Welsh college, as Jesus College has since been, without even as good results. Yet there was something to account for in the combination of two such men as Eveleigh and Coplestone. I never heard of anything that the former said or did out of the way ; whereas the latter was the most substantial and majestic and, if I may so say, richly-coloured character within my know-ledge of Oxford.   How could they work together on anything like parity of condition ?   But what had most moved my curiosity was that in my village and neighbourhood were many Eveleighs and that they showed a very strong family likeness to the portrait of the Provost.   The Eveleighs have all fair complexions and light hair ; they are mild, inoffen-sive, and unambitious.   There are yeomen and trades-men bearing the name, but all have the family features. They are all strangely fond of light blue.   The school children of the name—boys and girls—were sure to have blue about them, and I could not pass their cottages without seeing a blue rag on the road. Meeting a carpenter of the name in a neighbouring village, a jolly fellow of near seventy, I asked him about his relatives, and observed how fond they all were of light blue.   He replied he had never heard that said before, and had never noticed it.   I replied, ‘ Why, you’ve got a light blue neckcloth on yourself.’ At which, with a laugh, he succumbed.   I took the opportunity to ask Ellacombe what he remembered of his first Provost.   It was immediately clear that Eveleigh had left no strong or distinct impression on his memory.   This is what I should have expected. All he could mention was a line in some humorous verses by an undergraduate, describing the Heads of Houses, ‘ Here comes fair Eveleigh with his blue hose.’ This at once established his relationship.   Within memory a Miss Eveleigh, a lady, resided in Plymtree.

From another quarter I have heard that the Provost was shy of naming his birthplace. He used to say his family came from the North of Devon. No doubt they did, for the hamlet so named is there. Mr. Walkey, the Rector of Clyst St. Laurence, near Plymtree, had a servant of the name. He said to him, 'Don't you know, John, you've got a coat of arms?' John asked what it was, and whether it was worth anything, for he should be ready at once to turn it to account.

CHAPTER XI.

JAMES ENDELL TYLER.

JAMES ENDELL TYLER was so striking and so essential a picture of the college that he cannot be omitted, though at Oriel he was only a vivid memory when the movement began. His florid figure, florid address, and florid style, made him the centre of observation. As an undergraduate he had been Whately's contemporary and friend, and there were stories of their rustic appearance at a time when provincial fashion was more marked than it is now, and showed itself in colour as much as in cut. By the time Newman had taken Jelf's place in the tuition, Tyler was Coplestone's right-hand man. He was not a reformer of Churches or of creeds, but he was an able and effective lecturer. He was no genius, it used to be

said, but he could construe Thucydides 'through a
deal board.' He was on very good terms with most
of the undergraduates. His special fondness, however, was reserved for the Gentlemen Commoners,
above all for one 'dear boy,' who in after life became
the pet of the world, and who was probably indebted
to Tyler for no small part of his spoiling. This was
Charles A. Murray. Possibly a life-long devotion to
the memory of Henry V., native of his own town of
Monmouth, and member of his own college of Oriel,
may have implanted in his mind a deep veneration
for the noble and the gentle.

For eight or nine years Tyler held what was then
the perpetual curacy of Moreton Pinckney, in an out-
of-the-way part of Northamptonshire, near Canons'
Ashby, the seat of the Dryden family. He used to
run down there for a few weeks at a time, roughing it
as to accommodation, and making his presence felt
and appreciated by the primitive and half-gipsy
people. He would take down with him occasionally
some of his young Oriel friends, whose respective
statures, distinguished by their initials, remained many
years on the inside of a closet door. Some of these
men rose high in Church and State, and must often
have found recollections of a state of things rapidly
giving way to the ubiquitous and monotonous railway intruding upon them in the busiest seasons and
the most critical occasions.

Tyler left behind many marks of the interest he
took in the people and the place. I frequently came
on lists of classes he had had for instruction. He
had surmounted every gable in the church with a

stone cross, and had also put one on the stone ledge behind the altar, darkening the wall behind to give it prominence. A wretched old Quaker, surviving like a raven in the village, told me that had he been a younger man he would have pelted the out-door ones till he brought them down. Tyler had also added considerably to the old parsonage, no better than a labourer's cottage when he found it ; but for this his successors had to pay their share.

He had once had a singular mishap. He rode down upon an Oxford hack that had a trick of twisting its head about in such a way as to strangulate itself unless the halter was tied in one particular fashion. Arriving at Moreton Pinckney, and finding an invitation to Canons' Ashby, he availed himself of the poor beast to ride to dinner. He took good care to go into the stable and tie the halter with his own hands, as he had been directed. At ten the bell was rung for his horse, and was answered, ' If you please, sir, your horse is dead.' A groom had come into the stables, and seeing a halter tied in what he thought a bungling fashion, had set it right, and thereby enabled the animal to destroy itself. The unlucky hirer had to present himself at the livery stables on Monday morning with an empty saddle and bridle.

Tyler had a somewhat higher estimate of his position as Dean than was warranted by usage, or by the actual powers of the office. Perhaps he thought that with so great a man as Coplestone in the Provostship, even a second was as good as other firsts. He had to write a note to Gaisford, who, receiving it in company, read aloud, ' The Dean of Oriel presents his compliments to the Dean of Christ Church,' adding ' Alexander the coppersmith sendeth greeting to Alexander the Great.' This soon reached Tyler.

On the rare occasions on which he occupied the university pulpit, all the college went to hear him, even those who usually held loose to that obligation. He preached a now famous sermon on Naaman, the Syrian captain. Tyler was accused of conniving too openly at a pack of beagles kept chiefly by the Oriel noblemen and gentleman commoners, and this pack, it is hard to say why, had acquired the nickname of Gehazi. It was kept at Garsington, and as many mistakes were made in the spelling and pronunciation of the word, undergraduates hit at last on the common term of Gehazi, which was more easy to remember. Tyler must have known of the nickname. It may even have suggested his text. When the thread of the discourse passed from the prophet to his knavish servant, there ensued a great deal of tittering in the gallery at every occurrence of the familiar name.

Tyler preached the sermon in town. Lord Liverpool heard it, and was so pleased with the preacher, whose vigorous and energetic appearance went for as much as the sermon itself, that he presented him to the rectory of St. Giles-in-the-Fields. It was thought great promotion. Tyler accepted it at once, and thereby, to his long sorrow, lost his chance of the Provostship, which became vacant within a twelve-month.

His work in his new sphere was so appreciated that his parishioners did whatever he asked for. They

had to name a broad new street running from High
Holborn to the Covent Garden district, now a very
important and handsome thoroughfare. It passed
through the part where Tyler might be seen any day
or hour on his way from one parochial institution to
another ; and they wished to call it Tyler Street. It
was his modesty or some personal affection that
prompted the substitution of Endell Street. It is to
be hoped that the prebendal stall at St. Paul's, to
which he was at last presented, consoled him for
the loss of the Provostship, for which he would
gladly have given, so he is said to have declared,
all he possessed in the world.

CHAPTER XII.

HARTLEY COLERIDGE.

A REMARKABLE episode of Oriel history naturally
connects itself with Tyler. Entering heartily into the
new idea of collecting at Oriel the most interesting
and most promising elements of English society, he
was much pleased at the election of Hartley Coleridge.
This very singular being was son of Samuel Taylor
Coleridge, and cousin and contemporary of the late
Sir John Coleridge. He took his degree with high
honours in 1811, and it was possibly a mutual re-
silience between him and people of more orderly ways

that prevented him from standing at Oriel till some
years after. Tyler knew that the poor man, besides
constitutional weakness, was very eccentric, and he
was prepared to bear something.

Hartley Coleridge was of course fully aware that
he was on his trial for the first year, and that he had
to prove himself companionable and sufficiently
regular in his habits and ways. For six months, the
amount of residence required, this could be no great
strain. However, it proved too much for Hartley
Coleridge. He would not dress for dinner; he smelt
sadly of tobacco, and, indeed, was known to be
smoking all day. It was evident that he cared
little for the society of the Fellows, and it was known
that he was on freer terms than etiquette allows
with the people at his lodgings. He preferred
natural life to artificial. There was a certain drollery
about him which prevented these peculiarities from
being regarded as mere weaknesses. Being told one
day in the common room that he could not have
shaved for a whole week, he presented himself unmistakably shaven and shorn the next day. He
was then absent from the common room for a week,
in spite of repeated summons. He then reappeared
with such a growth on his face as clearly proved the
former charge of a week's neglect to have been a
gross exaggeration. The worst was that a glass too
much—nothing with a stronger man, or with a man of
less mercurial temperament—upset him altogether.

Sad stories reached Tyler, but he resolutely
closed his ears. If Coleridge could only hold out
decently, so at least as to elude absolute detection,

Tyler's generous nature would have been satisfied,
for he then would have handed him over to his
friends, and allowed him to choose his own associates,
remaining Fellow of Oriel. But Coleridge was not
the man to calculate consequences. He lived just
for the day, and no more. He got worse and worse.

Tyler found at last the case was hopeless, and he
either had a most wonderful vision, or he invented
one, to cover his retreat from an untenable position.
Perhaps the truth lies midway, and he had only
caught a whiff of poor Hartley's own dreamy temperament.

Midway on his ride home from a Sunday visit
to his Northamptonshire parish, at a point of the
road well known to Oriel men, suddenly road, hedge-
row, trees, and cottages disappeared, and he found
himself in Oriel Lane. A man lay in the gutter. It
was —— Tyler had steadily refused to believe
idle gossip, but there could now be no doubt of the
sad fact.

When Easter came the college and the probationer had arrived at the only possible conclusion—
that they were not likely to get on well together ; and
they parted good friends. It is a melancholy story,
and it is impossible not to ask whether the poor
youth might not have been saved by some friendly
and wise intervention. Perhaps the attempt was
made ; indeed, Tyler himself was the man to speak
at once kindly and strongly to anyone plainly in need
of guidance ; but it must be said that the wayward and
eccentric must and will take their own course, and
a university is sure to have a good many such men.

CHAPTER XIII.

THE VICARAGE OF TWERTON.

TYLER represented the ordinary fair and generous ambition which is a first step to the improvement of men and of institutions, whatever special form that ambition may finally assume. In his time the college was like some uncanny thing—say a cockatrice—the still undeveloped product of a long and restless incubation, unable to break its shell. Energy was flowing into it from various quarters, for besides its communication with Holland House, both the system of open fellowships and the careful selection of undergraduates attracted force.

But the college itself—the buildings as well as the men—was hidebound and shut in. It looked out on its principal approach, Oriel Lane, one of the narrowest and darkest in Oxford, on the slovenly and unfinished back buildings of Peckwater ; on the Provost's stables and offices, which could not be removed, for they were all that he had ; over a very narrow lane, on Corpus ; and on Magpie Lane, occupied by the college servants. But the north was the hopeful and debatable frontier. As common lay Englishmen understand law and equity, there could not be a doubt that St. Mary Hall was an appendage of Oriel ; indeed, some said the college was the appendage, for that St. Mary Hall was the origin and nucleus of the college. It was once proposed in the

common room to take the fire-irons and batter a hole
through the wall into St. Mary Hall, when they might
enter in a body and take possession. 'Johnnie
Dean,' the Principal of the Hall, was often threatened
with forcible entry. That, however, he took very
easily, for the maxim of his life, as appears by the
result, was 'After me the deluge.' The college had
thus no garden ; not space to add a single room, and
not much to be seen from the windows. Merton
College Chapel was a grand but a very noisy neighbour. Its big bells at certain times called a parish
which no longer existed to a service which was no
longer performed. In fact they did nothing but
disturb Tyler's very useful lectures and very good
temper. Its four weathercocks were creaking all
night, as bad as those which disturbed the sleep of
poor Catherine of Arragon as she lay in the Deanery
at Exeter, and which the Mayor of Exeter received
orders next morning to oil.

But in a still more important respect was Oriel
sadly handicapped for the race it had to run. Collecting and training the minds that were to control
the course of human affairs, it had no posts or outlets
for them except a dozen livings which were not only
divisible into poor, poorer, and poorest, but lay in the
most out-of-the-way places, far from the haunts of
fashion and the centres of thought. While fanatics
of any newly-invented dogma were busily securing
the seats of trade, the resorts of pleasure, and the
springs of health, the men of real thought were to be
banished to Salisbury Plain, to unknown villages
buried in dairies, orchards, and grazing-grounds, or

surrounded by fens ; purely agricultural, or barely relieved with some mechanic industry.

Could Oriel but tap the greater and higher world !
An opportunity offered.   There must have been some
very good years, for about 1824 the college. found
itself in possession of 4,000*l.*, to do what it liked with.
The living of Twerton was in the market.   Mr. Spencer
Madan, the incumbent, though a young man, was
dying, and neither the Provost nor Tyler, well informed
as they were generally, seems to have been aware that
the incumbent of a living on sale always is dying and
remains in a dying condition till the living is sold,
when he takes a new lease of his life, generally a long
one.   Twerton was described as an agricultural suburb
of Bath, pleasantly situated on the banks of the Avon,
twenty minutes' walk from the Pump Room and the
Abbey, combining town and country, and offering the
choice of a social and a literary career.   Should the
incumbent be a preacher as well as a pastor, his light
would not be hid under a bushel.

Bath was a more fashionable place sixty years ago
than it is now, when the railway has opened so many
other resorts more attractive to the young and enter-
prising.   The Duncans of New College, great men in
Oxford of those days, were of Bath.   Hampden had
Bath connections.   Devonshire and Wales were then
well represented at Oriel, and both those regions to
this day look with much respect on Bath, as being up
the country and quite in England.   The *genius loci* was
in favour of movements, at least supposed to be, for
it was at Bath that all last century His Majesty's
Opposition passed the winter to prepare for the next

Parliamentary campaign. Alas! *Fuit* Bath ; but it was still living in those days.

The bargain was concluded, and Oriel became the fortunate possessor of the living of Twerton. Soon did the illusion fade, and facts present themselves. Spencer Madan was reported in robust health, with every sign of longevity. In three or four years the college had notice of a railway that was to run right through the parsonage. This involved a new parsonage and a new glebe. The company offered 4,000*l.*, which would be handsome under ordinary circumstances, but there was a just apprehension that it might be insufficient in this case. Twerton occupies a rather narrow slip between the river and the hillside, and of this slip the railway would consume no inconsiderable part, thereby enhancing the value of the remainder.

In much trepidation it was resolved to send one of the Fellows to look about him and report. Charles P. Eden volunteered, and went down with a budget of cautions and instructions. Making immediate inquiries for some one who could acquaint him with all the circumstances, he had the good fortune to obtain an introduction to a very competent person, to whom he disclosed the whole case of the college. It was not till after several days that he discovered it was the local agent of the company he had taken into his confidence. The offer was accepted, and a moderate parsonage built at what was then the extremity of the ' village.' By and by there came another railway through the glebe, involving a claim for compensation.

For years Twerton was a matter for consultation and negotiation. The Great Western—for that was the first railway—came between the parsonage and the river. It brought factories and a population; Twerton rapidly improved in everything except the value of the living, which was fixed by the Commutation Act. The incumbent, if he did his duty at all, would have no time for walks into Bath, or for pulpit and platform demonstrations there. The living did not become vacant till the year 1852. At a moderate calculation of interest it had cost the college by that time not less than 12,000*l.*

Not a Fellow would take the living, with all its local charms and splendid opportunities. In the course of a generation Bath had somewhat receded in fashion, and Twerton had become a small manufacturing town, swarming with poverty and dissent. The Provost, clinging perhaps to the last plank of the old crazy speculation, but anyhow guided by a right instinct, and with a very happy result, persuaded his brother-in-law to reconsider his objections and take the living.

Buckle laboured there a quarter of a century, making excellent work, and earning a name for Twerton. But when, three or four years ago, he took a somewhat less laborious charge at Weston-super-Mare, the college, on public grounds, filled the vacancy with his meritorious curate.

Such was the commercial result of the investment, by a college which at present has not a pound to spare on its dilapidated buildings. Providence, that ordains all things for the best, has taken Twerton out of the hands of Simon Magus and his crew, and placed it in the care of conscientious and honourable patrons ; but it has not become, as was hoped for, the happy means of introducing Oriel's choicest spirits and special influences to the great world.

CHAPTER XIV.

TYLER'S TESTIMONIAL.

As soon as it was known that Tyler was going to St. Giles', it was taken for granted there must be a testimonial, which no man deserved better. The circle of noblemen and gentlemen commoners at once took the initiative. They had for their leader a man who, from first to last, was always great in small affairs—Norman Hilton Macdonald. They appointed a committee of themselves, drew up a suitable statement, and resolved on a service of dinner plate, which no one was so competent to select as Macdonald.

Having done all this, they invited the college to a meeting in the hall, and laid the matter before them. Phillpotts, a son of Henry of Exeter, and afterwards Archdeacon of Cornwall, came forward and spoke with characteristic plainness of the unwarrantably exclusive form and manner of the action taken by one small section of the college, who had no more interest in Tyler than the others and who could not more like

him and respect him than they did. It was, he
said, the very worst compliment they could pay him,
for it suggested the thought that Tyler had cared for
gold tufts and silk gowns more than for the college
generally. He waxed warm as he spoke, and rather
startled the freshmen, who had thought it was so
much a thing of course that the big men they saw dining
with the Fellows at High Table should take the lead,
since a lead must be taken.

The gentlemen commoners assumed an apologetic
tone ; pleaded something like a necessity ; and hoped
that the honourable jealousy now displayed would
show itself in the subscription. It did; but a sore
remained, and something more than a sore, for to this
day old Oriel men will remember Tyler and his high-
born or wealthy young friends. It is only justice to
the gentlemen commoners on this occasion to state the
simple fact that they were in a difficulty. The commoners had no circle of a representative character.
There were nobodies, and there were somebodies ;
there were good men and reading men ; there were
some strong individualities, and there were a few who,
for one reason or another, naturally attached themselves to the silk gowns—Samuel Wilberforce, for
example.

But among the commoners there was only one
circle of any numbers or prominence, and it was
of an exceptional, and therefore not representative
character. This was the 'Family.' It met every
night at the 'Bar,' which was said to be well supplied
with Scotch ale on tap, and whisky. The habitual
members were about a dozen including two sons of

Church dignitaries, several other sons of clergymen, a son of Sir Walter Scott, and a distant relation of the Provost, so I believe he was. Among these were good talkers and good listeners ; men of wit not always under just control, and men with some experience of public or high social life. Perhaps the literary and the philosophical elements were deficient. The meetings fell naturally into the class of *Noctes Ambrosianœ*, which I suppose implies a certain genial abandonment. There was an incessant flow of conversation in a good-natured tone, and the voices multiplied as the evening went on, indeed sometimes it was a Babel of sounds. There must have been more talkers than listeners.

For more than a year I was a Peri at the gate of this Paradise, for my rooms were on the same floor, and our doors opposite, about two yards apart. Most nights I was waked up out of my first sleep by the breaking up of this assembly. Yet I feel I had no reason to complain of my cheerful and lively neighbours. No doubt it was a great resource to some of the men, who might have found it hard to do anything better in the evening. Some of them have passed away, after lives of incessant struggling with scanty means in remote situations, with no society or support, spending the little money they had in church restorations, and getting into trouble with their parishioners on trifles of the hour. Such a club, for a club it really was, forfeited power and influence by its exclusiveness. It lived for itself, and could do nothing. The gentlemen commoners, on the contrary, had an open formation, and could not be called a close circle. So they naturally took the lead now, and did everything.

I should have let the 'Family' pass as one of the *arcana* of college life, did I not now look on it much more leniently and sympathetically than I then did, and attach to it an important bearing. If the college system is to be abolished, the Heads deprived of all power, the Tutors hustled out of work and out of the scene, and the university reduced to a mob of undergraduates and a crowd of professors, the vacant ground will possibly be occupied by private coaches and private tutors, and by combinations really deserving the name of families. Some organisation there will be, spontaneous if not authorised, and a time will certainly come when they that urge the present changes will witness the operation of the universal law, that a system once established does not follow the will of its authors, but takes a course of its own, and is, indeed, bound to adapt itself to the incessant change of circumstances.

In the matter of the testimonial the gentlemen commoners acted as they did in default of any other possible lead. They might have done better, which is much the same as may be said of all human action ; but upon the whole the event amply justified them.

Macdonald was necessarily a personage and a leader everywhere and in every stage. He was a very big, imposing, solemn fellow at Charterhouse. When in the first form, or sixth form as it is elsewhere called, not a dozen places from the top, Russell one day asked him his age. He drew himself up to his full height, which must have been six feet, and

said ' fifteen.'   Russell's expression was that of incre-
dulity rather than surprise, yet at any time of his life
Macdonald could easily have been supposed a good
deal younger than he looked. His father rode habitu-
ally in the Park a white charger that was said to
have brought a dozen bullets from Waterloo, and
when the animal died at last, there was a story that the
belief was found to be not quite without a foundation.

Macdonald was an imposing and constant figure
in the Union, making speeches so absurdly pompous
that they could not have been tolerable but for his
prestige, and a certain consciousness that he kept the
ball going.   Henry Wilberforce, early in his day,
used to rise in reply, too full of humour, for he could
do nothing but laugh at his own jokes before he
had developed them to his hearers.   His gusty mirth
and his broken phrases dashed like spray on the huge
rock before him and fell harmless, for Macdonald
was the last to see the point of them.

Macdonald became, almost as a matter of course,
a Fellow of All Souls, whence, at a University election or a Convocation, he would step over in his
dressing-gown and slippers, throw a Master's gown
over his shoulders, and give his vote, a perfect study
of indolence and indifference.   He held something
in the Foreign Office ; he accumulated a vast quantity of curiosities and bric-a-brac ; he had a very large
fashionable acquaintance, became enormously stout,
and was nicknamed ' Chaos,' as being without form
and void.   Void he was not, for he had an immense
knowledge of men and things, and without a good
deal of that knowledge the world cannot get on.

CHAPTER XV.

THE WILBERFORCES.

THE Wilberforces were the largest and the most interesting family group in this history. They brought
a great name, and also the name of a great party, for
William Wilberforce was the brightest star in the
Evangelical firmament. As the title of Evangelical
is one of the highest honour, except when monopo-
lised by a party or otherwise misapplied, it can only
be used with a continual protest in these pages. Such
a party, however, there was, and greatly did it stand
in need of the adventitious yet useful lustre of the
accomplishments which education and society can
give or improve. This was especially the case at
Oxford, indeed to an extent which amounts to a positive mystery. The Evangelical party there could not
show a single man who combined scholarship, intellect, and address in a considerable degree. The
public school men might not be anything else, but
they were not 'Evangelical.' Good men, and men
of good families, came from Scotland, and were of
course a little that way of thinking. If they had
brains, and a strong *physique*, they made their way, if
not they dwindled or retired. Oriel men of that
date must remember William Colquhoun, a fair and
promising lad, who tried one term, then another, but
proved incurably home-sick and went home. My
recollection of him is that he was always sitting at
his open window looking at the sky, which in his case
was eastward.

All watched with interest the course of the three already famous brothers. The result at this day is that Robert and Henry are both numbered by the Evangelical world among Newman's victims, while Samuel is partly admired, partly pitied, as a brand plucked from the burning, but with the smell of the burning strong upon him. No party in the Church claims him very decidedly, or would quote his authority upon any crucial question.

The real fact is that all three were already in a state of gradually increasing estrangement from the Evangelical party when they came to Oxford. True they were not of the High Church of that day, or of any other party, if there were any, for they knew little of the High Church, and that little could not be attractive. A long and bitter controversy with Theodore Williams, of Hendon, and weekly jests in the 'John Bull' newspaper, constituted nearly all their experience in the High Church direction.

It may seem absurd to name Theodore Williams, who was not only a very cantankerous but also a very ridiculous person, in any religious reckoning. Theodore was, however, a remarkably handsome man, with a most dignified manner, and he could be very gracious even to a stranger coming to him, cap in hand, to look into his church, or to ask a question his library could answer, for he was a fine scholar. He had all the metropolitan clergy on his side, for he contended against the right of anybody professing to be a churchman to assemble more than twenty worshippers over and above his own family, not being duly

ordained, instituted, or licensed, or placed under a
bishop or an incumbent.

The controversy with this champion of the Church
was twofold, or rather in two stages. It began in
the very great and natural desire of some of Mr.
Wilberforce's neighbours, rich or poor, to join his
family worship. This would generally mean his
Sunday worship. His morning and even evening week-
day worship—that is when the latter was possible—
was quite as long as that provided by the Prayer
Book, consisting of Psalms, a hymn, a portion of
Scripture, and a most eloquent extempore exposition.
Such a service, so conducted, must be supposed to
have had a great share in the education of his
children.

That it was possible to become weary of it is no
more than may be said of many good things. The
old butler took to absenting himself, first frequently,
then entirely. His master had that opinion of him
that he feared there was some serious spiritual impediment, and asked very tenderly why he could not
join family worship. The butler put himself into an
attitude, and said he looked into his Bible and found
written, ' To your tents, O Israel.' The master for
once was taken aback, or possibly thought it best not
to repeat what followed. Henry Wilberforce was of
opinion that it had something to do with tent beds.

The Sunday services would be longer and probably
more formal. It became known that outsiders, to
more than twenty head, or souls, as they are usually
called in this matter, were attending. Then began a
long, angry, and even scandalous attack, which ended

in some one having to count heads, and intimate to the twenty-first that he was one too many. It was succeeded by the project of a new chapel, and this was warmly debated at boards, in newspapers, and at all the religious houses of whatever side in London, and the country also. A chapel was built at last, but it could hardly have been before Mr. Wilberforce was leaving Highwood and becoming a wanderer. It must be borne in mind that the Church of England, particularly as represented by the High Church and by ecclesiastical dignitaries, was in those days one of the ' interests ' of the country. All those ' interests ' clung together, and made a common cause. The West Indian interest, the East Indian, and every other interest with the least monopoly or protection ; land-owners, boroughmongers, sine-curists—all were as one, and old Mr. Wilberforce, besides other liberal tendencies, had put himself in the front of the attacks upon two of these interests, slavery, and the monopoly of souls.

On the other hand, the Wilberforces had had a large experience of the Low Church, as it was called. First, they had had experience of many private tutors, and it was a very mixed experience. Some of these men, whatever their other qualifications, were not scholars, or men of common sense, or even quite gentlemen, or even honest in the sense necessary for the fulfilment of a positive and very important contract. Of the best of them the Wilberforces said that, after spending the whole day in his parish, and returning to a late dinner, he would take them just from nine to ten, when both he and they were good for nothing but bed. A scrambling lesson at any odd hour was the common rule. Robert's industry enabled him to surmount any difficulties, and he was his own teacher, but Samuel and Henry both found themselves very ill prepared in scholarship when they came to Oxford. Samuel was not the man to own this, or even to admit to himself that he was inferior to others in any respect; but it was plain to others, and in effect he never became a good scholar. He may now be placed by the side of Cobden, Bright, and many others as a proof that a man may be a great orator and a respectable administrator without being a scholar. But these clergymen had been engaged to make the young Wilberforces scholars as well as good Christians, and the pupils felt themselves and their father ill-used. Upon the whole, though perhaps an Etonian would say that he detected more than a want of high scholarship in the Wilberforces, it is difficult to deny that they stand to the account in favour of private education; even though they suffered their full share of its proverbial risks and mishaps.

Again, by the time the three sons were emerging from boyhood, the father was a man of broken health and strength, diminished means, almost out of the political world, a noble wreck and no more. He was no longer good for anything in the world's scale, and though he happily lived in heaven himself, his sons had not yet been educated to absolute resignation. Pitt had offered Wilberforce a peerage. It would have involved a good pecuniary provision of some sort, with the corresponding duty of a general support,

which Wilberforce was too conscientious to promise.
Had he promised it, Pitt's death would have set him
free while still young, and in possession of extraordinary powers, unequalled social charm, and the
most conciliatory manners. He would have been an
important member in a Ministry, perhaps Premier.
There were several instances of less men, within less
time, becoming marquises, in which case it would
have been ' Lord Samuel ' and ' Lord Henry.'

These were but poor imaginings, but when these
young men came to Oxford they found a great deal
to impress upon them that they had dropped far
below the level at which their father had gone to
Cambridge and entered public life. At this they
repined not, for they had the heritage of a name and
of a nature better than land or money ; but it also
brought before them the usage their father had received
from his religious friends. These people had always
been at him for some end of their own, and he could
hardly see anyone requesting an interview, or answer
a letter, without finding himself the worse off by a
round sum of money. At the sale of his effects,
when the family expected that the apparently large
library would be an appreciable item in the proceeds,
it was found that its bulk was very much owing to
tens and twenties, and even fifties of books of
sermons, poems, and devotional works that he had
been pressed to subscribe for and had never opened.
He had now been used, used up, and thrown away.

This may seem to ascribe to the Wilberforces
something of bitterness approaching to disappointment. It is not intended. The three Oriel brothers

had unquenchable spirits. They were always ready, both from principle and feeling to demand fair play for anyone professing a religious character. At Henry's rooms I frequently met the sons of clergymen and others well known in the religious world, and now recurring in religious biographies. One of them, who, as an undergraduate, was remarkable for pretension, foppery, and utter emptiness, died not long ago, and was described in a religious paper as one of the last survivors of the old school of truly pious clergy. He would have to undergo a great change before he deserved that character.

Facts, it is often said, are stubborn things, and, as a matter of fact, the Wilberforces found themselves moving adrift from the world they had belonged to. They had lived in large houses, abundant hospitalities, political and religious gatherings, and now they really were nowhere. Nobody knows what it is to lose such things but they that have lost them. ' The great use of a country house,' Henry would sometimes say, ' is to stow away things you cannot carry about with you, and do not want to destroy.' But what are these things ? They are the material making of a family— collections of letters, relics, heirlooms, portraits, ornaments, mementos of persons and events.

The truth is, both Robert and Henry Wilberforce were so without ambition in any practical form, that their friends out of Oxford used to urge upon them the duty of aspiring to higher society than chance or routine brought them at Oriel. Robert's very quiet and studious ways would be naturally proof against any such stimulus. Henry's nature was so little in

harmony with it that, on his return to college after a
vacation, he divulged at once with much simplicity the
exhortation he had received to go out of his college in
quest of better company than he found in it. He
said enough to give a little offence, but did no more.
At the end of that term he asked me to pay his
father a visit, and I declined, suggesting that I might
be better able another day. The next invitation came
in a more serious form in a letter from Bath, where
Henry was attending on his father. I was then tied
to my Northamptonshire parish and could not leave
it. It was a real concern to me that I could not com-
ply with the summons, because I had seen the father
at Oxford in a very helpless state a year or two before, and I knew Henry wanted some one with him.
It was only two or three weeks after that Henry
brought his father up to town, to die in a few days,
with no one else about him.

Culling Eardley Smith was then at Oriel, very
much the same ridiculous personage he always was,
and a flagrant tuft-hunter. He availed himself of his
high connections to cultivate Christ Church society,
and thereby got into a scrape. It is, or at least was,
usual for undergraduates to draw upon one another's
' battles' to meet the extra demands of a breakfast or
a lunch. But this could only be done when there was
a perfect understanding, and when a man was quite
sure that his friend would not want his ' battles.' An
undergraduate entering his room at breakfast or lunch
time, and finding that his 'battles' had gone elsewhere
to an entertainment to which he was not himself invited, naturally resented what was an injury as well

as a slight. There might be occasional mistakes and oversights, and, upon the whole, undergraduates are a forgiving race, squabbling like brothers and sisters, and shaking hands again. Culling Eardley Smith made this a regular practice, and, while showing his contempt for the country gentlemen's sons of his own college, was entertaining his grander out-college acquaintances at their expense. So one evening, when he had gone to a supper at Christ Church, the outraged gentlemen commoners of his own college entered his handsomely-furnished rooms, destroyed every article of furniture in them, heaped the fragments in the Quad, and, it was positively stated at the time, waylaid the owner, and left him for some hours tied up in a sack on the wreck of his own property. Somehow or other S. Wilberforce's name was prominently associated with this act of public justice—whether as instigating, aiding, or abetting, or simply conniving, was not very clear. If he did not enjoy the joke, he was the only man in college besides the sufferer who did not.

It may seem strange that so great and powerful a party, containing at least the most popular preachers and religious writers of the day, had none to lead them in their day of visitation. Newman was most loyal to his own early associations. I remember his speaking to me with pain of Pusey not being able to swallow a college lecturer of that school, a good man and an able man, and showing an unwillingness to be thrown into his company. My own wonder was, not that Pusey could not feel at home with him, but that Newman could.

It must be added that the Evangelical party was undergoing a rapid decomposition. Robert and Samuel Wilberforce had been seeing a good deal of Macaulay, who even then talked incessantly as nobody else could talk, and who had written off his article on Milton as fast as his pen could carry him. Macaulay had described to them his father Zachary's extreme disappointment when he declined the important service for which he had been destined and educated, the long desired Index of the 'Missionary Register,' or whatever the name of the father's periodical. Macaulay had also told them that there were not two hundred men in London who believed in the Bible. The Wilberforces were also acquainted with Gisborne, who, out of the same school, had emerged into the same freedom. Whatever speculative faith the 'Evangelicals' of that period had in their theory of salvation, their highest success generally was to make their sons clever men of the world.

CHAPTER XVI.

MR. WILBERFORCE AND SIR JAMES STEPHEN.

BUT there was something more. It will be contradicted, for it has been contradicted, but it must be said in the face of contradiction. Mr. Wilberforce, the father, was not so entirely without a sense of humour as some of his friends would have him. In his various religious and philanthropic operations, particularly as his basis was rather a broad one, he came in contact with a good many queer people, and with many queer things. In his own family circle he would frequently raise a smile by the seeming *naïveté* with which he described them. The smile and the cause of it stuck to the young memories about him closer than the matter and the men. All the four Wilberforces had abundance of humour, and they certainly did not get it from their mother, good woman as she was—in her way.

I said something to this effect, now many years ago, to a friend of the late Sir James Stephen, and, upon it being repeated to him, he took it up with exceeding wrath. It was utterly impossible, he said, that Wilberforce could smile at any of his friends. It was not likely he would smile at Sir James Stephen. But Sir James could hardly have maintained that all the hundreds and thousands of persons who got access to Wilberforce, generally for some little wants of their own, were as awful personages as himself. Again, there are smiles and smiles, and there are people who do not recognise a smile. Indeed, there are many smiles that address themselves to one order of intelligence and not to another.

Thus, in the late Bishop of Winchester's diary of October 16, 1858, are notes of a conversation at Haddo, in which the following is ascribed to Lord Aberdeen :—' I think *most highly* of James Stephen. He is a very first-rate man, and the most unpopular in Europe. I do not quite know why. Perhaps some-

thing in his treatment of inferiors was the cause. I
was never in that relation to him. I stood in the relation of an admiring master. His papers on the
Laws of the Colonies were admirable digests.' Now,
is there, or is there not, a smile in such commendation,
at once so high and so qualified in the very direction
in which Sir James Stephen himself would have wished
it unqualified ?

Certainly the Wilberforces had a good many
amusing stories of the persons their father had to deal
with, and of the meetings he attended and took a
part in.

These stories I cannot now recall. Perhaps I did
not pay much attention to them. I do remember
hearing several times of a plump, greasy little Dissenting minister, who was always invading the poor
old gentleman at the most inconvenient days and hours,
making long solemn speeches, and expecting the
whole stream of Mr. Wilberforce's time, interest, influence, and resources to flow through his own particular channel. One story has clung to my memory
because I have always suspected the incident described
to have been the outcome of some mischievous practice upon native credulity. At a great meeting a very
solemn missionary related his entrance into an African
city. It seemed almost deserted, but he was directed
to the market-place. There he found the whole population assembled, the army drawn out, the king, the
court, and the priests in the midst. There was a
hideous noise ; then silence. At a signal all fell
prostrate. The missionary was just able to distinguish the object of this awful act of adoration. It

was a cannon ball and three decanter-stoppers. The whole meeting burst into a roar of laughter. They had prepared their minds for a massacre, or at least some hideous idol, and the rebound was too much for them.

But it is impossible to look at the face in the familiar portrait, or at its reproduction in Westminster Abbey, without seeing that there is humour there, and that it must have found a vent somewhere.

The Wilberforces started with the immense and very rare advantage of perfect confidence and openness with their father. He was the joy of their life and the light of their eyes. Visitors have described, as the most beautiful sight they ever witnessed, the four young Wilberforces stretching out their necks one in advance of the other, to catch every word of the father's conversation, and note every change in his most expressive countenance. On such terms was he with them that a stranger might have thought their love and respect admitted of some improvement by a slight admixture of fear.

Sir James Stephen, who so warmly defended Mr. Wilberforce from the imputation of too much playfulness, I met several times, and I only wish I had met him earlier and oftener. With the care of near fifty Colonies always upon him, he could not have had much spare time for personal recollections ; but he might have told me something about old Wilberforce. When I did meet him he was expressing himself very strongly against all religious endowments. That this stern condemnation did not extend to other endowments he proved not long after by obtaining from Government the Professorship of Modern History, to the great disappointment of several resident Cambridge candidates.

Sir James was well known to have a temper, and to show it. I think I put it rightly when I say that Gladstone made Sir Frederick Rogers a second Under-Secretary in the Colonial Office, on the ground that a lawyer was wanted in the department. Sir James resented the imputation on his own career, and watched for his opportunity. An Indian judge sent home word that he desired to be relieved of his office, but would wait for the arrival of his successor. A successor was appointed and sent out, Sir F. Rogers, I know not why, being responsible for the regularity of the proceeding. It seemed to be quite safe because he was following the precedents. Sir James Stephen immediately made the discovery that the appointment was invalid, inasmuch as the Act prescribed that the successor could not be appointed till the place was actually vacant—a discovery he had never made before.

Upon the cessation of his long and laborious career, Sir James visited Rome for the first time in his life. Whoever wishes to see Rome should go there at once, for every year diminishes the power of mastering it. I came on Sir James as he was gazing most intently on the pilgrims crawling up the Scala Santa on their knees. He certainly looked as if he much wished to do the right thing if he could, and in the full belief that up these very steps our Lord ascended to the Prætorium. At least he was realising the fact that these steps had been so credited and so used for many centuries.

That evening a friend took me to his apartment,

It was soon apparent that he was jumbling up sadly the many objects of ancient and modern interest he had been visiting. The fifty Colonies were far clearer in his head than Rome. There came in a bright vivacious youth, who had everything at his finger's end, and his tongue's end too. He talked about everything with piercing clearness. As I listened with enforced admiration, I had my inner revenge. What is the use of knowing so many things if each is to occupy the mind two seconds, and then give way to another and then another equally transient object? As for Sir James, it was simply pelting him with Carnival missiles. The clever youth was, I believe, the present Head Master of Harrow.

CHAPTER XVII.

SOME RESULTS OF A PRIVATE EDUCATION.

ONE result of a private education on the Wilberforces was their truthfulness. A public school, and indeed any school so large as to create a social distance between the masters and the boys, is liable to suffer the growth of conventional forms of truth and conventional dispensations from absolute truth. Loyalty to the schoolfellows warps the loyalty due to the master. The world has had many a fling at Bishop Wilberforce's ingenuity and dexterity, but his veracity and faithfulness cannot be impugned. He said what he believed or felt, and was as good as his word—a fact that must be admitted by many that owe him little or nothing. But in those days, probably even more than now, very few came out of a public school without learning the art of lying. There was no confidence with the masters, and lads who would have shuddered at the bare idea of lying to a school-fellow thought nothing of inventing any false excuse, or even fabricating a story, to a master, whom they regarded as their natural enemy. Newman, who had many public school men among his pupils, lamented that they would not invariably tell the truth—for he knew they did not—although the only result of telling it would have been a gentle reproof, and a step higher in his confidence. He warned men not to acquire too much facility and cleverness in excuses.

On one occasion Henry Wilberforce had his truthfulness very severely tried. A man whose ac-quaintance he did not desire, and whom he had once, by mere accident, found himself in the same room with, sent him a card for a 'wine party.' He would not accept the invitation—in fact, did not go, but had no reason to offer except one that would have been offensive. The very morning after the wine party, upon entering the covered passage leading from the square of the Radcliffe to the Schools' quad, he en-countered the disappointed host entering the passage from the quad. They were *vis à vis*, and there was no escape. They came to a dead stand with their eyes fixed on one another. The other man waited for an explanation, and Henry had none to offer,

Something, however, was expected, and there was nothing but the bare fact. He delivered it in naked form. ' —— I did not go to your wine party yesterday.' The man waited for the reason why, and said nothing. Henry, after a pause, could only repeat, ' I did not go to your wine party yesterday.' After another pause of helplessness on one side and vain expectation on the other, he repeated a third time, 'I did not go to your wine party yesterday ; ' which said, both pursued their respective courses, and, it is needless to say, never recognised one another again.

It may be said that a public school boy, even if he cuts a knot with a good bold lie every now and then, on what custom holds to be the necessity of occasion, yet learns to manage the whole matter of truth better than he could at home or at a private tutor's. He learns better to distinguish between truthful and false characters, true and false appearances, the genuine and the spurious in the coinage of morality, the words that mean and the words that don't mean, the modes of action likely to bear good fruit, and the modes which only promise or pretend. Every public school boy can say how it was S. Wilberforce made some considerable mistakes, and how it was he acquired a reputation for sinuous ways and slippery expressions.

All three brothers would have learnt at a public school how to give and take, when all must offend more or less, and how to accept differences and even disagreeables with comparative indifference. A public school boy—indeed, a boy at any school of at all a public character—spends years in the society of boys from different families, places, conditions, and even classes. The varieties of character there presented are so marked as to have suggestive nicknames, and to furnish many an allusion more or less flattering. But it is all taken for granted and borne easily, and it is often combined with warm affection. All this is capital training for the world, where a man will often find he has to live his school life over again.

Robert Wilberforce was so diligent in his duties and in his search for knowledge and truth, he was so humble in his self-estimate, so modest in his expectations, and so kind, affectionate, and constant where he had a liking, that one is pained to write that he had some personal antipathies, which might have had excuse, but which could do neither him nor anyone else any good whatever. Now, a public school boy has his antipathies like anybody else, but he reduces them to a very small and very manageable compass, and he does not allow them to disturb his happiness or to clog his action.

Henry Wilberforce could defend himself promptly with resources adapted to the purpose, and he would carry on a little quarrel briskly, but it would soon pass away. He went with Newman to some public affair at the Theatre—a musical performance, I think it was—and they had to sit in the undergraduates' gallery, which is built in steps, each projecting about twenty-seven inches, if so much, from the higher one. Wilberforce soon found that he had directly behind him the tallest, longest-legged man in Oxford, Clough, a tutor of Jesus. His situation was most uncom-

I 2

fortable, for he had but a ledge of three inches to sit on. After a while he backed a bit to obtain more sitting-room, and found Clough's knee-caps sticking into his ribs. As this was intolerable, he drove back his elbows to save his ribs, and found them in contact with the aggressive knee-caps. This held out a hope of relief. He ground at the knee-caps with his very sharp elbows. Clough, who was a remarkably mild-looking man, turned to Newman and said piteously, 'Newman, is this a friend of *yours*?' Newman smiled in a way to express some sympathy with his tribulation, and I trust another solution of the difficulty was soon found. Wilberforce and Clough had a laugh over it afterwards.

One result of a private education in this case must strike all who can recall that period. The Wilberforces had a great love of natural history and of science, as far as they had been able to study it. Robert was much given to geology, and, upon joining the Church of Rome and consequently renouncing his Anglican Orders, he intended to devote himself to the study, but was not allowed to do so by his new masters at Rome. Samuel was always fond of trees and flowers. I once heard him and a friend alternately name Pines and Taxodia till they had got over fifty. I became rather impatient, and at a pause thought my turn was come. So I threw in, ' Yet the meanest grub that preys on one of these trees is higher in the order of creation than all of them.' Wretched man that I was! Instantly the Bishop looked me in the face. ' So you think a bucket of Thames water a nobler object of contemplation than Windsor Forest.'

I collapsed, for I never executed or even attempted a repartee in my life. I might have said that I would rather spend a day in Windsor Forest than in the House of Commons, or in Convocation, but that it did not follow I thought Windsor Forest higher than both of them in the order of creation. Henry Wilberforce had a great knowledge of insect life. His amusingly annotated copy of Pinnock's Entomological Catechism I cherished for many years. At classical schools of that period there was no such thing as natural history or science. From the age of ten or under till twenty-two it was Greek and Latin, Greek and Latin ; parsing, criticism, antiquities, composition, history—all Greek and Latin. Latterly the history itself vanished into criticism. True there were mathematics and a Mathematical Class List. Yet I once had a discussion with a mathematical second class who did not know the difference between the planets and the fixed stars, and who could not believe it possible that the planets revolved round the sun.

CHAPTER XVIII.

SAMUEL AND HENRY WILBERFORCE POLITICIANS.

SAMUEL and HENRY WILBERFORCE were both politicians, which, it is needless to say, is far from being the case with all churchmen, or even with all scholars, or all country gentlemen. It required a politician to preside over the Union, which Henry did for some time without reproach. He frequently made a gentle protest against the very strong language in which the exasperated Church people and Tories of the day spoke of the revolutionary action of the Parliamentary Reformers. 'It's either Parliaments or pitchforks, gentlemen. Take which you please.' In the very infancy of the Union Samuel Wilberforce had had to stand some persecution for his constitutional principles. Neither in his Life nor in that of Hook do I find an incident that at the time caused some amusement and some indignation at Oxford. Hook and a friend chanced to be on a visit to Oxford one night that the Union met, and went in unobserved. The question happened to be substantially the case between Charles I. and his antagonists. S. Wilberforce made a speech which I did not hear—indeed, I think I was not yet a member—but which I have been told was a very fair statement of the points at issue, not wholly condemning either side. Hook at that time was full of the High Church antipathy to the very name of Wilberforce, and sent off an account of the speech to his uncle, the Editor of the ' John Bull.' It was published with suitable comments to the effect that the young Wilberforces might be expected to take part in any revolution or treason. Hook and S. Wilberforce became in due time the most affectionate of friends, and if the latter would ever have prescribed limits to the royal prerogative, the former had his eyes on episcopal usurpation. On the other hand the apologist of Parliament became a courtier and a bishop, while the champion of the Presbytery became the historian of the Archbishops of Canterbury, and died spending all he could earn, and with it probably some years of a strong vitality, in the restoration of a cathedral and the rebuilding of its tower.

Hook preached a great sermon in St. Mary's. All Oxford was there. Of course it was on the Church, and treating the State as an aggressive and dangerous rival. In the afternoon St. Mary's was again crowded to hear James Anderson, a well-known Evangelical preacher from Brighton. I had to give careful attention to both sermons, for I had then the correction of the sermon notes. The Provost commented on the morning sermon to some members of the college with much energy and some warmth. He concluded, 'After all, there was something in the morning sermon ; in the afternoon sermon there was nothing —nothing at all.'

I have to thank S. Wilberforce for the kindest intentions to myself, though continually thwarted in one way or another ; such being my folly or my fate. In 1826 he pressed upon me to become a member of the Oxford Union, and offered to propose me himself. I consented, and was elected ; almost a matter of course in those days. But there was also a half engagement that I was to speak, and in order to bind me to this S. Wilberforce proposed that I should undertake a subject. He suggested several. I chose the Seizure of the Danish Fleet, an event then only twenty years old. As S. Wilberforce suggested the subject I asked his own opinion on it. He had none except that it was anyhow a very strong act, and required defence. I took the patriotic side. England can do no wrong. Moreover necessity knows no law. This was a case of self-preservation. I was not of much service to my country on this occasion. I read about the matter, wrote a speech, and committed it to memory, not quite, but sufficiently as I thought. But in my anxiety I had been sleeping little and eating little. On the day itself I had hardly been able to swallow a mouthful. I went to Pearson's rooms, in Baliol, where the Union met that evening. My name was called. I rose and delivered two or three sentences, which my friends told me afterwards promised well. Then all vanished from me ; the Danish Fleet, patriotism, necessity, and everything. I tried to recall it, but in vain. I did not quite faint, but I had to be taken out of the room, and the debate proceeded, whether in the lines of patriotism or of eternal justice I cannot remember. It was one of many like failures. I have had to leave public speaking and debate to others, and fortunately there is never any want of men both quite ready, and fairly competent, to undertake these duties. Among the subjects suggested by the Wilberforces was one which involved a question frequently recurring in those days, almost antiquated now. ' Do you hold the doctrine of Divine Right ? ' I had to answer that I did. ' Then that settles the question.' I could not take that subject. What was said implied that the royal prerogative had a large place in the mind of all three brothers, but that they could not go all lengths with Charles I. and his advisers.

In the subjects of debate at the Oxford Union

enumerated by S. Wilberforce's biographer, I see that with only one exception he took the Liberal side. A few words about this. The Wilberforces were intensely filial. They worshipped their father. He had been now for many years the principal object of Tory aversion. Toryism, in those days, included all the ' interests : ' the West Indian, then very powerful ; the boroughmongering ; the Church monopoly down to its grossest forms and most flagrant abuses ; and generally speaking, the right of any authority or power to do just what it pleased. The Wilberforces were fighting for their father, still not so as utterly to preclude reconciliation with what was then the opposite side. They were fighting for him all the more valiantly in that he was himself now retired from the war, and yet was the object of much ungenerous attack.

In Dr. Hook's Life, by his son-in-law, there is a letter so remarkable and so interesting that the bio-grapher had no choice but to publish it, for it is Hook's own account of a meeting and a discussion with old Wilberforce. Though it was bound to see the light, yet there are comments to be made upon it such perhaps as would not have become the biogra-pher. The date is June 4, 1827. In October of that very year Newman and, my impression is, one or both of his sisters, paid a visit to old Mr. Wilberforce at Highwood, and I have always understood that he had then to be treated very tenderly, and was not in a condition to argue with. My own brief experience is a year or two later. I sat by old Mr. Wilberforce at St. Mary's, when he was as helpless as a child, though paying fixed attention to the sermon. The day after, when I was in Oriel Library, Robert brought his father in, and introduced me, asking me to get out some books. I spread out some of the show books; Smith's 'Mezzotintos,' Stewart's 'Athens,' and Gell's 'Pompeii.' The old gentleman turned over the leaves as if looking for something worth his interest, but said hardly a word and asked no questions. He could scarcely creep along the floor.

But if such was old Mr. Wilberforce about that time, what was Dr. Hook? He was twenty-nine. At that age he was assuming the familiarity of mentioning Mr. Wilberforce by a shortened form of his name. I do not remember to have heard it, but I do remember that almost all surnames were abbreviated or travestied in those days. Time had done its worst with 'Hook,' which I suppose was once Hugo, but even monosyllables did not escape, either at school or at college, in my time. Only two or three years before this Hook had been foraging, and most probably writing, for the 'John Bull,' the Editor of which was his uncle Theodore, young enough to be his brother. The style of the letter is redolent of 'John Bull.' The argument was about the new 'London University,' as it was then called, in Gower Street. Since it would not be of the Church of England, was it better it should have some religious instruction—say the 'Evidences'—or none at all? Hook credited himself with taking the Evangelical side of the question, and proving old Mr. Wilberforce a pseudo-evangelical, because Mr. Wilberforce wished for some religious instruction, in the hope that it would lead to more, whereas Hook himself wished there should be none, lest it should tend to worse.

Such a discussion was a joke and nothing more. Was it pious, was it decent, was it humane, to attempt to drive old Mr. Wilberforce out of his life's path, when he had been so consistent to it, and it could not be said without the warrant of a great success?

In my own recollections of the 'John Bull' about that period, there survive three topics repeated till they were stale enough. The first was 'The Cowkeeper,' that is Mr. Wilberforce's eldest son, who had been persuaded by the religious secretary of a Milk Company to take its stock, and who had been ruined by an unexampled drought. The next was 'Silly Billy,' that is the Duke of Gloucester, who was a dabbler in science. The third was 'Stinkomalee,' that is the university which Hook at this time was so anxious to secure from heresy that he would prefer it should have no religion, or approach to religion, at all, than mere elements or evidences. Was Hook in a position to enter on such an argument? The difference between the two disputants is plain. Wilberforce had, as he always had had, a simple and unaffected love of souls, whom he would feed anyhow. Hook contended for orthodoxy, to be maintained at any cost, leaving the souls to take care of themselves.

CHAPTER XIX.

CONTRAST BETWEEN S. AND H. WILBERFORCE.

MANY years after that period, when Henry had gone over to Rome, the two brothers, Samuel and Henry, gave a singular illustration of their respective shares in the wisdom of the world. They made a trip to Paris. Immediately after they had left their hotel to return home, there came an invitation to the Tuileries. It was telegraphed down the line, and brought them back to Paris, when they spent an evening at the Tuileries, and had a long talk with the Emperor. The Archbishop of Amiens was there, and engaged them to a reception at his palace, offering them beds. It was a very grand affair ; a splendid suite of rooms, brilliantly lighted, and all the good people of Amiens. The bedchambers and the beds were magnificent. Putting things together, and possibly remembering *Timeo Danaos*, the Anglican bishop came to the conclusion that his bed had probably not been slept in for some time or aired either. So he stretched himself down upon the coverlid in full canonicals, had a good night, and was all the better for it. Henry could not think it possible a Roman archbishop would do him a mischief, and fearlessly, or at least hopefully, entered between the sheets. He caught a very bad cold, and was ill for some time after.

Henry had many a good story of the consequences sure to arise when a simple man attempts to act the part of a perfectly sensible man. At his curacy in the New Forest he soon found it necessary to consult economy, and about that time he received a great encouragement and assistance in the new coinage of 'fourpenny bits,' so pretty, so lustrous, and so cheap. It occurred to him, for it had been in fact one of the motives of the coinage, that there were occasions in which it would be thought handsome in a squire or a rich incumbent to give sixpence, in which therefore it would be at least sufficient for a curate to give a fourpenny.

Chancing to meet his banker, a natural association of ideas led to his mentioning this unexpected boon. But how was he to get a stock of fourpennies? 'Nothing more easy,' the good-natured banker said. 'Have you a sovereign about you? Give it me. Go to the bank, and tell them to give you that in four-pennies.' Henry was much pleased, and took the first opportunity of walking into the bank and giving them his order from their chief. The clerk said he had nothing to do with that. His duty was to hand nothing over the counter except for an equivalent. Mr. Wilberforce had better take a sovereign's worth of fourpennies in the usual way and state it to the banker, who would of course repay the sovereign which had been paid him irregularly. Henry fell in with this suggestion, and thereby parted with the sovereign he had reckoned on for settling some small accounts. A few days after he paid a bill for twelve or thirteen shillings in fourpennies, having no other money about him. Meanwhile, though he was giving away his fourpennies more freely because they were only fourpennies, ostlers looked hard at them. In this country, though kings no longer levy poll-tax, that is the rule of ostlers, and of beggars of all kinds, including societies and institutions. With them, a gentleman is a gentleman, and they expect as much from 200*l.* a year as from 20,000*l.* Henry never renewed his stock of fourpennies, and, what was worse, he never had the courage to tell the kind banker that he had been obliged to pay for them over again at the counter. He thought it not unlikely the banker had forgotten all about it.

Henry Wilberforce occasionally went to public meetings for which he had received the usual circular invitation, and was frequently late. He was sure that, had he been in time, he would have been asked to take part in the proceedings, and as he was never without something to say, he was sorry to find himself in a crowd of listeners, perhaps disappointed listeners. He noticed, however, that his brother Samuel, though quite as liable to be behind time as himself, nevertheless was always on the platform, and always a speaker. How could this be ? Samuel explained it straight. He was perfectly sure that he had something to say, that the people would be glad to hear it, and that it would be good for them. He was also quite certain of having some acquaintance on the platform. So immediately on entering the room he scanned the platform, caught somebody's eye, kept his own eye steadily fixed upon his acquaintance, and began a slow movement in advance, never remitted an instant till he found him-

self on the platform. The people, finding their toes
in danger, looked round, and seeing somebody looking
hard and pressing onwards, always made way for
him. By and by there would be a voice from the
platform, ' Please allow Mr. Wilberforce to come this
way,' or ' Please make way for Mr. Wilberforce.' Such
a movement of course requires great confidence, not to
say self-appreciation, but anybody who is honestly
and seriously resolved to do good must sometimes
put a little force on circumstances. I should doubt
whether Henry ever tried to follow his brother's
example.

I can give another testimony to the Bishop's command over his eyes. Crossing the Channel together
in a wretched French screw-steamer, we had to wait
the tide off Calais. The vessel rolled incessantly like
a log, and we were told we must expect two hours of
it. The Bishop secured his hat with a string, and then
leant against the bulwark, fixing his eyes on the horizon, his recipe for sea-sickness. The sailors did not
like to see a Bishop commanding the waves, so they
watched him with intense interest, hoping to see him
succumb with the majority of his fellow-passengers.
He kept his own to the last, and landed as if nothing
was the matter. He had with him then his daughter
and his future son-in-law. To the former he was very
affectionate, but I could not help noticing that he
always addressed her as ' Miss Wilberforce.' There
might be some special reason.

At Grindelwald the future son-in-law was gone, and
Archdeacon Wilberforce was in his place. On Sunday
we had service at the hotel; the Archdeacon reading

the prayers, the Bishop preaching on the duty of English people showing themselves Christians in a strange country. In the afternoon I and those with me were sitting at the windows commanding the half mile of road leading up to the parish church. The congregation came out and came down the road in a dense black mass, but obliged to tail a little. Before long, and long before the mass neared the hotel, we heard a deep sonorous utterance. Then we perceived two figures leading the column, and occasionally turning round to one another. These two were the Bishop and the pastor. The former had attended the service, and, upon its close, had introduced himself to the latter, and entered into conversation with him. It probably took the form of a discussion. The congregation gathered round them, and, upon their leaving the church, had accompanied them right up to the hotel. One could not but be struck with the courage of an Englishman entering into a controversy with a German, in German, for such I suppose was the language, in the midst of his own people. The Bishop gave us an account of the conversation as if it had been all in English.

Two or three years before his death, when his health and strength were sadly failing, Henry Wilberforce was advised to try a winter in the West Indies. It must have chimed in with his heart's wishes, for he was the one who most identified himself with his father and his father's work. He and his friends had fixed on Jamaica, he told me shortly before his voyage, and he expected to see a good deal that would be interesting in Negro life after so many years of perfect freedom and almost unexpected prosperity. He thought he might have some experience worth publishing. Going there with the best introductions, he saw the island, at least what he did see of it, under favourable auspices. Immediately on landing he was taken up to a house in the mountains, where he had everything he could desire, and felt himself getting better and stronger every day amongst the kindest of friends. But the Blacks he found inaccessible. They did not like to see anybody looking at them, or at their cottages, or at their ways. It was partly that they did not want to be advised or criticised, and partly that they were always expecting some new tax or fiscal regulation. They had generally squatted on the ground most convenient for them, without caring to ask whose property it was ; indeed so much property had been abandoned that it was excusable to think property no property at all. Henry Wilberforce thought if he had stayed longer he could have got at the people ; but he had to come home, and so far, it was one of his many disappointments. But his daughter Agnes, who accompanied him, will be able to say more about it.

———————

K

CHAPTER XX.

THE SARGENT FAMILY.

HENRY WILBERFORCE'S want of a public school touched him in another way. A public school is a male commonwealth. As regards the older boys it is a monastery, and the results are about as mixed as in the monastery of old times. But one result is that the young men learn to exist, for a time at least, without female society. At that period there was no female society in Oxford, except that of the ladies of the Heads of Houses, and their families, if any there were. A public school boy, indeed any schoolboy, coming to Oxford for a two months' stay, did not feel utterly banished and desolate because there was not a pretty face to be seen or a sweet voice to be heard. It was part of his education. When Henry Wilberforce returned to college, especially after the Long Vacation, he was heart-sick, insomuch as to give the college generally to understand that their society was utterly distasteful to him. He had been amongst the four still unmarried Miss Sargents, or other young ladies as pretty and agreeable. He was a very charming fellow; they could not but make much of him, and he could not but return their attentions. Forced back to Oxford he was shut out of Paradise, and in another place altogether. It was but loyalty to those he had left behind to tell us so. Golightly, I remember, did not see all this. He felt he had legiti-

mate and solid claims to love and respect that no
amount of pretty girls could justly interfere with. This
fit of nostalgia generally lasted about a fortnight, for
then Henry Wilberforce could begin to look forward
to the end of term.

In 1829 I met all the four celebrated sisters together at breakfast at Robert Wilberforce's, and looked
at them with a strong mixture of curiosity and admiration. Mrs. S. Wilberforce was a bride in her first
year. The brighter constellation must have eclipsed
the brothers from my memory, for all I remember of
Samuel was his springing up to remind the party they
had a great deal to do and must set about it. They
were to divide, and I was to assist.

First we lionized our own college, lingering a long
time in the common room. I have always found the
common room the thing ladies are most interested
about. That is quite natural. A common room is a
male drawing-room. It should exhibit the Fellows at
their elegant ease or their dignified state. What can
they do there ? How do they arrange themselves ?
In a circle, or all about in separate parties ? Do
they leave their work or their books about ? What
are the ornaments ? What sort of carpets and cur-
tains have they ? This was before Denison beautified
the common room, and it was looking rather dingy.
However, the ladies on this occasion were charmed ;
they looked out of the windows into the quad they
had just left, and all agreed it must be a very happy
place.

The next day I talked over them with Henry, and
chanced to say that I admired Mary's 'cool' expres-

sion and manner. I meant calm and self-collected, but I never heard the last of that unfortunate word, remembered half a century after. The youngest seemed a mere child, indeed she hardly looked more when I saw her at Hanbury, in Staffordshire, seven years after, as Mrs. George Ryder, a very sylph in form and in feature. Mrs. S. Wilberforce I met again, not two years before her death, at Canon James', at Winchester. She was still beautiful, but her strength was evidently declining.

I met Henry Sargent, the surviving brother, at a common room breakfast at Oriel the day of his matriculation. His life was watched by many who had heard of the old saying that no heir to the Lavington estate had ever succeeded his own father. He seemed to me in health and strength, and he talked cheerfully about Oxford. I did indeed note the peach bloom of his cheeks, but saw no harm in it. A fortnight after that he was gone.

This delicacy of complexion I think must have come from the mother's side. A first cousin of hers, Mosley Smith, one of my younger friends at Charterhouse, was remarkable for it. So also was an elder brother of his, in the bank of Derby, a very good-looking man, but a little too pretty to be handsome. He was a good deal quizzed for the pinks and lilies on his round cheeks, and was known everywhere as Sweet Pea Smith. To burn off the bloom he would often walk in the hot sun to Burton and back, but in vain, for it would persist in returning.

Mosley Smith, my young Charterhouse friend, was, by the Birds, second cousin to the Wilberforces,

as well as first cousin to Mrs. Sargent. My chief
recollection of him is that once on our return from
the holidays, we had neither of us done a translation
into Greek Iambics which had to be sent in next day. I
offered to do his for him, and, setting to work at once,
very shortly completed a copy which I thought good
enough for him. My own copy I had to send in unfinished, and of course it was nowhere. The finished
copy had a respectable place.

CHAPTER XXI.

JOHN ROGERS.

WE had all of us one sad business with Henry
Wilberforce. We were much in fault, myself I fear
first and most, but he resented it too warmly and
quite needlessly. He had a very dear friend and
former fellow-pupil, for whom I also had a great regard, though the rest of our set did not care much for
him. They pronounced him solemn and drawling.
This was John Rogers, of Baliol, a fine but rather
dreamy figure, with a rich-toned voice, a set utterance,
and a large store of knowledge. He had deep religious
feelings, but upon the whole his training had been
more secular than traditional.

I had long walks and long talks with him. One
argument, or rather friendly comparison of ideas, must

have lasted two hours, and seven miles, or more.
'Which is best—a thoroughly well-defined sphere of
knowledge ; everything known exactly and in its
place ; or one less compact and certain, with a large
fringe losing itself in the indefinite, with glimpses or
guesses of the far beyond ?' If I have not put the
question in a way creditable to John Rogers, it is my
fault. He chose the former ; indeed, it always had
been his choice. I the latter. As I had a hazy subject, no doubt I did it hazily ; all chiaroscuro and
nothing more, like Turner's pictures in his tenth or
twentieth style. May I give here an instance of the
separableness of an essence from its surroundings, and
the possible transformation of an individuality, or
what is next akin to it, hereditary character? As I
was staying at a Lincolnshire parsonage some callers,
the Sollys, came with a little girl two years old. I
instantly said that must be a relative of John Rogers.
She was his cousin.

Some of our people at Oriel were a little jealous
of John Rogers' place in Henry Wilberforce's affection. They were Damon and Pythias. I and another—I forget who—went into Henry's rooms one
day, and not finding him in, looked about for a slip of
paper to leave a note. We were not quite so unlucky
as a parent who had shortly before come to see his
son, and not finding him at home had written a
note. On folding it he saw it was a 'bill delivered for
cigars, 80*l*.' The young gentleman had been making
his rooms a divan for the use of his friends. Our eyes
were caught by a row of cards, with lists of names,
stuck up on the mantelpiece. These were evidently

arrangements for a series of wine parties, some of the
names recurring in various combinations. One of the
friends was represented by the figures 14 ; and it had
the singular honour of appearing in every combination.
We were amused, and we had the folly to ask some
of the rest to share our amusement. Of course they
called John Rogers No. 14, and spoke of him to
Wiiberforce by that denomination ; and it always
elicited some strong remarks on the treacherous and
ungentlemanly habit of prying into a man's private
memoranda. As well pick his pocket, &c. Wilberforce kindly looked over the heads of the chief de-
linquents, at those who were adding insult to injury.

There was not the least reason in the world why
he should be offended, for he had only been doing
what everyone does, and is bound to do, though it is
not usual or advisable to publish one's plans. But
Henry Wilberforce never put anything away. I
doubt whether he ever possessed a key for a longer
time than was sufficient to lose it in. Some people
leave everything about ; their cheque-books wide
open ; their tradesmen's urgent reminders. They
would leave their Will on the table, if they had ever
made one. Recalling the whole of our Oriel circle,
not a large one, I can understand their want of sympathy with Wilberforce's inseparable friend. It was
the Darwinian element in my own education that gave
me access to his mind, and made us mutually interested. But No. 14 was a perfect gentleman, and a very
nice fellow ; and, as I believe, a very good Christian.

CHAPTER XXII.

A COLLEGE FOR STUDY AND ACTION.

IN the year 1828 Newman's hands were beginning to be full. Besides such a devoted body of pupils as Oxford had never seen since the chiefs of the northern or southern faction or the heads of rival scholastic systems moved about with little armies, he had succeeded Hawkins in the vicarage of St. Mary's, the University church. Even to fill that pulpit and reading-desk as well as the new Provost had done would have been no slight honour and no mean engine of usefulness. The services, however, were necessarily parochial, and for a small parish, and they had not much chance of competing for a congregation with the university.

But in point of fact there was soon a large regular attendance at St. Mary's, and the sermons occasionally flew over the heads of the High Street shopkeepers and their housemaids to a surrounding circle of undergraduates, who now went to hear the University Preachers sometimes, the Vicar of St. Mary's always. Newman was thus what might be called a popular preacher, little as he coveted that distinction, for several years before he ever published a sermon. Indeed he repeatedly maintained that for a parish priest to publish his addresses to his flock was as shocking as it would be for a man to publish his conversations with his wife and children, or with his intimate friends.

To St. Mary's was attached the hamlet of Little-more, three miles from Oxford, on the lower London road. There was no church there, or within two miles of it, and the want had to be supplied, as far as one thing could supply the place of another, with house to house visiting. Newman walked or rode there most days ; almost always with some young friend, who greatly valued the privilege.

Immediately on his acquiring a parochial position, his mother and two surviving sisters came to reside near Oxford, first at Horspath, as I have stated above, then in the village of Iffley, afterwards at Rose Bank, on the slope between that village and Oxford. They attended to the schools, the charities, and the sick people of Littlemore, which though without a church, and at that time with scarcely a genteel resi-dence, had more care bestowed on it than many a village furnished with all the outward symbols of parochial completeness.

Up to this date, and for some time after, it could not be said that there was any open breach between Newman and the Low Church party. In the familiar conversation and correspondence of the circle, the difficulty of describing and naming the parties in the Church was got over by a simple expedient. The Evangelicals were always designated by the letter x, High Churchmen, or High and Dry as they came to be called, by the letter z. No doubt this practice arose out of the unwillingness to use a good word in the ill sense of denoting a party division. Newman was from the first very anxious to ascertain the position of the party claiming this title, and how he stood in regard to them. If they neglected, and indeed depreciated, large parts of Revelation, they were to be respected for that they still held.

It was not, however, till after the completion of the 'Arians' that Newman felt so strongly he was parting company with his old friends that he set seriously to work on the character and tenets of the 'Evangelical' school, as compared with the Church of England and the great Anglican divines. For this purpose he wrote an elaborate comparison of it, particularly as to its subjective character, with the more objective system of the Primitive Church and the Church of England. It was put in the form of heads for inquiry. This he circulated in manuscript among his friends, including some who had been his pupils, and it was done so fairly, in so neutral a frame, that such Evangelicals as chanced to see it accepted the account of themselves and were thereby the better pleased to remain as they were. I showed it to some acquaintances brought up in the teaching and under the personal influence of Dr. Chalmers, and they entirely acquiesced in the description of the two sides, without seeing in it any reason to reconsider their position.

The copy I made at the time lies before me, and I have lately gone over it again. I have also read in the 'Apologia' Newman's account of the successive developments of feeling which led him to Rome. A comparison naturally suggests itself between an apology for leaving the 'Evangelical' party and an apology for leaving the Church of England. That comparison, however, is rendered difficult by the former being an act contracted by circumstances into brief limits of time, and the latter the religious history of a life. I speak therefore diffidently and under correction. In the former of these documents Newman was describing Evangelicals as a school of mere feeling, with an evident tendency to lapse into rationalism. It was not necessary to his immediate purpose to describe the tendencies of the Church of England. In the 'Apologia' it does seem to me that Newman returns a long way towards his earliest religious impressions, and shows himself more at home with the Evangelical party. He relates the spiritual history of his soul, and records an impression, continually increasing till it becomes irresistible, that the Church of England is an external affair, out of the sphere of the soul, and incapable of being taken into it, but condemned to be always outside. I can only say I should like to see the comparison put better, for it is above my *métier*.

It is a significant landmark in the development of Newman's opinions that in a large Bible for family use presented to his mother, with a most affectionate inscription, on March 28, 1828, he had the Apocrypha placed last of all, after the New Testament, in order to indicate how low he then rated these books in the scale of Inspiration. This was rather an unpractical way of carrying out his purpose, for everybody knows it is the first and the last parts of a volume that are most read—the middle the least. Nay, there are readers who read a book backwards, and even some who read the index and nothing more.

This was not long after the time that Newman gave his influence in favour of Hawkins over Keble, and it may contribute to explain what some have thought unaccountable. Did not Newman at that time agree with Hawkins more than with Keble, with whose strong political feelings, the result of his country education and associations, Newman never had much sympathy?

At the beginning of 1829 Sir R. Peel suddenly produced his Roman Catholic Relief Bill, and, by resigning his seat, appealed to the university to give him its deliberate support. The Test and Corporation Act of the previous year had looked the same way, but had been stoutly defended on the ground that it could not lead to anything else. However that might be, the present appeal was met. Forty came, reduced by a single defection to thirty-nine, assembled in a common room, opened the Oxford Calendar, turned to the list of Christ Church gentlemen commoners. stopped at the first unexceptionable or indeed possible name, that of Sir R. H. Inglis, and took their stand there. The name was one to unite all Church parties, and so it did on this occasion. Lord Ellenborough, writing either after the date, or with singular prescience at the time, speaks of the '700 Oxford firebrands' that turned out Peel; but the greater part were in no aggressive mood.

Newman's feeling was that, since the world was going one way he would go another, and that the world had no right to complain if it compelled counter-action. The universities and the Church of England were rendered ridiculous in the eyes of the

British public by a sudden order from headquarters
to wheel to the right about. To men with the least
independence of spirit it was equivalent to leaving
them for the future to consult their own honour and
their own best and highest interests. Peel had outraged and lacerated the feelings of the Church and
the universities. His statecraft was commercial and
military ; not properly political, religious, or social.
Whoever bound themselves to him might any day be
called on to unsay all they had been saying and undo
all they had been doing.

Yet in 1830 there were no other leaders or parties
in the kingdom that Oxford men could look to, for
the volcano of Reform was already heaving and
roaring on the eve of a grand eruption. With clouds
and darkness about him, and the ground itself
treacherous, not even knowing whither to direct his
steps, Newman felt that he had those about him that
heard his voice, that were sensible of his guidance
and grateful for it.

This was Oriel College, many a university
friend, and the congregation that flocked to St.
Mary's. What if he then conceived the idea of
forming the college, of reviving the college of Adam
de Broome, or of Laud, or of making it such as they
would have made it in the present altered circumstances ? What if he dreamt of a large body of
resident Fellows taking various parts in education,
some not very much part, pursuing their own studies
and exchanging daily assistance in brotherly love
and confidence. The statutes still implied residence
and bound the Fellows to it, as also to theological

studies. In theory no Fellow could leave the
college or return to it without the Provost's leave.
Nor was the idea simply mediæval or ecclesiastical.
Lord Bacon zealously advocated colleges for study
alone, and in these days the endowment of research
holds a prominent place in the programme of the
advanced party. Newman had now been Fellow six
years—a long time at Oxford. He had seen considerable changes, and had Froude and R. Wilberforce at his right hand, both ready to go through
fire and water with him, the former only likely to
quarrel if the pace was too slow.

So far as I can remember, from my election at
Easter 1829 to Newman's return from the Mediterranean at Midsummer 1833, his main idea, still rather
a dream than a purpose, was the reconstitution of
the college in the old statutory lines. Religious lines,
I should add, but no Fellow of Oriel can ever forget
that he is bound by the statutes not to become
religiosus, that is a member of any Order. At the
time of which I am writing—that is on the eve of the
Reform Bill—it was held almost necessary to a high
type of character that a man should have his life's
dream. Books were written to urge it. At Oxford
it was currently stated, truly or not, that the Sunday
after Hawkins came from Merchant Taylors to St.
John's, he made a tour of the university and walked
into Oriel. He could not be struck by the beauty,
the amplitude, or the picturesque features of the
college, for it is one of the homeliest and closest ;
and already at that time it was falling out of repair.
Yet something about it took his fancy, and when he

heard that its fellowships were open to the university, he instantly resolved that he would be Fellow of Oriel, and Provost in due time.

If true, this was thought most honourable, and was adduced to show the power of a defined and proper ambition. Surely then it was not less honourable to resolve, upon the persuasion of extraordinary circumstances, to make a college what it was founded to be, and to put it thereby in the form best qualified to counteract the vicious tendencies of the age. It might not be possible, but that could only be ascertained by trial, and meanwhile, even with the possibility of failure, there would be a certain benefit in setting minds upon the pursuit of a good object, which is indeed the usual plan of moral education.

For several years the notion of a large body of resident Fellows, occupying their own college rooms, and engaged in religious studies, was steadily maintained as the *beau idéal* and the true purpose of a college. When a Fellow gave up residence at the end of his year of probation, he was looked on as a deserter, and rallied accordingly.

But a college formed on such an ideal would require something like homogeneousness in the Fellows. Within reason they must be of one mind Even that idea was so far from being new at Oxford at that time, that it was really the rule. With very few exceptions, including notably Baliol, elections to the foundation had become appointments, made almost invariably for personal or domestic reasons. Each college had become a domestic and a social circle, of course working in harmony, always pleasantly,

sometimes even usefully. Nay, in Oriel itself, cosmo-
politan as it was, there was occasionally a most
desperate resistance made to the choice of a meritorious and distinguished candidate, on no other
ground than that he would not be found a uniformly
pleasant companion.

Mere social compatibility, however, was not the
kind of thing Newman had in his eye in his dream
of a regenerated college and university. Yet a fair
prospect of assimilation was certainly likely to affect
the choice of the future Fellows. How far it affected
the vote of Newman and his friends could only be
found by a special and minute inquiry conducted
under the not trifling difficulty that the virtual
election is secret. Much, however, may be easily
guessed. Perhaps it would be found that during the
next ten years after the Roman Catholic Relief Act
the college made some very indifferent or useless
elections in an excessive anxiety to resist Newman's
lead, while every single election made in accordance
with that lead justified itself by its results. This of
course is a personal question, in which it is not to be
expected that all will agree. A man may think an
election a very good one, when the Fellow never
does anything that the world knows of except make
a competency, marry, have children, and die. He
may think it a very bad and improper election when
the candidate elected spends a long life in continual
services to the Church and to the State, attended
with some success and large appreciation. But Newman at that date certainly had an eye to the formation
of the college.

CHAPTER XXIII.

TWO CANDIDATES.

AMONG the undergraduates who had become Newman's pupils and friends were two who might be
expected to stand at the Oriel election in Easter
1829. They had taken their degrees in the previous
year. Of these one was John Frederick Christie, a
sound and elegant scholar. He was one of a very
good batch of sixth-form men, including Claughton,
sent to Oxford by Dr. Wooll, before Rugby gave itself
up to historical and philosophical speculations. He
was a man of·extensive reading, for he read all the
novels and all the poetry of the day, and he took to
Tennyson, it may be said, at first sight. He was a
poet himself. His prize poem on ' Regulus' might
have a place in any collection. There was a reasonable prospect of his election.

The other was myself. Besides being not well
grounded, I had been self-willed and perverse. I
had indulged from my boyhood in a Darwinian dream
of moral philosophy, derived in the first instance from
one of my early instructors. This was Mr. George
Spencer, Secretary of the Derby Philosophical Association founded by Dr. Darwin, and father of Mr.
Herbert Spencer. My dream had a certain family
resemblance to the ' System of Philosophy' bearing
that writer's name. There was an important and
saving difference between the two systems, between

that which never saw the light, and perished before it was born, without even coming to wither like grass on the housetops, and that other imposing system which occupies several yards of shelf in most public libraries. The latter makes the world of life, as we see and take part in it, the present outcome of a continual outcoming from atoms, lichens, and vegetables, bound by the necessities of existence to mutual relations, up to or down to brutes, savages, ladies and gentlemen, inheriting various customs, opinions, maxims, and superstitions. The brother and elder philosophy, for such it was, that is mine, saved itself from birth by its palpable inconsistency, for it retained a Divine original and some other incongruous elements. In particular, instead of rating the patriarchal stage hardly above the brute, it assigned to that state of society a heavenly source, and described it as rather a model for English country gentlemen, that is upon the whole, and with certain reservations.

I had, however, more or less consciously, some points in common with the younger philosophy, for I had derived straight from the elder Spencer a constant repugnance to all living authority and a suspicion of all ordinary means of acquiring knowledge. From him I had learnt to believe that what you were simply taught you did not really learn ; and that every man who wished to know things really must rummage them out for himself in all sorts of ways, the odder, the more out of the way, the more difficult, all the better. As well as I can now state in a few words, such was my dream from the Ivory Gate, and many years was I dreaming it.

I used to read Bacon, and giving nobody the opportunity to correct me, I took for granted that my system was Baconian induction. The proposed mode of induction was such a steady contemplation and careful comparison of all sayings, laws, rules, maxims, or what not, as should gradually and completely gather and harmonise all into a system, wherein each would have its proper place and proportion, and thereby a fixed mathematical character. Mr. George Spencer looked forward hopefully to the time when all words, ideas, and sentiments would be stripped of their drossy and fallacious accretions, coined into a universal currency, and made amenable to mathematical calculation. He used to insist on the propriety, indeed the honesty, of always employing the same word for the same thing, and not attempting to please the ear of the hearer or the reader by the use of words not really synonymous as meaning the same. In this he anticipated the Revisers of the Authorised Version, though not with the same intent. They desired to follow the original ; he to reduce morality to mathematics. I recognise in the younger Spencer a continual attempt to persuade himself that he has established new ethical principles as incontrovertible as that two and two make four, and that the three angles of a triangle are equal to two right angles. It is needless to say that my dream was moonshine. It amounted to nothing less than a very serious mental disorder, for though it is said every man ought to be mad upon something, at least now and then, this was a madness with almost sole and continual occupancy.

It was exclusive and tyrannic, for it always asserted the right of possession against every fact, every opinion, and every sentiment that books could offer. It was much favoured by my personal defects. From infancy I had been slow and inarticulate, and as I took much time to say what I had to say, this was a bar to instruction by the ordinary method of lessons. The quicker ones were always before me. Thus my 'system' was a consolation for continual defeat, but being a consolation, it made me on all *vivâ voce* matters a beaten man. Such I was under my successive masters till I came to Oriel, when I was not so much beaten as self-confident and rebellious. I would not give up my dream, which I confidently believed to be the secret of all knowledge and wisdom. For everything that offered itself I had one reply, 'I know a better way than that.' Of course I had only to open my eyes to see what nonsense it all was. It had nothing to do with actual life or with daily events. Its completion and operation, if any, was in the far future. It admitted of no argument or comparison of ideas ; it was hardly of earth, and I could not honestly have said that it was of heaven ; it had no more to do with the Christian revelation than with anything else in the universe ; it was not a rule of life or a moral guide in any sense directly applicable to the present difficulties. By repudiating authority and resting on experiment, it left everything really unsettled. Being thus without sanctity or awfulness of any kind, it became a refuge and a harbour for all sorts of follies and weaknesses. In a world of my own I could do what I pleased.

Early in my acquaintance with Henry Wilberforce, I had let out something about Mr. George Spencer and his views. I must have spoken of him as a very interesting man and original thinker; indeed as a strong character, and as inculcating high principles and proper independence, besides a vast amount of ingenuity, As to the last point I may as well mention that he was an early teacher of Sir Charles Fox, besides other since prominent characters; and that he was great in such ideas as the Crystal Palace, long before they came to be realised. I had, as I supposed, saved myself to H. Wilberforce, by protests on moral and religious grounds. Spencer never recognised any religious authority. He held that social worship ended inevitably in degradation, and was fundamentally untruthful and unreal. He was known uniformly to disappear on the Sunday. As a boy I credited him with field preaching, and felt a sort of reverence for him on that account, though holding it a mistake. That he went into the fields on Sunday I think likely enough, but, in the matter of religion, I should now be surprised to hear that he had ever advanced beyond the contemplation of things in general, with a careful avoidance of the revealed solution.

Henry Wilberforce had detected that Spencer had a deeper hold on my mind than I chose to acknowledge, and that there was an inward conflict, and consequently a sore point. So, when he had nothing better to do, he would make some apparently casual remark implying that I had the profoundest reverence for Spencer, and might be regarded as his disciple, and consequently incapacitated from sharing higher feelings and convictions. He was sure of drawing out an indefinite, perhaps a peevish, protest, and an explanation which he could object to as not quite satisfactory. I said what I felt, but the mental disorder I knew to be still within.

For many years I thought it impossible I should ever give up this insanity. It was part of my nature, and my one chance of emerging, or even having a solid existence. It gave me a self-esteem which naturally imposed on some of my friends. The strangest thing is that I now find it impossible to say when, and how, and by what means the dream departed from me, for it is gone, and its place in my mind is not to be found. I suppose that every time I did an act of duty or plain necessity ; every time I engaged myself in such a healthy pursuit as an inquiry into facts, or testing opinions by consequences, or learning a lesson thoroughly, I was unwittingly encroaching on the ground of my system, undermining it, and sucking away such strength as it had. It died at last easily and without a struggle, so that I knew not that it was dead. I was under the spell all the time I was at Oxford. For the 'Rhetoric' and the 'Ethics' I could find no resting place in my system ; so, as they could not rest, they flew away. All my deep and serious convictions were from my dream. To everything included in the Oxford course I could only give superficial regard.

Of course I gave up all thought of honours, for I was too proud to try, except for the highest. In my last term Newman told me I must get a 'Third' at all events, or I could not otherwise stand for Oriel. This was a bit of encouragement, I added some extra books to my list, and I was duly gibbeted, like some other illustrious offenders, in the third class.

A few days after taking my degree I was pressed to do something for my brother James. He had been sent very early to Grantham School, on the recommendation of Archdeacon Bailey. Andrews, the master, was a good scholar and a diligent teacher, but of violent temper and brutal manners. Like most people of that sort, he made a special set at any lad who showed spirit, as some lads cannot help doing. At the age of thirteen matters came to such a pass, that upon James's repeated entreaties my father took him away. Could my brother have borne it a year longer he would have come in for a gentler master, as Andrews had to be removed. From that time he had daily lessons from James Dean, a clergyman, a Hulme exhibitioner and a good classical scholar. He was also having many a long argument, on the pretence of mathematical instruction, from George Spencer. But it was not like being at school, and my father had a conviction which grew every day, and gave him much pain, that James was wasting his time and doing no good. So, at the request of the family, I wrote to Arnold, lately come to Rugby, stating the whole case, and asking admission for my brother. The answer was kind, but decisive. My brother was then three months past fifteen, beyond which the governors had decided there should be no admission. Arnold closed his reply with the words, ' From what you say of him, I am very sorry that we are unable to receive him.' My friends at Derby were not satisfied, and wrote again next February, only to

elicit a much longer and stronger denial. Both letters
are before me, and show in their composition and
penmanship a remarkable contrast to the slip-slop
notes which some distinguished personages are said to
have tossed off at the rate of thirty an hour, from
vestries and railway carriages.

This was one of many disappointments, for my
brother had before this been very nearly elected at
Corpus, and had passed a good examination for
Wadham.   I am now quite satisfied that he was not
admitted to Rugby.   Two years before this he had
translated large portions of the Iliad into very good
English verse, and he would not have been content to
be in any lower form than the highest, that is Arnold's
own ' Twenty.'   But his hesitative manner of speaking,
which showed itself most in construing, would have
made him very much in the way there.   It is a question of time, and a very serious one.   Twenty are a
small class, compared with the classes of fifty or sixty
common in those days. Russell had always a hundred
and twenty before him, that is, the first, the second,
and the upper third.   Even in the very moderate case
of twenty, each boy has only three minutes out of an
hour, and if he unfortunately requires ten minutes to
do what boys with far less brains but quicker tongues
do in three, he reduces the time available for the
others to little more than two minutes and a half a
head.

Moreover, there were some points of fatal resemblance between Arnold and my brother. Both
were independent in their opinions and quick in
their tempers.   It was only sixteen years after this

that my brother published in the 'Christian Re-
membrancer' an exceedingly able and interesting
review of Arnold's 'Life and Correspondence,' by
Stanley.

CHAPTER XXIV.

COLLEGE ELECTION OF 1829.

AT Christmas I became the tutor of a nice little
fellow, now Lord Doneraile, a representative Peer of
Ireland, and a master of hounds. I was to have
gone straight to the family seat in county Cork, but
her ladyship had spent the last winter in Ireland
with all the lower windows boarded up, and she had
now had to read at breakfast every day the reports
of spies, to the effect that immediate and sudden
death awaited both her and her husband on their
return home. So she would take Cheltenham in her
way. There she at once filled her drawing-room
with bulbs timed to flower at various dates, and
announced her intention of staying till she had seen
the last of them out. The very best of them, a rare
and beautiful specimen, was not to be in its perfection
till near Easter. The devoted husband had to bear
as well as he could the sickening perfume in the long
spring evenings, for it gave him a continual head-
ache, which he tried in vain to walk off on the
Cotswold Hills. This he confided to me, enjoining

me not to give the least hint to her ladyship. From the first he had been longing to be back to his dear native country. He would have to dodge blunderbusses, but that was better than having nothing to do at all, the usual fate of a country gentleman weather-bound at an English watering-place.

Meanwhile I was in daily communication with the other expected candidate, living at Cheltenham, a hundred yards off, and I discussed with him the chances of myself standing so frequently and so coolly that he became very nervous, and his father seriously ill. The pupil's parents also were rather worried about it. At last the question depended on one vacancy or two. The one undoubted vacancy had arisen from the death of William Churton, who had passed away in the prime and sweetness of youth, after taking the highest honours, after making many friends, and becoming private chaplain to Archbishop Howley. The other vacancy was doubtful. Edward Pusey had become Professor of Hebrew and Canon of Christ Church, and he had just married or was about to marry. Ten days before Passion week I learned from Oxford that there would not be a second vacancy. I at once told my friend and my pupil's parents that, this being the case, I should not offer myself. All were set at ease, and the pupil's mother shook hands as much as to say that it was a positive engagement to stay. However that might be, the shake of the hand was never forgotten.

At last all started in the family coach, with four posters, northward, stopping everywhere, and always allowing daylight enough to explore towns, churches, castles, and city walls. I and my pupil raced round Chester and up and down its arcades, and up Wrexham Church tower and into the crowd of round hats and red cloaks in its market-place, and round Shrewsbury.

At the last place an evil suspicion entered my mind. We were all staying with Colonel Leighton, a relative of my pupil's parents, and Lord Doneraile had a good deal of talk, confidential it sometimes seemed, with the colonel's son, who had taken his degree in the same term as myself, the late Warden of All Souls. I thought I perceived an increased security and cheerfulness of tone in the parents, as if they had been told that it was quite out of the question I could be Fellow of Oriel. This touched my pride. I had been making too much of myself, perhaps enhancing my services by talking idly of other prospects. But it did not change my intention not to stand.

About an hour before dinner time we arrived at Norton Priory, near the Mersey, and just within sight of the shipping of Liverpool, whence we were to cross the Channel. Sir Richard Brooke had a very large company and a grand banquet, including a musical performance, ready for our party. But in the course of the morning Henry Wilberforce had arrived from Oxford with a message from Newman to say that Pusey's Fellowship had been declared vacant, so that now there would be two vacancies, and I must stand. Immediately after dinner I parted from my pupil and friends most sorrowfully, and, travelling all night, arrived at Oxford the next morning. I was too late for some formalities and for the first part of the examination, but under the circumstances this was excused. I and my friend Christie were both elected, out of thirteen candidates, though there were some who were very indignant, as there always will be.

The election cannot be alleged to prove that Newman and his friends were packing the college with their favourites, or with men just of their own views. Nor were these views determined at that date. This was Easter 1829, and Newman was only twenty-eight. He frequently said that a man ought to decide his course and his opinions at thirty, as if it might be better he should not decide till then. He was still more of an Evangelical than of a High Churchman, while Froude was a Tory and a bit of a Jacobite and Nonjuror. Newman looked forward to spending many years in the college, and, unreasonable as the hope was, he looked to have the society of men with the same plan of life and the community of feeling requisite for it.

Seven years after this I was glad of the opportunity to make a very small return to Henry Wilberforce for his long journey in my behalf. He had been reading for the Denier's Theological Prize, the subject of which that year was 'Faith in the Holy Trinity.' It was a Friday evening. The Essays were to be sent in on Monday, and Henry had not put pen to paper. It was vain now to think of attempting it, as he was due for his Sunday duty at Bransgore, at the other end of the New Forest. So I offered to take the duty for him. On my return to

Oxford late on Monday, I found, to my delight and surprise, that Henry had actually completed and sent in the Essay. The prize was awarded to it.

CHAPTER XXV.

THOMAS BENJAMIN HOBHOUSE.

OF the eleven unsuccessful candidates some were good and likely men. Isaac Williams must have been elected, but that it was known to make little difference to him, as he was sure to be elected Fellow of his own college in due time. Vaughan of Baliol was a first-class man. He has been for many years a useful clergyman and acceptable preacher at Brighton. Several of the candidates might have saved themselves the trouble of standing. Walter Mant might, but probably his father had put it on him.

Two of the candidates had been with me in the same house, living in the same room with me, several years at Charterhouse. It was a rough system there, no separation either by day or by night. In our house, which was a small one, thirty of all ages lived in the same room, down which ran two deal tables, from breakfast to bed-time, doing all our work there, however elbowed, jostled, dinned, and distracted. These two candidates were old competitors. They had always beaten me in *vivâ voce*, and I had had generally the advantage on paper.

Thomas Benjamin Hobhouse was half-brother of Sir John Cam Hobhouse, tall, with a good figure and fine features, but with a singular want of repose and self-possession. He and I were Monitors, that is, bound to keep the boys in order. Charles Childers, for half a century the well-known chaplain at Nice, was Monitor Præpositus, nominally over us. Hobhouse and I had for several years interminable wrangles, almost one long wrangle, for there was always a tail left for the next day. Towards eight o'clock, if we were not more than usually busy, he took his station with his back to the fire, and threw out some challenge, when I took my station by his side. He very shortly became angry, insulting, and abusive. He foamed at the mouth, and had a strange trick of striking the grate with his heels, even if there were ever such a fire in it. Doing this continually he burnt off the calves of his trousers, reduced his shoes to slippers, and wore away the heels of his stockings. He would walk slipshod for months in consequence.

We disagreed about everything, but politics were the staple. He held everything to be vicious and corrupt—court, aristocracy, institutions, laws—no good to be done without rooting out and turning upside down. I held that all these things had a right to stand till found hopelessly bad, and that in all questions where they were concerned the turn should be in their favour. One point we had in common, though perhaps I did not see it so plainly then as now. It was that all these institutions, comprising nearly all the old state of society, were in favour of the weak and dependent elements—that is, for the help of those who could not sufficiently help themselves. So far we agreed, but no further. With all forms of this class I had an excessive and foolish sympathy. Hobhouse had none. He despised and hated weakness in every form. I must add that though he swore freely, he was not otherwise profane or irreverent, and he was entirely free, both in language and in mind, from the worst of the moral plagues that wretched schoolboys are addicted to.

Childers struck in sometimes into our discussions, not to arbitrate, but on some side issue. He must have thought us all bad, for he had out his Bible every night and read a chapter to himself, which nobody else did. I do not think he talked to anybody for his soul's good, and he was the only one at all likely to do it.

However, to return to my nightly antagonist. The Criminal Code was being ameliorated, and it gave us plenty to disagree upon, for at that time I was likely enough to defend capital punishment for forgery. In the year 1823 we had a bitter discussion in chapel, during one of Archdeacon Hale's sermons most probably. The question was, could a man now be hung for picking pockets. We all sat, almost in the dark, in a remote corner of the chapel, with an immense pier before us, and we all did just what we pleased. Hobhouse got very exasperated. I said there was no occasion to be angry, as we could soon find out how the law stood. Yes, but I was so shifty, he said, that I was likely to deny having maintained what I did, if I found I was wrong. So he took my Prayer Book and wrote on a fly-leaf, distinct and large, 'Hobhouse says that a man who picks another man's pocket of a handkerchief is liable *by law* to be hung. Mozley denies it.' It is only the other day that I lost the Prayer Book with this interesting record. It will be found, if ever, in some cottage in Devonshire.

To secure better behaviour during service the governors of Charterhouse added an aisle to the chapel, projecting into the 'Green.' It was done in stucco, with Gothic windows of the period. Here was a new point. Hobhouse declared the building detestable, such as the commonest mason ought to be ashamed of. I said that it was homely, but fit for the purpose, and that if there had been any ornament it ran a chance of being destroyed. He said I could not possibly have an atom of taste. The building was not homely but vulgar, which was a different thing. This was a rather early protest against Churchwardens' Gothic, for at that time there was no other Gothic in the country. For the matter of having a taste I felt inwardly fortified by the fact of my having recently copied on a very large scale, for the performance of Pyramus and Thisbe, a coloured print of the Acropolis in Hobhouse's 'Tour in Turkey and Greece.'

We played at chess. When Hobhouse won there was no end of cock-crowing. We all had colds; with the usual result of cracked lips and sore noses. A kind friend sent Hobhouse some lip-salve. The rest of us resorted to the tallow-candles. This gave him a great advantage. 'There was no accounting for tastes. Some liked smearing their faces with tallow, some did not.' The balance of propriety, however, was not always in his favour. He betted me one day that he would drink ten mugs of water in ten minutes. Each mug held half a pint, so this was five pints, a good day's allowance for a labouring man. I thought it impossible. He pressed me to accept the bet, which I did. After the first mug he left the room and returned. When he had done this several times it dawned upon me how the feat was done. By tickling his throat he got rid of the water as fast as he drank it. I became frightened for the consequences of such a disturbance of the regular course of nature, but he must and would proceed. He won the bet, and covered with his exultation any sense of shame he might have felt. Whether it was impecuniousness, to which all schoolboys are liable, or the desire to get a triumph out of me at any cost, I never knew.

Though a Whig, Hobhouse was most arbitrary and tyrannical to the little boys, insomuch as to drive me to the other extreme, for I was far too easy-going. He was not cruel, but wanton, and even violent. Dicken, the master of our house, was having some friends to dinner, and this made the servants rather slack in their attendance to us. The candles had been called for, and they did not come. Hobhouse called out, 'Go all you unders, and call for candles till they come.' Instantly there started twenty boys, little and big, only too charmed to have the opportunity of making a row without being responsible for it. Crowding into the passage, a few feet from the dining-room door, they set up a tremendous and continuous shouting, to the dismay of the little dinner-party. Dicken's pride must have been touched at this exhibition, for on his finding that Hobhouse had caused it he complained to Russell, and Hobhouse was flogged.

This was done so speedily that I did not hear of it till after morning school, when I was shocked and grieved. Hobhouse was not a fellow to flog, and bully as he was in a certain harmless way, every boy in the house would have protested against it had he been consulted. It has occurred to me that Russell had been watching for an opportunity. He had called one day for an authority for the quantity of the second syllable of *victoria.* Of course he wanted the passage in the Satires, but no one had it. He passed rapidly a score or so. When it came to Hobhouse he rapt out, ' *Jamque manu viridem tendit victoria palmam.*' Russell looked queer, and asked where it was. Hobhouse answered, 'Lucan.' It was impossible to stop the school and make a search, so Hobhouse took twenty places, and was in great delight, boasting, however, not his memory but his ready wit. Russell no doubt felt himself grossly imposed upon, but he had to let it pass.

The Toryism of those days relied much on the army. Besides an old and natural alliance, it had then the bond of a great necessity, for there was hardly an institution of the country that could have stood as it was without the aid of physical force. Military glory was then all the glory possible ; at least all that was recognised. Even Hobhouse shared this enthusiasm. With much solemnity he and I one day tried the *Sortes Biblicæ.* It was, I fear, the only time I opened my Bible that term. The seventh verse, in the first column, in the first, that is the left-hand page, was to be decisive. My verse made me unmistakably a man of war, with multitudes of men and horses at my command. Hobhouse's as clearly made him a man of peace. He was thoroughly disgusted, and did not try it again.

Hobhouse left Charterhouse before me, and went to a private tutor, I think Arnold. Then he came to Baliol, and soon made his appearance in the Union. I was told to my surprise and concern that he was drinking too much, and that he primed himself for speaking, in which, however, he had not much success. His mind was still running on the Criminal Code, and he had resolved to make a stand somewhere, for he put up, 'The necessity of retaining Capital Punishment for Murder.' I went, and there was a large muster.

Hobhouse rose with a slip of paper in his hand, which he kept flourishing in his usual nervous manner. He felt quite easy and confident in supporting the proposition before the meeting, because it rested on a natural and immutable foundation. If people chose to divide land and to build houses ; to make goods and chattels and to coin money, then we had to see that they did not encroach too much on common right, and exceed the bounds of humanity in protecting from man the rights which man had made. But your life was a natural and inalienable property, and in this case the danger was not lest you should guard it too much, but lest you should not guard it enough. The

most precious of possessions had to be protected by
the greatest of penalties. That was equal and fair.
But he would go to the oldest of all law books, the
foundation of all jurisprudence. There was a good
deal in that book which was limited to place, time,
and circumstance, but there was no place, time, or
circumstance to limit the character of murder, or the
justness of the penalty. He wished with all his heart
England had followed the law of the Bible in its
mercy, and he therefore had the less hesitation in appealing to its justice. The ancient and eternal law of
the Bible in the case of murder had been expressly
delivered to save mankind from reverting to its former
stage of violence.

He had taken care to write it. Nothing could be
more express, and it took no lawyer to explain it.
'Whoso sheddeth man's blood, by him shall man's
blood be shed.' The roar of laughter that followed
this enunciation only stirred Hobhouse to greater
earnestness. He did not expect to have the Bible
laughed at in a company of gentlemen, least of all at
Oxford. He had always respected it, even if he had not
read it as much as he might. 'Well, but the text?'
they called out. 'Call it a text if you like. It is a
law binding on all the world. Here it is, and I wish
all laws were as plain : 'Whoso sheddeth man's blood,
by him shall man's blood be shed.' 'Read, read,
read,' they cried out. So he took the paper, stretching
it out with both hands, and read it again, with a pause
before every word, and a tremendous emphasis on the
words 'by him.' Whoso, sheddeth, man's, blood, by
him, shall, man's blood, be shed.' But he was again

drowned with laughter, when a friend took the paper away from him and pointed out his mistake. 'You all knew what I meant,' he exclaimed. 'Then why didn't you say it?' 'What signifies the mistake of a word?' 'But it does signify who is to have the right to kill us all.' When the storm had subsided, Hobhouse went on with his speech, and made a good finish.

In due time he went into Parliament, was member for Chatham for some years, afterwards for Lincoln; spoke occasionally and well, but not to much purpose; was very unpopular in the House, and, in effect, did nothing.

CHAPTER XXVI.

GEORGE ROBERT MARRIOTT.

GEORGE ROBERT MARRIOTT, the other candidate from Charterhouse, and from my own house there, was the son of a Chairman of the Middlesex Sessions well known in society. He was a cousin of Charles Marriott, not yet come to Oxford. He must always have had a hard battle for life, for he was very small and slight, and he had a strangely malformed head. So little breadth was there across the temples, and such a mass of fluffy hair that would not lie down, that he was, not very appropriately, nicknamed 'Cocoanut.'

Of the genius that takes the form of ready wit he had more than all of us, and he was never at a loss.

Boy's wit is nothing if it be not sarcastic. Seeing me making a map, he glanced over my work with the words, Μὰψ, ἀτὰρ οὐ κατὰ κόσμον. I would have given five shillings to have said it myself. Besides his wit and his scholarship, he brought to our house a vast knowledge of the London world, at least of a very important part of it. At thirteen or fourteen he knew all about all the courts of law, an utter mystery to most country lads even up to man's estate. He knew by name and character all the judges and leading lawyers. He talked familiarly of Lord Kenyon, Judge Richardson, Sir John Bayley, 'Fred Pollock,' and many others I had never heard of.

He was himself intended for the law. The father had been compelled by failure of health, or physical weakness, to limit his own ambition to a moderate career ; he no doubt looked to the next generation to retrieve his own shortcomings. He must have looked with much hope on his precocious, spirited, nimble-witted boy. Yet he could not have looked on his long, narrow face without misgiving. Parents who urge their children to rise in the world sometimes succeed only in making them proud and discontented. The child acquired a contempt for small and even for struggling people ; for ladies who were their own housekeepers, and who had been seen giving out sugar to the servants ; for 'pigging,' as he expressed it, in a cottage, and for humble associates. From mere pride he was saucy in his food, and would not touch rice-pudding with currants, because the boys at his 'totherum,' that is his last school, had nicknamed it fly-pudding. All knowledge he measured by its power to raise a man in life, and to make him a figure in the world.

His ambition, or his love of great people, made him the slave and the toy of a very big fellow, the son of a Cabinet Minister, in our house, who could do anything with him, and be forgiven the minute after. I once saw this fellow take up Marriott, and by main strength lay him on a shelf, seven feet above the floor, so narrow that had Marriott moved an inch he must have rolled to the floor, most probably headforemost. There the poor child lay for near half an hour, entreating in vain to be taken down. At another time his tormentor took him out of bed and hung him by the heels out of a four-story window. The people of the mews behind hearing cries and seeing something very extraordinary, came round and rang the bell. There was an inquiry next day, and Marriott gave Dicken a very mild version of the affair dictated by his tyrant.

At another time the latter had some oysters sent him. They must have a supper. Marriott was pressed to go out and buy a couple of pounds of butter. Of course he would have to be flogged if he were seen, but he only escaped that for a worse fate. He brought the butter enveloped in cabbage leaves. His friend put his nose to it. ' Capital,' he said, ' it seems quite fresh.' ' Only in this morning, they assured me,' said Marriott. ' We'll have a jolly tuck in,' said the other. Whereupon he seized Marriott as in a vice between his knees, and slapping the butter hard down on his bushy poll, worked it into his hair, till it became a foaming stream, blinding his eyes,

filling his nose, and saturating his clothing down to
the ground.   After enduring this and a great deal
more, I should doubt whether Marriott ever got a word
or a line, or even a thought, from his tormentor, from
the time that one went into the Foreign Office and
the other to Oriel.

· Marriott could be obliging even when there was
nothing to be gained, and all in that house owe him a
debt of gratitude for his helping much to enliven its
dull hours.   Will these debts ever be paid ?   Nay,
rather, how can they ever fail to be ?

It was very soon found that Marriott could im-
provise stories.   Accordingly, when the candles were
out and all were in bed, there arose the cry, ' Now
Marriott, tell us a story.'   He started immediately and
well, but by the time he had got the travellers, after a
long journey, into a deep lane, with the moon sometimes showing itself, sometimes hidden, and the sound
of hoofs in the distance, he would fall asleep.   After a
pause there was a cry, ' Go on, go on,' with vitupera-
tive comments, and a shower of missiles would descend
on him.   He had utterly forgotten his story. ' Where
was I ? '   ' In a dark lane, with the sound of hoofs in
the distance.   Go on.'   Marriott would take up the
thread of his tale, till the most importunate of his
listeners had fallen asleep and he might do the same.

When Marriott came to Oriel he became one of a
trio of constant friends, equally sharp-witted and
men of the world.   The two others were Joseph
Richardson, son of the Judge, and Charles B. Pearson, son of the Dean of Salisbury.   I saw much of
all three.   Richardson, taking pity on my shyness and

awkwardness, coached me through the first wine party I had the courage to give. Some years after I entertained him at Moreton Pinckney, gave him some direction and information when he was going the round of the county as Commissioner of Inquiry into the administration of the Poor Laws. I often think of a saying of his at college, 'Cut me in two, and you'll find me a rotten apple.' I believe I might have said the same, but I wasn't used to express myself in that slapdash fashion. He died young, attended by Tyler on his deathbed, and well reported of by him.

Marriott was sadly disappointed at the result of the Oriel election. Relying on our old familiarity he said to me that it was a case of favouritism. 'Why didn't they let it be known they intended to elect you?' I was too sorry for him to say a word, for I knew it was his only chance at Oxford. It was, however, partly his own fault. He could easily have taken a first class, and in that case the college would have found it difficult to pass him over. So, at least, I think. He had a short and sad life, for in a few years he went out of his mind, and in that state he died.

CHAPTER XXVII.

WILLIAM DOBSON.

IN the wake of these two Carthusians I take leave to bring in a third as different as can be imagined,—a being all smoothness, ease, and grace, without malice or guile, entirely destitute of ambition. William Dobson had nothing to do with Oriel College, or with any movement or cause, but he became Principal of Cheltenham College, the maker of that college as some say ; and some even go further, the maker of the town as it now is. Dobson came to Charterhouse in 1822 from Richmond, then enjoying a high reputation from being Canning's first school. Tate was said to be a first-rate scholar. In that same year I was appointed to teach a form.

This will puzzle some readers. Russell had adopted the plan of mutual instruction, the Madras system as it was called, imported into England by Dr. Bell. It was supposed to be economical, by enabling fewer masters to do the work, and accordingly we had only eight masters for nearly five hundred boys ; that is one to sixty boys. Some of the masters, too, were little better than boys themselves. A boy had to teach a form satisfactorily for at least six weeks if he would rise from the fourth form to the third, and the same condition was required for a rise from the third to the second, and again from the second to the first. If, as sometimes happened, as it did happen in my case, he did not teach very efficiently, he had to teach a form another six weeks. I spent a whole year in teaching and nothing else ; except paper work. Russell did not seem to think it a matter of serious consideration that when an indifferent teacher was remitted for a second trial, the unfortunate and guiltless form put under him had the largest share of the punishment.

I found Dobson in my form, a very nice fellow of thirteen, with black hair, dark eyes, well moulded, mildly expressive features, and a soft pleasant voice. Not two years before this, that is on returning from the Long Vacation in 1820, I had just learnt the Greek alphabet for the first time, and now I was to take a form in the Iliad, and teach it critically too. I very soon found that Dobson knew a great deal more about it than I did ; or to speak more correctly, that he knew a great deal, while I knew nothing. I really felt it a providence. I kept him steadily at my right hand. He coached me every word, every aorist, every elision, every dialectic difference, matters on which a scholar may make a volume out of the first ten lines of the Iliad. All this he did quietly, concisely, and clearly. After a consultation with Dobson every other line, I faced my form manfully, and sustained the credit of my position. This went on for two months, and they are an oasis in my life.

Some will ask how this could go on, and why did I not report Dobson as fit for a higher form. No teacher that I am aware of ever did that ; nor do I think it was expected of him. The masters of the lower school, dropping in now and then, and hearing a lesson, were expected to manipulate the classes. It was they who looked over the 'exercises,' and a good scholar might be idle out of school.   This indeed was the fashion.   'Exercises' interfered with games and conversation.   There was a certain selfish, designing look in extra care given to them, as if a boy was trying in that way to steal a march on his school-fellows.   But here was Dobson, I am quite sure, fit for the first form in 1822.   By Easter, 1823, I was in the first form, and Dobson down among the dolts and dummies of all sorts in the lower school.   At Easter, 1824, he was still only in the third form, where I find his name close to that of R. A. Reynolds, who had such a row with Lord Cardigan.   What could he be doing all that time, and what could his masters be about ?   He and I became friends, not that we had very much to say to one another, for he was just a schoolboy and not much more.

It is plain he ought to have been taken by the hand and seated in the higher room.   His example brings out the fault of the system as concerned the lower school, while the upper school had quite as serious faults of its own.   At Cambridge Dobson was First Class, and became Fellow of Trinity.

When the present Bishop of Truro had been some time head-master of Wellington College, he was de-sired by the governors to make inquiries on certain points at other large schools.   He came to Chel-tenham, and was pleased with the Principal.   He was particularly anxious to know the spiritual and moral relations of the Principal to the scholars. 'That,' said Dobson, 'is the great advantage of my

position. I've nothing to do with the boys out of
school time. The lessons over, I am a man at large.'
Benson failed to appreciate this limited responsibility. Perhaps he did not consider what it would be
for the Principal to have a hand in the theological
imbroglio of the place.

Dobson however could enjoy ease, and no doubt
his nature required it. When Cheltenham, upon his
retirement, offered him the choice of a testimonial,
he did not ask for a service of plate, but for a handsome and comfortable brougham and pair. The
town, however, must have his portrait, and it would
have been a pity if so handsome a face had not been
duly perpetuated. I saw the full-length portrait at
the Royal Academy. It was a very good picture,
and it also showed that Dobson had at sixty or so
the same features, the same expression, the same
complexion, as at thirteen. But what would Russell
have said ? At Charterhouse every boy was bound
to stand always in the 'first position.' To cross
one's legs was a high crime and misdemeanour.
And here was Dobson handed down to posterity
crossing his legs and leaning against a table.

I was myself the very opposite of Dobson—no
scholar, but very ambitious and very desirous to gratify
my friends at home. It would have suited my case to
pay less attention to my exercises and more to the
preparation of my lessons. Had I done that I should
have remained longer in the lower school, and in the
lower forms of it. It would have been a trial to me
to be amongst boys of inferior intelligence, but that

one might have borne. Being 'Monitor,' too, in my house would have made the lower classes less tolerable.

One act I cannot remember without shame and something like remorse. It must have been in the hot summer time of 1821, when Russell unexpectedly presented himself one afternoon in the lower school. It was fearfully hot and close. There were between a dozen and twenty forms going on, and if, as was likely, they were not being kept well in hand, they were all talking. Russell proceeded to examine form after form angrily, bestowing savage looks on the assistant and under masters. The latter had been complaining of the size of the forms, which were beyond the control of the teachers.

Suddenly Russell strode to the desk, took a slate, and by striking it against the desk several times gave the usual summons to attention. He ordered the whole school to form one long line, or rather *queue*, round the room, about 350 boys. Beginning at the top, he was rapidly dividing them into twenties Slow as I usually was, I was quicker than he on this occasion, and found that I was the first of a twenty. This would be no good to me, for I might be the last of that twenty before the end of the day. To be the first of a twenty was a step gained. A few days before this I had bought in the streets a knife with a dozen blades of one sort or another. I immediately offered it to the next above me, if he would change places. The poor fellow caught at the bait, and in half a minute more I had gained a promotion. I am quite sure it would have been better for myself at least not to have interfered with Russell's process, rough as it was.

If Sir William Fitzherbert, Bart., of Tissington Hall, still lives, and reads these words, he may remember the Jacob that got this much of his birthright out of him.

CHAPTER XXVIII.

MEETINGS FOR THE STUDY OF SCRIPTURE.

IN Michaelmas term, 1829, Newman and the other Fellows and Probationers named or alluded to above began to meet twice a week for the study of the Scriptures. There had been various gatherings of this sort at Oxford for some time, not very unlike those which the Wesleys and their friends had held exactly a century before, seemingly with little forecast of the outcome. These meetings were bearing their fruits in Oxford. About this time not less than a dozen men of good university position and respectable abilities went out of the Church of England in different directions, agreeing only in a hasty and presumptuous opinion, as we may certainly call it, that the Church of England was incurably wrong and finally doomed. These seceders were so good in their way; so amiable; so well-intentioned and single-minded, as far as one could see without a close analysis of character, and in some cases so distinguished, that the loss was much felt, all the more because it augured greater losses to come.

The choice of the subject for our meetings belonged rather to the time than to the men that made it. Prophecy was much preached and written upon in those days. For years before it had been debated all over the land whether Napoleon or the Pope were Antichrist, for one of them it must be, and the downfall of the former had decided the question for, that is against, the latter. It was everywhere held to be of vital importance to have a right understanding on this question, and Newman was doubtful. It was decided, apparently without much forethought, to read the Revelation of St. John with the best commentators. I had Joseph Mede, but I did not make much progress with his book, which is in Latin, nor was I much called on. It served to impress on me that there is a grammar of prophecy, a matter generally little known, or much overlooked.

The only conclusion come to, as far as I can remember, was that Antichrist was not the Church of Rome, but Pagan Rome, the spirit of which survived Paganism and the Empire, and, as it were, haunted and partially possessed the Church, especially the Roman Communion. It was the spirit of old Rome. This was a comfort to me, because while I had never been able quite to reject the great article of faith held in those days as all but necessary to salvation, that the Church of Rome is Antichrist, still I had an insuperable repugnance to the notion for more reasons than I could number here. My good friend

Golightly had often quoted the saying of some witty Anglican divine, that ' if the Church of Rome be not Antichrist, she hath ill-luck to be so like him.' For the matter of that I reflected that Antichrist must be expected to be not only like the Church of Rome, but like Christ Himself—nay, that Christ Himself had been condemned for being so far like the Roman Emperor as to pretend to take his place. The truth is likenesses have to be interpreted.

There was then hardly such a thing as Biblical scholarship in the university. Of course it could have no place in the much crowded, much circumscribed preparation for the schools. Our Oriel tutors gave exceptional attention to our New Testament lectures, but these consisted almost entirely in our construing the original and having occasionally to be corrected on some point of mere scholarship. I remember being told as an incident of that very morning that the very learned tutor of a neighbouring college had not opened his mouth once during the whole ' lecture,' except to observe on the words ' Draw out now,' in the miracle of Cana, ' Whence we may infer that the Jews used " spigots." ' I leave it to better scholars than myself to say whether the inference be just, for I doubt it.

For the degree of M.A. and for all the degrees in theology and in law there was then no more examination than there is for a bogus degree at Philadelphia. In point of fact they were bogus degrees and nothing more. The Regius Professors of Divinity did their best to revive theological studies, but when Lloyd collected a private class it was to study the history

and original sources of our Prayer Book, and when
Burton took his place in that practice it was to
study Eusebius and the Primitive Church. When
any preacher went out of the text of Scripture it was
generally for some paradox or some oddity to strike
and fix the attention, or a sort of five minutes
wonder. Tyler had a decided turn for the picturesque
and quaint. To illustrate the absolute sanctity with
which the Jews regarded the Temple, he quoted a
strange Rabbinical story. Along all the lines of the
cornice and roof there were wires in such complete
communication that not a sparrow could light on any
part without setting 6,000 small bells tinkling. As
may be supposed, a responsive titter rose through St.
Mary's.

Newman might be supposed to have really believed the English translators inspired, for any critical comment he ever made on the Authorised Version:
as if he would rather have every defect in it implicitly
swallowed than that it should be made the sport of
scholarship such as scholarship was in those days. It is
true the Authorised Version was being frequently questioned, as it had been all last century, by well-known
divines. Even village preachers, after reading some
disquisition on a corrected text, would air their newly-
acquired scholarship to the poor rustics before them.
But the practice was discountenanced by serious
people of all schools.

In one respect there was a great difference between
Newman and Keble, Froude occupying a point between
them. All three had the same strong antipathy to the
moral tone ostentatiously displayed by many men of

science, flattering themselves that they had beaten
'Revelation' out of the field. Froude was too ardent
for all real science not to stand up for its right to its
own just conclusions. Keble, on the contrary, once
had an argument with Buckland on a coach-top all
the way from Oxford to Winchester, in which he
finally took his stand on the conceivability and indeed
certainty of the Almighty having created all the fos-
sils and other apparent outcomes of former exist-
ences in the six days of Creation.

Newman at that time had nothing to say to any
such physical questions. Yet he could not but be
stirred by the vulgarity of the triumphant *savans*.
The British Association brought a number of Cambridge men to Oxford. Buckland, always coarse, was
emboldened to unwonted profaneness. A very distinguished Cambridge professor having to deliver a
lecture to the ladies in the Radcliffe Library, congra-
tulated them on the thirst for knowledge they had
inherited from their great-grandmother Eve. Oxford
men in those days were rather jealous of Cambridge
men. It is not so now, when any Cambridge man is
as welcome at Oxford as a sea-lion or a chimpanzee
in the metropolis. This jealousy, of course very unreasonable in itself, led to a general suspicion of Cambridge men. Froude, writing from abroad, says, 'How
these Cambridge men quote one another ; such a one's
lectures, such a one's articles, &c.' The result on the
occasion just mentioned was a deep disgust at the
Cambridge invasion. Let each university have its
own and take its own course Newman felt.

At that time the course of Oxford was plain.

Newman so often spoke of Laud as seeing and hearing all that was going on, and actually walking about Oxford, that he seemed to realise it as a fact. At all events, Why not ? Who could possibly say that Laud was not there, as well as all the good men who had fought the good fight of faith at Oxford since its foundation. It is impossible to disprove such beliefs, and hardly wise to question them.

Yet the argument must have its reasonable limits. At my own table once, an unhappy gentleman, not in his right mind, handed to the servant the plate of mutton he had just been helped to with the words, 'Take that to the poor old man at the back door.' His brother in charge of him exclaimed, ' Now you know there is no old man at the back door.' ' How can you possibly tell there is not an old man at the back door ? ' the poor lunatic rejoined ; and there was no reply, none at least that he could have apprehended.

Up to this time, that is to the end of 1829, all was going on smoothly between the four tutors, *i.e.*, Dornford, Newman, Wilberforce, and Froude, and Hawkins the newly-elected Provost. Newman, besides being a tutor, was parish priest and preacher ; a great reader, and a writer on rare occasions. If I may say it, the relation of tutor led the way. Newman was first tutor, then preacher and pastor, then writer. Charity begins at home, and the home in this case was the room in which then, and for many years, Newman had quiet talks with his younger friends.

The reader must excuse an illustration from natural history. I once put out a mare to grass in

Blenheim Park for the Long Vacation, and had some talk with the people there. The horses, some hundreds of them, divided themselves into herds of about forty head. In every instance the nucleus was a mare and foal. A new horse would be sure to attach himself to them, and so the ball would grow.

The interest felt by Newman for his pupils and by his pupils for him was contagious, for young men are certain to find out quickly who really cares for them and has interests in common with them. There were plenty of college tutors in those days whose relation to the undergraduates about them was simply official and nominal. Newman stood in the place of a father, or an elder and affectionate brother. There were indeed intractable subjects at Oriel as there are everywhere, but some of those very men became in after years repentant and ardent admirers.

His pupils would generally agree in the recollection that the best work he did with them was in private, in conversation, in revising the essays or biographies he had set them. From the most ancient times there had come down the practice of 'disputations' and 'themes,' the former upon questions admitting of an affirmative and a negative side. These exercises, as may be supposed, were mostly done in a very perfunctory manner. Newman asked much more than this from those who were at all willing to work for him. But whatever the exercise his first care was that the pupil should know what he intended to say, and what his words stood for. Finding, for example, the expression 'principle of evil' in one of my compositions, he pressed hard for an explanation of what I meant by it, whether a person or thing, and what was the nature of the evil.

Of 'verse,' in whatever language, he was a severe critic, and had a fastidious ear. After one of the first examinations for the 'Ireland,' Keble, one of the examiners, lamented to find so much scholarship and so little poetry, and this was very much Newman's view of the scholarship of the day.

Newman entered early into university office. He was examiner in the Classical School in 1827 and 1828 ; he was Pro-proctor for a year. There was before him, in all human likelihood, a high university career, with its usual consequences in the larger field of the Church.

CHAPTER XXIX.

THE 'EVANGELICAL' SCHOOL.

THE religious state of the country, prior to the Oxford movement, is a matter upon which more and more questions are asked, and more and more answers given with increasing positiveness. The younger people are, the more they think they know about it. But even the oldest must speak with diffidence, for they speak from experience, and experience cannot but be local and personal. However, a moderate observer and inquirer may contribute a large body of recollections on this point. I believe I could, but space only admits of a few. My own deep impression at that time, left on me by all I saw and heard, was there was a good deal of religion in the country at the beginning of this century, but that it had little opportunity of showing itself, or of taking concerted action for any good purpose ; that the High Church found its scope in the regular exercise of the pastoral office, and the Low Church in preaching its peculiar tenets, and in meetings and demonstrations of one sort or another.

The difference of practice was quite as wide and distinct as the difference of doctrine. The High Church clergyman was seen daily in his parish ; he was visiting sick folk, or calling upon the genteeler ones ; once in the thoroughfares he met everybody and exchanged a word with everybody. There was no appearance of pressing business about him ; he was not bound to an appointment, booked for a meeting, or on his way to a coach-office. He might sometimes seem to be at an idle end, and even too accessible. But you saw him. If you wished you had a talk with him ; and if you wished more, a serious talk. He was well read, that is in comparison with his ordinary parishioners. He would sometimes be a polemic, and if so a peppery one. He would have small quarrels, and would look on dissenters invidiously and helplessly, not knowing what to do about them, and finding vent for wounded susceptibilities in peevish expressions. When Sunday came he delivered a cut and dried sermon ; if he was a big fellow and had a strong voice, *ore rotundo* ; if not, in a monotonous tone, as much as to confess that what he was

saying was hardly worth your attention.   Yet there
were very good and very energetic High Church
preachers in those days, but most of them were in
rural districts.

In the prevalent estimate of the clergy of that
period and of the preceding century, they are most unfairly charged with what they could not possibly help.
It was not their fault that thousands of livings were
without parsonages, and with incomes so small as not
to admit of building or even of renting.   It was not
heir fault that non-residence was almost the rule in
some districts, and that even the pastoral duties of
which all clergymen are capable and which are always
welcome, were discharged intermittingly and cursorily.
It was not their fault if the church fabrics fell into
disorder and even decay.   It was not the fault of the
clergy generally that bishops and dignitaries made
fortunes, and used their patronage for private purposes.
There was a broad line between the rich and the poor
clergy in those days ; but in truth the poor clergy represented the Church, the rich clergy her oppressors
and plunderers.   Nevertheless, whether rich or poor,
there were scattered here and there many who did
their duty under increasing difficulties.   The public
are plentifully informed of those who went about
preaching and speaking ; who started movements,
whose lives furnished events, and who co-operated
with many like-minded men.   But it is only in local or
family traditions that they live who did their work, that
is their bounden duty, quietly at home, and were
better known among their own cottagers than in
strange churches, town halls, and newspapers.   It

was the High Churchman who was pastor. The two things went together naturally, for the High Churchman assumed all in his parish to be his flock, all to be Christians—all on the road to heaven, though requiring much help, guidance, and stimulus. Of course he had to work quietly. There was no one to report or publish his talk. His best things were said to one at a time. A hard day's work would not be known even to the next parish. Talking daily with poor country people he became more and more like them, for we all grow like those we are most with. His sympathies preyed on his purse as well as his strength, and after a long spell of this work even an able man would become fit for it and for nothing more.

The part of Evangelical preacher was the very opposite of all this. The great mass of the people committed to his care he assumed to be utterly bad or hopelessly good, that is hopelessly trusting to good works ; or perhaps waiting for the day and hour when the divine call was to reach them. Anyhow, he could discard them altogether from his consideration. He had delivered his message and that was enough, for him at least. He could thus reserve his attention for a few, and would naturally consult his tastes and preferences in the selection. Relieved thus from the dull reiteration of house to house work, and from close parochial duty generally, he became mobilised. He preached and heard preaching ; he spoke from platforms and heard speeches ; he came across missionaries, philanthropists, and the flying staff of societies. He saw something of the higher, richer, and more educated classes. He was in the world, and he daily acquired more and more of that knowledge and of those manners that in the world make the chief difference between one man and another. The Evangelical preacher very soon discovered that his vocation was not in cottages and hovels, or in farm-houses, or in garrets and cellars far up or down, in dirty lanes and courts. Very soon, too, did he discover his own great spiritual superiority to the rank and file of the Church, consigned to the only drudgery they were capable of.

These clergymen were known, while the others were unknown. Evangelical preachers were announced and paraded. The corners of the streets and the newspapers proclaimed their appointments and invited listeners from all quarters. They sought the most capacious and best situated churches, and long before the Oxford movement rich partisans were fast buying up the most important pulpits for them.

The doctrine thus everywhere preached was simple enough. Its fortunate discoverers and propagators rejoiced in its simplicity. Simple I say it must have been, for it excluded everything else. You were to be quite sure not only that you had received a special revelation that Jesus Christ died for you in particular, but also that your salvation was now such a certainty as to place you above all further anxiety. You might have your faults, but you were saved. Your neighbours might have their virtues, but, wanting this personal assurance, they were not saved. They were not even one step on the way to salvation.

I sat myself under this sort of preaching for many years of my boyhood and early youth, indeed up to my ordination, whenever I joined the family circle at Derby, and I feel certain that the impression I acquired of it is sufficiently grounded. I feel that all the more because I liked some of the preachers personally, and much respected others whom I had not the opportunity of liking more. The impression of the system on my mind, after many years of such sermons, nay thousands of such sermons, with hardly any relief whatever, was that it put the character of Jesus Christ entirely out of account, and that it reduced the Sermon on the Mount, all the discourses of our Lord, and all the moral arguments and exhortations of St. Paul and other Apostles, to mere carnalities that no real Christian need have anything to do with. All that is tender, all that is touching, all that appeals to our higher and nobler feelings, all that by which Jesus Christ is the object of unbounded love and adoration even to those who shrink from the attempt to fathom the mystery of His being, was thrown aside, behind I should rather say, trampled upon, as likely to lead us astray from the real point at issue, viz. whether we ourselves are personally saved to our own certain knowledge.

As to the effect of this preaching, repeated Sunday after Sunday, it was simply none. Hundreds of times have I looked round on a congregation specially moral and respectable—for it had none of the political element to be found in the principal church, and none of the operative element to be found in no church at all—to see how they took the final and irreversible sentence of eternal doom sounded continually in their ears. As often as not everybody was asleep, except a few too stupid to be ever quite awake

or quite asleep. The sermon was *brutum fulmen.*
Humanity and common sense revolted against such
teaching, and it could really no more reach the understanding than so many letters of the alphabet shaken
out of a bag upon a table. A fanatic indeed may
swallow what a sane man and a good man will not;
but we were not fanatics there.

CHAPTER XXX.

TWO CLERGYMEN OF THE PERIOD.

DURING all the period I speak of, which extended
from the Battle of Waterloo to the Reform Bill, there
were two clergymen at Derby placed by their circumstances far above the rest. Charles Stead Hope was
in all respects a big man, with a sonorous voice, a
commanding manner, and a quick temper. He was
of good family and undeniably a gentleman. He
held both the corporation churches, All Saints with
little income, and the better living of St. Alkmund's
to eke it out. He was a High Churchman after the
fashion of that day, and a Tory of course. Old
members of his congregation noted, without a murmur,
that they heard the same sermon very often. He could,
however, write a good sermon, and his powerful utterance made every word tell.

He had one great occasion, and as it resulted from

a combination of events for which history can present few parallels, I will relate them as they bore on one another. In June 1817 there was a rising of poor stockingers and handloom weavers in the north of Derbyshire and Nottinghamshire, very like some former outbreaks. The men had no work, or wages they could not live on. Though simple, they could read the papers, and their leader had made an important improvement in his machine. They believed that their misery was owing to high taxation and corrupt government. These indeed were the universal topics of the day. A band of these men, never amounting to a hundred, some armed with pikes and swords, went about demanding bread and arms ; and they seem to have thought that they might be strong enough in a few days to march upon Derby or Nottingham, where, they were told, the soldiers would not fire on them. Coming to a farm-house, and being refused what they asked for, the leader shot a man through the kitchen window. Already the wildest rumours had been circulated as to their designs, and this made the matter look very serious. The most serious part of it, however, was that the population of Derby generally, and most of the people interested in trade and manufacture, heartily agreed with the insurgents, only differing from them as to the means to be employed. Charles S. Hope was Mayor, and immediately took the proper measures for the defence of the town, calling up the Yeomanry and the Militia, swearing in constables, and patrolling the approaches. The insurgents were surprised and routed by the Hussars from Nottingham, but were lodged in Derby gaol. A

special Commission was issued, and opened at Derby
in October. The trial, however, did not take place till
the middle of November. The grand jury had already,
at the previous assizes, returned true bills on the indictment for high treason against all the men. Meanwhile the whole town was very much moved. The
charge of high treason was trumped up, people said,
for political effect. The leader, it was true, was a
fanatic and talked nonsense, but the rest were work-
men and wanted bread. The Liberal party, which
included the corporation generally, had the mortifica-
tion of witnessing two serious desertions from their
ranks. One of these was Copley, afterwards Lord
Lyndhurst, who had now taken a brief from the
Crown. The other was William Jeffery Lockett,
clerk of the peace for the county. He was the leading lawyer of the town, a tall, grave figure, with very
marked and prominent features, and a perfectly sallow
complexion. He had been a corresponding member
of the French Revolutionary Convention. He was
known to be at heart a kind and generous man. But
he was now to be solicitor for the Crown. He lived
next door to us, and I now often saw him and Copley
walking arm in arm ; himself the taller, solemn and
saturnine ; Copley bright, ruddy, and mercurial. The
trial once begun did not take very long. Denman
exhausted his eloquence in vain, but deeply impressed
all hearers. The facts were undeniable ; one or two
guns and some newly-cast bullets in stockings, were
produced and handed about the court. So, too, some
strangely-written proclamations. An example must be
made. The leader and two others were sentenced to

be executed after the barbarous old fashion. When the warrant came down it was found that His Royal Highness had graciously remitted the 'drawing and quartering.' A week was given them to prepare. The day before the execution I and my older brother went to the blacksmith's to see the instruments ; a ponderous axe, a small and handy one, and a large knife, all beautifully finished, and sharp as a razor. We tried the edges on our fingers. When the morning came, all good people, whether as a protest or in mere disgust, were to keep indoors. But there was still an undefined hope of some intervention, not probable, hardly possible in those days. The execution was fixed for twelve ; the London mail was to come in at eleven. As the clocks struck, it drove up in the middle of the town. There was no reprieve, but the Princess Charlotte with her babe was dead. In a few minutes everybody in the town knew it, and everybody asked whether it was possible the execution should take place after that. But there was no possibility of stopping it. My father, after some changes of mind, felt it a public duty to witness what no doubt would be variously described. There was a vast crowd. The hangman's work was then a very ordinary business and made no sensation. There was then a long pause. One of the poor creatures was lowered, and something was done behind a low screen. In matter of fact a young London surgeon did the work with a knife. A grim fellow then stood up, and raised high with both his hands the head of the chief criminal, pronouncing thrice in different directions 'the head of a traitor.' At that hideous spectacle the whole crowd, with a confused cry of horror, reeled and staggered back several yards, surging against the opposite houses. My father came home sick and faint. For many days after the small shop windows contained coarse and vivid representations of the scene. We had a memento of the execution always in sight. Mr. Lockett soon after considerably enlarged and beautified his house, throwing out a handsome stone portico. It was speedily named 'Brandreth's Gallows,' after the unhappy ringleader.

The terrible news of the morning seemed the end of all things, so completely had the foreground of hope been occupied by the newly-married pair. Nobody knew with what expectation to fill the gap. The Duke of York was Tory enough, but the Liberals had now no fear of him. What else was there? Though the deceased Princess had taken her mother's side, none knew how to estimate her loss in the political reckoning. Only thus much was certain ; the dynasty was now in peril.

In less than a fortnight followed the funeral. There was to be one service, late in the evening, for the whole town at All Saints. The corporation met at the Town Hall, and went in procession with a long train of flambeaux, headed by Hope, both Mayor and Vicar. The crowd rushed in with them, and the church, a very large one, was immediately a sea of heads still heaving and eddying. I remember seeing my own schoolmaster, Edward Higginson, the Unitarian pastor and teacher of the Strutts, beckoning to friends and clambering over the pews. The best lighting in those days was gloomy and fitful. But one could see the town was

there. Many indeed heard that day their first and last
sermon. Hope was almost the only Tory in the
corporation, and he had just taken a strong side for
the powers that be. The past was full of sores ; the
future a very blank. He had all the world before him.
A man of greater genius or inventive power might
have failed. He rose to the occasion, and seemed
quickened by the sense of difficulties. This was a
blow that fell equally on the whole nation, on all
classes and parties, that confounded all calculations,
and united all in the common sense of an inscrutable
visitation. I was just eleven when I heard the sermon, and the feeling of national prostration it left on
me has not wholly departed to this day.

The temptations of such a position are obvious,
otherwise they that are in the world, and have to use
the world, would not be so emphatically warned not
to abuse it. I believe the clerical Mayor, who it
should be considered, was surrounded by open foes as
well as candid friends, was said to be too free with his
tongue, and to sit too long at the table on convivial
occasions.

There are those who would say at once there is no
more to be said about such a person. Yet there are
simple tests to which even the discharge of the ministerial office is liable. There can be no just claim to
spirituality when there is no action or appearance at
all. Even when there is both appearance and action
we have to look sharp to our definition of spirituality
before we can say positively it is not there. We have
to be quite sure what spirituality is. The High
Church Vicar was always in the presence of his people.

I could not walk through the heart of the town without it being more than an equal chance that I met
him somewhere between his two churches, or in their
neighbourhood. He could not walk ten yards without
exchanging greetings, or fifty yards without being
stopped for a talk. This was early and late, for I
often saw him walking through the town before breakfast with a garden tool in his hands. There was no
man or woman in the whole town who was not familiar with the rather imposing figure of 'Old Hope,' or
'Charley Hope,' as the older ones called him. He
resided constantly in his only parsonage in one of his
churchyards, just under the church tower. He noticed my brother James and recognised him again and
again from the time my brother was barely two years
old. It was a case of mutual admiration. In my
oldest recollections of Derby I see him moving along
the thoroughfares, and hear him thundering the Commandments from the altar of Gibbs' largest and hand-
somest church. I see him laying, with masonic rites,
the first stone of St. John's, the first entirely new
church built in Derby after the Reformation. Well,
there is something here, even if it be matter to be well
sifted.

Now for the Evangelical counterpart. This was
the Vicar of St. Werburgh's throughout the same
period, and for many years after. He was a nominee
of Lord Eldon, as a good many other Evangelical
clergymen were. He resided in a pretty villa, surrounded by extensive grounds, out of his parish,
and a good step out of the town. I am certain that
neither I nor anybody else ever saw him in his parish

except when he drove in to take part in the Sunday services, or upon some very special occasion. He knew absolutely nothing of his parishioners.

At the time of the Irish Famine of 1825, or some like occasion a little after that date, there came an urgent appeal to the ministers and churchwardens to canvass at their own houses those parishioners who were at all likely to contribute. It had been apprehended that a collection in church would not produce much. My father was churchwarden. He took care to provide himself with a list. However, it was proper to suppose that the Vicar had one of his own. My father asked to see it before starting on the round. The Vicar drew a dirty slip of paper from his pocket and opened it. There were about twenty names. The first three or four had been dead long ago ; others had left the parish. There were not more than three or four to the good. The paper had evidently been made out at the Vicar's induction into the living many years before, and he had never corrected it or made another.

Of course he had curates ; but the whole matter of these curates, their selection, their management, the doctrine they were to preach, and all they had to do, he deputed to a wealthy tradesman of the strongest and bitterest 'Evangelical' principles. Being a man of business, and so far a man of the world, with much natural shrewdness, this Gaius of Derbe, as his friends called him, made a good selection within his own lines, and entirely escaped the unhappy selections which the best clergymen are apt to make. But if these men had wished to preach the Bible or the Prayer Book, they would not have been allowed to do it. This censor sat over them, and if their tone had once faltered into mercy and grace, they would have been sure to hear of it.

What they preached under this dire compulsion was nothing more than the coarse blasphemies of the market-place put into longer words and strung into sentences. It meant about as much as what the fellows say in the streets, and was taken at that value by the generally sleeping congregation. It may be said that this was an exceptional instance, but it is not my own experience that it was exceptional, nor is that the result of the inquiries which even then I was making.

It was openly avowed that this was not the doctrine of the Prayer Book. A hundred times did I hear, ' I don't go by the Prayer Book. I go by the Bible,' the fact being that the one was treated much in the same way as the other. When a chapel of ease, not then with a district, was built in the parish, a clergyman of these opinions and of a good county family took it, as he proudly avowed, because it did not involve baptisms, burials, and marriages, none of which services he could conscientiously perform. Of course, too, in the same view of pastoral duty, he had no occasion to enter any house or exchange a word with anybody, except in his own theological circle. Generally speaking the Evangelical theory was held to relieve the clergyman of his pastoral duties altogether. All he had to do was to declare his message every Sunday. They who accepted it were saved ; they who did not were damned. That concluded the matter. What more could he say or do? The younger and more active clergymen of the school were to be seen flourishing about everywhere and heard everywhere, except in their own parish. When heard of in their own parish it was not among the weak and maimed lambs of the flock, not among the aged, sick, and dying.

In the year 1827 I was told by a Fellow of St. John's, Cambridge, as a simple matter of fact, that Simeon, the prophet of the school, having the charge of an important parish in that town, gave up the whole pastoral work to Robinson, afterwards Archdeacon. Robinson, in his turn, and for the same reason, viz. a feeling that his call was rather to preaching and committee work, passed on the whole pastoral duty to another clergyman. This other clergyman found pastoral duty as little in his line as did his superiors, and the result was the whole pastoral charge of a parish for which three clergymen were thus answerable, was consigned with a small gratuity to a very humble member of one of the college choirs.

Yet I know well there are men who stand on the Prayer Book and yet are untrue to it; and in like manner there are men who can be happily untrue to the most foolish dogma ever invented by man. There is that which never fails, notwithstanding the changes of appearance and form. Ten years ago, one winter's day, I stood by the bedside of a village patriarch more than ninety years of age. He had cleaned the shoes of a Rector who had been Fellow of Oriel in the middle of last century. Finding him cheerful and seemingly stronger than usual, I took the opportunity to ask what he remembered of old times. 'Was the world better now than he krew it eighty years ago?' He collected his thoughts and said solemnly, 'There were bad people then and there are bad people now. There were good people then and there are good people now.' That evening I was stepping out of a cottage into the dark, and was awe-struck to hear a knell. I thought of this or that, but becoming conscious of some one nearing me from the village, I asked whom the bell was tolling for. It was for the old man who had given me his dying testimony to the perpetuity of the true Church.

CHAPTER XXXI.

COLLEGE COURTS.

BEFORE the impending dispute on the tuition, New-man, Froude, and Wilberforce—it was hard to say which took the lead in it—tried a revival which was at least very agreeable to the younger Fellows. It might be called the sweet infancy of the 'Oxford movement.' Oriel College has estates and manors within easy distance of Oxford. It certainly was advisable that as many of the Fellows as possible should have some acquaintance with this property.

Some of them had a great deal to learn about agricultural affairs. It was long after this that a

Fellow of the college, being driven over Salisbury Plain, was so scandalised at the operation of paring the turf, burning it, and spreading the ashes for manure, that he got into a warm argument with his driver, and finished by denouncing the act as a sin against the majesty of nature and the ordinances of God.

The Provost was the only college official who could be called permanent. The senior Treasurer might give up his fellowship any day, before he had learnt his duty. The visitation of the estates and the holding of the manor courts, if held at all, was left to the Provost and the Treasurer, perhaps more generally to the professional steward. Yet all the Fellows, from time to time, were called on to vote upon questions of rent, renewals, fines, rebuildings, or what not.

I remember that at some college meeting at the Provost's house, he entered the room with a document in his hand, observing that he had just concluded a matter dating from about the Reformation—he gave the very date. Of course it was a lease on lives, and this would be the determination of a lease that had run for three centuries. None of the Fellows seemed to know more about the matter than I did. This alone would show how much depends on the life of the Head of a College, happily so often almost preternaturally prolonged. Perhaps the little revival I am now speaking of might be ascribed chiefly to the comprehensive idea of restoring the college to its old form and old ways. However that might be, the Provost, half-a-dozen of the Fellows, and the steward, made some pleasant visitations.

The college was very proud of Wadley, near

Faringdon. At the beginning of last century, a gentleman who held it on an old lease from the college, and had a freehold estate of his own adjoining, thinking the leasehold as good as freehold, built a large family mansion upon it. This possibly led to the college raising its fines for renewal. Anyhow there ensued a lawsuit, the progress of which was watched with much interest by all concerned in this sort of property all over the kingdom. The decision was in favour of the college, which celebrated a great victory.

In 1830 the mansion had been some time unoccupied, except that it was occasionally used for Yeomanry and county balls. We held a court there. The Provost and Fellows put up their horses at the stables, roamed over the house, and opened the court in the servants' hall. The business was not such as to require a large attendance.

The Provost, however, had received applications from a number of labouring men at Littleworth, a hamlet on the property, asking for cottage gardens, or pieces of land to cultivate as they pleased. As luck would have it, under the instigation of some local agitator, they had used language which indicated a theoretical right rather than an appeal to benevolence. This promised sport. The Provost had taken care to invite the presence of spokesmen both at the manor court and at the hamlet itself. The men presented themselves, looking not very like labourers, but more like outcasts from a town.

The Provost and senior Fellows had their case ready. A labourer's best chance is wages. His time and strength are due to his employer. Land above the scale of a garden is an encumbrance. Who is to pay rates and taxes upon it? What is to be done when the holders increase and multiply? It was fortunate that neither Whately nor Bishop was there, or the discussion, one-sided, would have lasted long enough. The labourers could only repeat that they would like some land to do what they pleased with, and that they had been told manors were for the poor as well as for the rich. Oriel College was a very great body. It had taken Wadley House from the builder. It could do anything.

From the court the college rode to the hamlet, a couple of miles off. It was not a very natural looking place. The people might have been squatters, speculating on the generosity or forbearance of the college. But the argument was resumed, and being reinforced by numbers became rather loud at one or two wicket gates.

Whether the college ever tried the experiment of a little Ireland I cannot say, but some years afterwards C. P. Eden, a Fellow of the college, devoted himself to the building of a pretty little church at the place. He had to go to Cambridge and fight a hard battle with Simeon, whom he described as a Hebrew of the Hebrews, but he finally secured the patronage for the bishop, and Littleworth, which includes Wadley, now makes a proper appearance in the Clergy List.

The college held another court at a village beyond Ensham, in the north-west of Oxfordshire. There was not much to be done, and there were no episodes to enliven it or spin it out. Froude, and one or two

others, including myself, made their way up to the
bell-chamber of the church tower, in the hope of
finding old bells and quaint legends. The bells had
been recast two years before, and bore the date and
the names of the churchwardens. The port provided
at the village inn was not drinkable. Accordingly
two of the Fellows, neither the oldest and wisest nor
the youngest and least wise, took the bottle, minished
by a single glass, filled it up from the contents of the
cruet-stand and the saltcellar, recorked it, shook it
well up, and left it for the next customer.

Had the college extended its visitation some
twenty miles northward, it might have held a court
where it was really wanted. A large village had become a reproach, a nuisance, and an eyesore, from the
fact of anybody with the requisite amount of money
and impudence seizing on any bit of the common
he fancied, and building a cottage or a public-house
upon it. The main street of the village itself had
been twisted and constricted, and rendered dangerous
as well as dirty, by lawless fellows who did what they
liked, and could not be restrained because the only
authority was the lord of the manor. This was
Oriel College, that never went near the place, and
only knew of the state of things through a clergyman
who had complained so long and so often that nobody
listened to him.

But we had many other riding expeditions. In his
earlier Oriel days Newman rode a good deal. The
use, and still more the possession of a horse, was then
one of the principal charms of a Fellowship. Froude
was a bold rider. He would take a good leap when

he had a chance, and would urge his friends to follow
him ; mostly in vain.   Anyone who has seldom been
on the back of a horse till the age of twenty-two had
better not try bull fences.   The two elder Wilberforces, properly accoutred, rode to London and
back, or to the South Coast.   It was possible in those
days to do either of these journeys on roadside turf,
with frequent commons and open heaths.   Froude
delighted in taking his friends for a gallop in Blenheim
Park, to the no small peril of indifferent riders, for the
horses became wild, and went straight under the low
hanging branches of the wide-spreading oaks.

Newman rode well enough to come to no mishaps.
Besides taking his chance of the Oxford hacks, he had
for some time a rather dangerous animal, Klepper, a
pretty creature with Arab blood, which had been
brought over from Ireland by Lord Abercorn, then at
Christchurch.   It was said that she had been bred in
small square enclosures, where she had to get her
living by picking up what she could on the rough
edges of the ground.   In such a place, when she
chose to take a run, she had to turn at a sharp
angle every two hundred yards.   The tendency remained, and involved some strain on the rider's
attention, and nerve also.   Newman had always a
difficulty in keeping her straight and saving himself
from his own momentum.   Klepper became mine,
and I lent her one day to C. P. Eden, duly warning
him of the creature's dangerous tendency.   On his
first and last attempt to ride her, he found himself
lying, sadly contused, on the turf of Bullington Green,
and Klepper nowhere in sight.

CHAPTER XXXII.

SOME CHARACTERISTICS.

BUT what was Newman in the Oxford world at this time? How did he stand to his university sur-roundings, and how were they mutually affected? His appearance was not commanding to strangers. It never was. Henry Wilberforce, from the first, used to speak of him as 'O Μέγας, but he knew the inner as well as the outer man. Newman did not carry his head aloft or make the best use of his height. He did not stoop, but he had a slight bend forwards, owing perhaps to the rapidity of his movements, and to his always talking while he was walking. His gait was that of a man upon serious business bent, and not on a promenade.

There was no pride in his port or defiance in his eye. Though it was impossible to see him without interest and something more, he disappointed those who had known him only by name. They who saw for the first time the man whom some warm admirer had described in terms above common eulogy, found him so little like the great Oxford don or future pillar of the Church, that they said he might pass for a Wesleyan minister. John Wesley must have been a much more imposing figure.

Robust and ruddy sons of the Church looked on him with condescending pity as a poor fellow whose excessive sympathy, restless energy, and general unfit-

ness for this practical world would soon wreck him.
Thin, pale, and with large lustrous eyes ever piercing
through this veil of men and things, he hardly
seemed made for this world. Canon Bull meeting
him one day in the Parks, after hearing he had been
unwell, entreated him to spare what fibre he had for
a useful career. 'No ordinary frame can stand long
such work as yours.'

His dress—it became almost the badge of his
followers—was the long-tailed coat, not always very
new. There is a strange tendency in religious schools
to express themselves in outward forms, often from
the merest accident. It has been said that the long-
tailed coat—morning same as evening—which pre-
dominated at Oxford sixty years ago, was a tradition
of the Eton Oppidans ; and it was so long kept up
by the new Oxford school as to be likely to become
as permanent as the distinctive garb of the Quakers.
Newman, however, never studied his 'get up,' or even
thought of it. He had other uses for his income,
which in these days would have been thought
poverty.

When the Duke of Wellington had come forward
to form a Ministry, at any cost of trouble or risk of
failure, on the occasion of an unexpected breakdown
of the Whigs, Keble, Froude, and other Oxford
Tories got up a subscription for a statue of Wellington to be given to the university. The appeal was not
responded to by the country clergy as Froude thought
it ought to be, and a bust was now all that could be
hoped for. Newman took the part of the clergy.
'They can't afford it,' he said. Froude replied,

'They can do with one coat less a year.' 'Perhaps they are doing that already, and can now do no more,' Newman answered.

It became the fashion of the party to despise solemnity of manner and stateliness of gait. Newman walked quick, and, with a congenial companion, talked incessantly. George Ryder said of him that when his mouth was shut it looked as if it never could open ; and when it was open it looked as if it never could shut. Yet he was never so busy or so pre-occupied but that he had always upon him a burden of conscientious duties to be attended to, calls of civility or kindness, promises to be fulfilled, bits of thoughtfulness carried out, rules of his own to be attended to.

Genius and a high vocation are sometimes pleaded as an excuse from the common drudgery of life. There are people too much in the clouds to trouble themselves about accounts. Newman used to astonish the High Street tradesmen with the rapidity and the infallible accuracy with which he went through the parish accounts. He was surpassed, it must be said, in the college accounts by Coplestone, perhaps also by Hawkins. Every term the Provost and several of the Fellows used to meet in common room to add up the weekly 'battles' of all the undergraduates and other resident members. Each bill would consist of eight or ten sums in pounds, shillings, and pence to be added up. Coplestone rapidly passed his finger up the central column once and declared the sum, which was always correct. This was to add three columns, nay more, at once, each step involving several carryings. Whately as a boy was an arithmetical prodigy. When he became a scholar, a logician, and a good deal more, he lost his powers of calculation. In one point, which to Newman was of no practical importance, he was deficient. He had not much measure of length, breadth, height, and capacity. It led him into no mistakes, for he could state what he wanted, and that was a bare sufficiency.

He never complained of any unexpected addition to his work or any interruption. I had undertaken a Saint's-day sermon. An hour before the time I presented myself a defaulter. I could not do it. Newman threw aside the work he was busily and eagerly engaged in, and wrote a sermon, which, when delivered, might indicate days of careful preparation.

He always claimed to have been substantially the same from first to last, only in progress and development; under heaven-sent guidances, impulses, and assistance. It was the fashion of that day to speak of utter and complete change from one type of character into another as possible, and indeed ordinary, by the influence of education, or association, or new, circumstances, or a sudden call. Most young people believed in this possibility, and trusted to it; while some of their elders demurred.

On one occasion, when Newman was on a visit to Derby, my father quoted the saying of a wise old Yorkshire schoolmaster, that men never change. I thought myself bound to protest against a maxim which seemed to preclude hope and discourage exertion for the improvement of others, not to speak of oneself. Newman, not to come between father and son, turned round to me, shook his head and smiled, as much as to say there was too much truth in the maxim for it to be hastily put aside.

Newman looked out inquiringly, expectantly, and believingly for the special powers and intentions of his younger friends. They generally agreed that his fault lay in believing and expecting rather too much of them. He would easily accept a promise, and interpret silence itself favourably. This is common with 'movers,' for they interpret others by themselves. But Newman had also another faith in accord with his own career, and that was in the existence of a particular part and a special work to be accomplished by everybody, in accordance with his powers and his circumstances. In his own case he was always consulting the auspices, so to speak, to guide his course and to decide some question which he found it impossible to decide simply on its own merits. An unexpected act, or word, or encouragement, or a check, the appearance of a book or an article, pleasant or otherwise, a meeting, a separation, came to him with the significance of an intervention.

Whatever happened he interpreted it as providentially designed. We really have no choice but to do this, though we may carry it too far, and may do it by no rule but the merest fancy. His powers were often taxed. Why was it ordered that such a one should suddenly withdraw, perhaps turn round? Above all, there occurred very frequently in the course of a long and large career the always mysterious phenomenon of a man in the infancy or in the maturity of his powers, with golden hopes, and work in hand, being suddenly withdrawn from the seen world to the unseen. One of Newman's common interpretations was that such a one had done all the good work he could do or was likely to do. He was withdrawn because he would do no more, or could do no more. He had said his say in writing or in the pulpit, he had put a parish in order, he had built a church, he had started a local movement, he had left a name behind him—more he was not likely to do, for the work was thenceforward too much, and he might possibly have lost in it what he had gained before.

He would warn his young friends who had done something to see that it was not the whole work of their life. They might read in its very completeness the completion of their own career. He had something of the Highland idea of an extraordinary exuberance of spirit before departure, the dying note of the swan. He once gave a humorous illustration of it. My servant drove him in a pony trap from Cholderton to Salisbury—eleven miles. The poor man, who was gardener, and always had a good deal to say about the country and things in general, talked the whole way. The next letter from Newman ended with, ' Pony went well, and so did Meacher's tongue. Shoot them both. They will never be better than they are now.'

CHAPTER XXXIII.

NEWMAN, KEBLE, AND FROUDE.

As Newman kept careful account of his pupils, witn occasional allusion to their spiritual progress as well as their other acquisitions, he would now and then bring to their remembrance the great law so emphatically laid down by Butler; the vital difference between the active and the passive reception of truths and impulses. Whatever we do on the call of duty we do easier next time; whatever we fail to do we find more difficult, that is we are still less disposed to do it. We fall back on the sure law of habit. Having not done it, we continue not to do it. That may not be as Newman expressed it, for he reverted to the topic often, with a great variety of illustrations. One of these I heard repeatedly, for it described what was then the universal danger. It was the unhappy maid of all work, who has to light the kitchen and parlour fire, to sweep the floor, to dust the furniture, and to prepare the breakfast, but not knowing which to begin upon, goes to bed again. Another occurs to me: 'You can't eat your cake and have it,' he would say of those who used up too rapidly their powers and opportunities in the idle expectation of possessing them still for better purposes.

Newman found in human character the same variety, the same matter for contemplation and research, that others do chiefly in the works of nature.

He had this at least of the traditional Jesuit about
him. There was in those days, and there still is, a
great deal of speculation about character, but it is
apt to take the turn of mere moralising, rapidly
degenerating into unprofitable satire. Newman, early
hoping to move the world about him, and having no
means for the work except such human agencies as
Providence might bring in his way, considered well what
any man was good for, and had his eye on the metal
rather than on the dross. Crabbe, as is well known,
was one of his favourite authors, and nowhere can be
found such generous and discriminating appreciations
of human character as in Crabbe's poems.

Though Law's works generally were in great
favour, with Froude at least, the 'Serious Call,' the
most entertaining of them, was never mentioned at
Oriel in my time, to my recollection. I have seen it
lately described as a much overrated book. That is
easily said. Five or six successive generations of
readers and admirers are now dead and gone, and, it
is quite true, their place is not supplied. My own
copy I lent or lost many years ago, and have not
replaced it. If I now looked into the 'Serious Call,' it
would be for criticism, which I don't care to bestow
on a book so valued in its day. It would, however, be
worth the while of a 'serious' writer to point out its
deficiencies. Perhaps I should say from memory that
it calls attention too much to externals, and thereby
takes the form of caricature, at once odious and useless. It would enable anybody to ticket and cata-
logue his neighbours, rather than divest himself of his
own follies. What Froude and the others discussed

continually was ἦθος, the dominant moral habit or proclivity. Newman several times put before me a question which I know I shall not state well. No doubt, too, it is well put somewhere in his writings. All therefore that I can say with certainty is, that such a question he did put to me, and probably to his other young friends, for their serious consideration :—Which does Scripture present to us as the ruling motive, and that most contributing to form the Christian character and life—the sense of sin, or τὸ καλόν, the beauty of holiness and of high moral aims ? The two motives are necessarily presented to us, both in succession, and also as continual and co-operating ; both as severally applicable to classes, to characters, and to stages, and also as universally applicable. They contribute the one to the other. But it cannot be said that they move only by mutual dependence. In fact the one motive becomes often much more prominent than the other. Men begin, or at least they ought to begin, with penitence. The Saints began with penitence, often in exaggerated and grotesque forms ; Churches begin with penitence ; divines lay down a solid foundation of repentance from dead works. But when these necessary preliminaries have been executed, and the rough foundation laid, all go off into spirituality, perfection, piety, holiness, decorum, sweetness, and all the qualities that figure in biographies, funeral sermons, and epitaphs. One might suppose that most of the good people one hears of had never done anything to repent of, except some trifle, just sufficient to give occasion for the first stage of Christian growth.

The proportion of the two motives cannot but vary with the constitution and character, for there are those whose tendency is to be happy, and those whose tendency is to be miserable. Their religion must and will take the constitutional form. There are also stages of life, and circumstances, in which it would be very idle work to attempt to impress so deep a sense of guilt and unworthiness as to keep down the more ambitious sentiment in even its most secular forms. What would be the use of telling a number of young men, in health and spirits, with their programme of studies and amusements fixed for days and months to come, that they ought to have the constant feeling that they are miserable sinners, unworthy of a moment's happiness? Even especially Christian operations, such as the building of a fine cathedral, would be unduly hindered by too much prostration of spirit. I do not pretend, however, to elucidate Newman's meaning, but to inform my readers that he repeatedly touched on some such comparisons, indicating himself no preference, but leaving it to us to feel more that there were two classes of motives, neither to be undervalued.

Was it ever in Newman's thoughts to derive from the school of nature the proper proportions of the gay and the grave? I several times heard him notice that the sounds of nature—the wind, the water, the poor beasts and even the birds, were all in the minor key; as, too, age itself, in comparison with youth. Energy, contest, glory, and triumph were in the major key. But as Newman had to think well over it, I suppose this comparison may admit of some qualifications.

One striking peculiarity in Newman's character must have been often noticed by his walking companions. It was his admiration of the beauties of earth and sky, his quickness to observe the changes overhead, and the meaning he put into them, sometimes taxing the patience of a dull observer. Flowers, especially certain flowers, he was as fond of as a child could be. He could seldom see a flower without it reviving some memory. Old English forest trees he delighted in.

On a visit a few years ago to my Devonshire parsonage he compared the garden, much to its advantage, with those he had seen at several other parsonages better known and more largely endowed. Those were surrounded by walls. This contained a grove of oaks, elms, and ash trees. There were three ancient and lofty poplars, covered with moss, and the ground rising round their stems. 'I never cared for a poplar before,' he said, 'but I like those. I shall like poplars now.' He looked wistfully at a large bed of St. John's wort. He had tried several times to make it grow at his Retreat, near Birmingham, but it would not.

The walk from Oxford to Littlemore, especially if taken every other day, might be thought monotonous, but it never palled on Newman. The heavens changed if the earth did not, and when they changed they made the earth new. His eye quickly caught any sudden glory or radiance above; every prismatic hue or silver lining; every rift, every patch of blue; every strange conformation, every threat of ill, or promise of a brighter hour.

He carried his scenery with him, and on that

account had not the craving for change of residence, for mountains and lakes, that most educated people have. Unless his voyage with Froude to the Mediterranean in 1832 be excepted, he never made a tour for pleasure sake, for health sake, or for change sake. He did move about a good deal, but it was to the country parsonages to which so many of his friends were early relegated. He had much to say ; he had to advise, to direct, and he had occasionally a note to make. He looked for progress of some sort or other. These visits sometimes took him into districts singularly wanting in the features constituting ' scenery ' and ' landscapes.' But even in Salisbury Plain, where there are no trees, no hedges, no water, no flowers, no banks, no lanes, and now not even turf, and seldom even a village or a church in sight, he would walk or run with a friend as cheerfully as the prophet ran bef..:e the king from Carmel to announce the opened gates of heaven to Jezreel.

I must give Salisbury Plain its due. It has its flowers, though they escape the eye by their minuteness, or by their shy habits. In 1831 I traversed the Plain in a walk from Oxford to the Isle of Wight, in the very agreeable company of Neptune, S. Wilberforce's dog, whom I deposited finally at Brightstone. It was a time of great heat and long drought, and the Plain was as hard as iron, with about as much to be seen on the surface as there is on a not entirely worn-out Turkey carpet. Poor ' Nep,' a genuine Newfoundland, walked as gingerly as he would on a cook's ' hot plate.' I sat down, keeping my open palm, accidentally, flat on the ground for a quarter of an hour.

On removing my hand I was struck by the exact impression left, and on further examination I counted twenty-five different species of vegetation in that very small area.   On going to Cholderton, five years after, I remarked on the want of flowers to Walter Blunt, the curate in charge.   Without saying a word he went to a shelf and took down an album containing in his own writing the Flora of the parish—340 species.

Newman never went into architecture, though very sensible of grand effects, and ready to appreciate every work, of whatever style, good in its way.   He much admired the restoration of the interior of St. Mary's, executed in his predecessor's time, and recently threatened with utter effacement by the more fastidious taste of the present Dean of Chichester.   He used to mention in a pathetic tone the fate of the young man who designed it, completed it, and died. It will be seen that when he finally withdrew to Littlemore, he simply utilised a long row of stables and sheds, and would not add a single architectural feature.   He asked me to give my ideas on the subject, and I sent some suggestions of a sort to redeem the utter plainness of the existing walls, but they made no appearance in the result.

Froude was most deeply interested in architecture, but it is plain that he was more penetrated and inspired by St. Peter's than even by Cologne Cathedral. After spending three days with me in taking measurements, tracings, mouldings, and sketches of the interior of St. Giles at Oxford, one of the purest specimens of Early English, he devoted a good deal of time at Barbadoes to designing some homely Tuscan addition to Codrington College.

Keble was a latitudinarian, if not a utilitarian, in architecture. He could see a soul in everything if he could only be allowed to enjoy the illusion. Travelling with me on the top of a coach he came in sight of the west front of Lichfield Cathedral, and fell into raptures. 'They do nothing like that in these days.' I let him go on for some time, and then had the wickedness to tell him that only a year before I had seen the entire front chopped and chiselled away, sheets of copper laid on the rough wall, big nails driven in, tarred cords stretched from nail to nail, and all the niches, saints and angels of the old work reproduced in Roman cement upon this artificial backing. I received a very sharp rebuke indeed for not letting him remain under an illusion, which had been honestly intended, and which had contributed to his happiness. 'What good could it do to him to know how the thing was done?'

A few hours after, on my taking him into the market-place of Derby, he was at once struck with the very graceful and airy Ionic portico then standing before the newly-finished Town Hall. 'It seems to take the town under its protection,' he said, which was indeed the effect. Municipalities have lost favour with advanced Church-people latterly, but Keble was far too much of a scholar not to reverence the institution which formed the central point of so much ancient virtue and piety.

Many years after this, at the consecration of one of his new churches in Hursley parish, he said to me

'Come this way, and I'll show you something very unpleasant.' It was the side of the church away from the public road, where, for economy, brick had been used instead of flint or stone.

I think we all of us found it easier to admire, and even to criticise, than to design. Keble, Froude, and Ogilvie undertook a memorial of William Churton, to be placed in St. Mary's. It was to be simple, modest, and unobtrusive, like the subject. Whether the result carried out this idea I leave others to say.

———

CHAPTER XXXIV.

JOHN KEBLE.

JOHN KEBLE was at this time the sun of this little world. Most of its happy members knew the 'Christian Year' by heart. There were interesting questions as to the meaning of a few passages, and some of the transitions could be variously accounted for. But a meaning there must be, even though ordinary men might not be able to penetrate into it. For some years after the publication of the 'Christian Year,' and its intimate reception into many thousand hearts and minds, there was no other published work whatever that could be called the distinctive literature of the new Oriel school, taking the place of the 'Noetic' philosophy. Not only did Keble lead, but he was alone as an author. Had Keble remained quite as he was for two or three years more, and had the others been content to preach and to talk, half Oxford, and a great part of England, would have been called Kebleans to this day most probably.

But Keble's shy, retiring habits must have always disqualified him for the difficult task of getting many men to work together in some practical fashion. From all I could hear, he spent his earlier years in what may be called the sacred seclusion of old English family life, among people enjoying a perfect harmony of taste and opinion. His nature, indeed his very appearance, was such as to move the affection of all about him, and he could hardly ever have the least need of those rebukes and contradictions that pursue ordinary people from infancy to manhood, indeed later still.

From the time he was known to write verses, he could not go anywhere without finding that he must leave a blessing behind him in the form of some contribution to a lady's album. At least he must read something he had written elsewhere. Some months before the publication of the ' Christian Year ' in 1827, it was reported that Keble had been persuaded to collect and publish his stray pieces. Several of the Sundays had had to be composed very hastily, in a morning's walk for example, to complete the series. This must be all the foundation for the stories of Keble going to this or that house, and reading the whole ' Christian Year ' before publication.

Such a training had not that admixture of roughness which is necessary to fit a man for the work of this rude world. He could only live in a calm and sweet atmosphere of his own. He had not the qualities for controversy, or debate, which are necessary for any kind of public life. He very soon lost his temper in discussion. It is true there were one or two in our college who might have tried the temper of an angel, but there really was no getting on with Keble without entire agreement, that is submission. This was the more lamentable in that some very small matters came in those days to be raised into tests of loyalty and orthodoxy.

Keble was evidently shrinking from the general society of the college in my time, though a large part were devoted to him. But here was a puzzle, which often occurred to me, then and after. How had he managed to get on with the old Oriel school? Was it that the theological question was less developed then? It was not till his deathbed that Keble would give up the famous line in the 'Christian Year' that gave so much offence to his High Church admirers. Was it that all scholars, and all divines, and all who read their Bibles through, had been thrown together by a common necessity to defend faith, truth, godliness, and common sense against infidelity on the one hand and Simeon on the other? No doubt scholarship created a community of feeling, for Coplestone and Keble might have much to say to one another without approaching theology or any Church question.

When Keble's favourite pupil, Sir William Heathcote, then member for Hants, and afterwards for the University, invited him to Hursley, he created the most beautiful picture of English society that this

century can show. Away from the garish metropolis,
the proud cathedral, and the restless university, Keble
pursued quietly that sublime life of pastoral duty
which is so little esteemed in these days. The great
poet of his Church was content to spend himself in
those humble ministrations which noisy pulpit adventurers proclaim to be utterly beneath their notice,
not to say their contempt.

But there are inevitable drawbacks in any earthly
position. People felt, not unjustly, that Keble was,
as it were, a little smothered in the embrace of a not
very large-minded or open-minded section of the
aristocracy. Landowners cannot help being very
sensitive on points that affect, as they think, their
very existence, and this tenderness they cannot but
impart to their sympathising surroundings. I remember one of Keble's curates, a strong, healthy
man, bursting into tears as he related that Sir
William would probably have to put down one of his
equipages on the repeal of the Corn Laws. Well,
Keble would not have done this, yet it was impossible
not to feel that his sympathies were very one-sided,
and not enlarged or corrected, so to speak, up to the
actual state of things in the Church and in the world.

Moreover, people who have found a quiet harbour and made up their minds to remain there, are
not quite the best advisers for those who are still
struggling with the currents and storms of life. Keble
induced a number of his neighbours and friends to
sign a protest against Her Majesty choosing a
Lutheran Prince for one of her son's godfathers. It
must immediately occur to any reasonable person that

the Vicar of Hursley had nothing at all to do with it, and that if anybody had a call to interfere it was the Primate. But Keble can hardly have considered the certain consequences to the signatories. He had himself renounced all hope of promotion, but there might be some of them to whom it was almost a necessity. Moberly was kept at the grindstone for many years after his strength had begun to fail, and his soul to desire refreshment, through his compliance with this most unnecessary, indeed unjustifiable act.

Keble had not the art, only to be attained by the best natures, assisted by the best breeding and the most propitious circumstances, of being quite ready for any occasion and meeting it perfectly. If one heard nothing at all about a man, except the very trifling incident I am about to relate, one would call him very absent, or awkward, or something of that sort.

On one of the few occasions on which I was at Hursley, we spent the evening in the drawing-room ; Keble and I on one side of the large round table of the period, and Miss Coxwell, afterwards Mrs. Peter Young, on the other side. We were talking. The young lady was at some needlework that required both the two candles to be brought close to it. The candles, like all the candles of those days, rapidly acquired huge chignons. Keble made a long arm, drew the candles across the table close to the edge on his side, and deftly applying the snuffers, restored the wicks to their proper form. But he omitted to replace the candles, and the young lady was even worse off than before he had come to her rescue.

When sufficient time had elapsed to disconnect the reclamation of the missing candles from their abstractor, she stretched across the table and replaced them close to her work. In a quarter of an hour the same double process was repeated, and so it went on all the evening. I think we all three failed in this matter. Keble of course did, in not completing his well-intended kindness ; the lady might have asked for the return of the candles in a way to impress by its prettiness ; and I might have amused Keble and the young lady too by pointing out what he was doing.

Such matters, small as they are, nay the more because they are small, are a school for important matters, often ill done from want of ' manner,' that is an address at once genial and plain. The art of making really good capital out of such light stuff as 'chaffing' or persiflage is best learnt at public schools and in good society, so as it be not the society just of a parish or a clique. But of course there are those who never learn it, for it requires a man to be quick of tongue, simple and kind.

One little way Keble had which must recur to the recollection of those who knew him. It was his habit of suddenly rousing himself, shaking himself rather, throwing his shoulders back, and raising his head. Perhaps his friends, in view of George Herbert's consumptive habits and early death, had often cautioned him against stooping. Perhaps it was the heroic element struggling against the downward tendency of a weak frame. When I last saw Keble, past seventy, he was brisk and upright, though reading and writing more than most people. The trick I have mentioned, which was indeed a spontaneous convulsion of the whole frame, reminded me of George Herbert's quaint appeal to England, to spit out her phlegm and fill her breast with glory. If people would but observe some such *Sursum corda* every quarter of an hour, they would be able to make a better resistance to the weight of years, and whatever else time and decay are sure to bring.

CHAPTER XXXV.

FROUDE.

NO one, even then, would have said that Newman was simply the greatest man among Keble's admirers. He was no more that than he was an 'Evangelical' of the St. Edmund Hall school, or a destructive logician of the Whately type. He has repeatedly said what he was at all times. He was always for a thorough religious conversion, with a real sense of it ; a deep sense of the necessity of doctrinal truth, and an absolute devotion to its claims. No wonder that even when Keble might have heard him in the pulpit many times, and must have had many talks with him, alone or in company, and must also have heard common friends discuss him freely, he still saw the trappings of his old Calvinistic harness hanging about him.

But what was there—who was there—that may have contributed much to determine the direction of this great movement? Robert Wilberforce, besides being a scholar and a theologian, was a conscientious and most laborious man; and, with his youngest brother Henry, was no inconsiderable power. He was also a very good college tutor, with the special qualities for instilling philosophy, poetry, and scholarship into ordinary minds. But he attained not to the foremost rank of the little body now about to shake the Anglican world. If there ever could be any question as to the master spirit of this movement, which now would be a very speculative question indeed, it lies between John Henry Newman and Richard Hurrell Froude.

Froude was a man, such as there are now and then, of whom it is impossible for those that have known him to speak without exceeding the bounds of common admiration and affection. He was elder brother of William, the distinguished engineer, who died lately, after rendering, and while still rendering, most important services to the Admiralty, and of Anthony, the well-known historian, the sons of Archdeacon Froude, a scholar and no mean artist. Richard came to Oriel from Eton, a school which does not make every boy a scholar, if it even tries to do so, but which somehow implants in every nature a generous ambition of one kind or other.

As an undergraduate he waged a ruthless war against sophistry and loud talk, and he gibbeted one or two victims, labelling their sophisms with their names. Elected to a Fellowship, and now the com-

panion of Newman and Pusey, not to speak of elders
and juniors, he had to wield his weapons more reverentially and warily. But he had no wish to do
otherwise.

His figure and manner were such as to command
the confidence and affection of those about him. Tall,
erect, very thin, never resting or sparing himself,
investigating and explaining with unwearied energy,
incisive in his language, and with a certain fiery force
of look and tone, he seemed a sort of angelic presence
to weaker natures. He slashed at the shams, phrases,
and disguises in which the lazy or the pretentious
veil their real ignorance or folly. His features readily
expressed every varying mood of playfulness, sadness, and awe. There were those about him who
would rather writhe under his most cutting sarcasms
than miss their part in the workings of his sympathy
and genius.

Froude was a Tory, with that transcendental idea
of the English gentleman which forms the basis of
Toryism. He was a High Churchman of the uncompromising school, very early taking part with Anselm,
Becket, Laud, and the Nonjurors. Woe to anyone
who dropped in his hearing such phrases as the dark
ages, superstition, bigotry, right of private judgment,
enlightenment, march of mind, or progress. When a
stray man of science fell back on 'law,' or a 'subtle
medium,' or any other device for making matter its own
lord and master, it was as if a fox had broken cover ;
there ensued a chase and no mercy.

Luxury, show, and even comfort he despised and
denounced. He very consistently urged that the

expenses of Eton should be kept down so low as to enable every ordinary incumbent to send his sons there to be trained for the ministry. All his ideas of college life were frugal and ascetic. Having need of a press for his increasing papers and books, he had one made of plain deal. It must have been Woodgate who came in one day, and finding some red chalk, ornamented the press with grotesque figures, which long were there. Froude and Newman induced several of the Fellows to discontinue wine in the common room. As they had already had a glass or two at the high table, they did not require more. There was only one objection to the discontinuance, but it was fatal at last ; and that was its inconvenience when strangers were present.

This preference of tea to wine was no great innovation in Oriel. When I came up at Easter, 1825, one of the first standing jokes against the college, all over the university, was the ' Oriel teapot,' supposed to be always ready ; the centre of the Oriel circle, and its special inspiration. How there ever came to be such an idea I cannot guess, but wherever I went, when I passed the wine, I was asked whether I would not prefer some tea, much to the amusement of the table.

Self-renunciation in every form he could believe in ; most of all in a gentleman, particularly one of a good Devonshire family. His acquaintance with country gentlemen had been special, perhaps fortunate. He had not been in the north of England, in the eastern counties, or in the midlands. It was therefore in perfect simplicity that, upon hearing one day the description of a new member in the Reformed Parliament, he exclaimed, 'Fancy a gentleman not knowing Greek!' I chanced one day to drop most inconsiderately that all were born alike, and that they were made what they are by circumstances and education. Never did I hear the end of that. No retractation or qualification would avail.

When Mr. Bulteel, a Fellow and tutor of Exeter College, mounted the pulpit of St. Mary's, denounced the university and the Church of England, took his name off the books, married the sister of a pastry-cook in High Street, and set up a meeting-house behind Pembroke College, Froude went about for days with a rueful countenance, and could only say 'Poor Bulteel!' He had married a housekeeper, no doubt, Froude thoroughly believed, to chasten his earthly affections and show what a minister ought to be. Nor was Froude's faith in his fellow-countryman much shaken when it turned out that the pastry-cook's sister was still young, accomplished, rather good-looking, not at all dowdy, and that she had a good fortune of her own.

Not to speak of Froude's laborious researches into the history and correspondence of Thomas a Becket, the writer most on his table and his tongue was the above-mentioned William Law, of the second school of Nonjurors, the author of the 'Serious Call,' the antagonist of Hoadly, and the 'most honoured friend and spiritual guide of the whole Gibbon family,' of whom Warburton says that 'he begat Methodism.'

CHAPTER XXXVI.

THE TUITION REVOLUTIONISED.

IN 1831 Newman had finally ceased to be tutor, and to explain this important and to him very painful deprivation, it is necessary to go back a year or two. When he, Wilberforce, and Froude had been working together in the tuition for some terms, and bestowing on their pupils as much time and trouble as is usually only expected from very good private tutors, they proposed to the Provost some improvements in the course of lectures, the selection of books, and the formation of the classes. Dornford was still tutor, but that would have been no difficulty, for he would have had the choice of profiting by the new arrangement, or, if he should prefer it, having his own classes and his own books, by the old routine.

The discussions on these points extended through the year 1829, and were concluded early in 1830. Not to speak of the introduction of modern books to be compared with the ancient classics, as, for example, Butler's Analogy to be read by the side of Lucretius— an innovation claimed for Hampden by his biographer —the principles of the proposed arrangement were an exacter regard to the character and special gifts of each undergraduate, and a closer relation between him and his tutor. It was a large and novel proposition in those days.

The Provost received it with a suspicion amounting

to dismay. He felt that the tutors would thereby have the tuition entirely in their own hands, and that he might find himself left out of the actual course of studies and out of the current of college thought and feeling. It might be all well, he said, while those three men were the tutors, but supposing a tutor with an ambitious spirit and revolutionary views, how was the Provost to control him?

There was also an immediate and practical difficulty of which Hawkins must have had experience the very first year of his Provostship. The three tutors named were even then lecturing in new books, such as the minor Latin poets. Three times a year, at the end of each term, every undergraduate in his turn was summoned to the Tower, that is the room over the college gateway, and examined in all that he had been doing. These Collections, as they were called, were formidable enough to idle students ; not so to the examiners, who had gone through the books often, and who would select their own passages and ask their own questions. But if the tutors were to be always introducing new books, the Provost would have to get them up also, or would have to be content with taking little part in the examinations. Hawkins was about as equal to such an emergency as most men would be. In his own lectures he would occasionally save himself the trouble of laborious preparation, yet detect the omission of it in the class. Thus in reading the Tusculan Disputations he once turned over several leaves and said, ' Please go on there, Mr. ——.' The unhappy man immediately came upon the word Equuleus, and rendered it ' a

little horse ; ' nor was anyone in the class wiser. It is
' a rack of torture.' So ancient is the practice of giving
fond names to diabolical devices.

I do not think the Provost can have objected to
the moderate introduction of modern classics for
illustration and comparison with the old. His edition
of . Milton's ' Paradise Lost,' published before this
date, illustrates with a great abundance of quotations
the classical allusions in the poem, just as the school
editions of Virgil give the passages from Hesiod,
Homer, Aratus, Theocritus, and Columella. But I
should think it likely he would insist at least on a
veto in the selection of modern authors.

The proposals of the three tutors, however, went
beyond the selection of books, for they amounted to
a new organisation of the college, as far as the studies
were concerned, and they were likely to include the
discipline also. There ensued a controversy as to
the academic position of a college tutor, to which the
Provost would not allow a substantive character.
His idea was the French king's—'*L'état, c'est moi.*'
As the three tutors persisted, the Provost announced
that no more undergraduates would be entered to
their names, so that in three years they would have
no classes at all, and that meanwhile he would find
lecturers to do the work.

There were younger Fellows coming on, and the
future was no difficulty. The present emergency was
serious, and the Provost met it with an expedient
which was a great shock to the old college traditions
of Oxford. Hampden, a former Fellow, a man of
ability and university distinction, was then residing

with his family, and taking private pupils at the other end of St. Giles's, and the Provost invited him to give the lectures, for which his learning and his intellect undoubtedly qualified him. It was not a popular step, and it was not successful ; but if the Provost was to hold to his declared views, there was nothing else to be done, and he could hardly be blamed for availing himself of a good instrument found at hand in the hour of need. The tutors finding their classes dwindling, soon left the Provost in sole possession of the ground, but only to find the rising tide of academic revolution bringing on changes far greater than those he had resisted.

In some respects the points contended for by the three tutors were singularly prophetic. They asked for subjects, rather than particular books ; they asked for properly composed classes ; and they asked for the fittest men to teach each class, though it does not appear that they distinctly recognised that the last demand would be likely in time to interfere with the monopoly hitherto possessed by the college tutor. Few can see the inevitable consequences of their own acts. The Provost certainly did not see that he was breaking up the college system, upon which his own exclusive claims over the teaching of the under-graduates depended, when he invited a married lecturer to visit the college just for his hour's work and no more. Little, too, did he see that by insisting on his rights he was hastening the day when the younger members, alike of the college and of the university, would obtain their share in the government of both, and by their greater activity and aptitude for new formations would in effect leave their elders behind.

Nevertheless it cannot be denied that the Provost seemed to be justified by the event in not virtually resigning the education of his college into Newman's hands. He foresaw the consequences of Newman's policy, though, happily for his present comfort, he did not foresee the consequences of his own.

There were men, however, who might have been consulted, and who ought to have been consulted, and who could have told the Provost that the three tutors had both right and the public interest on their side. Arnold was now conducting Rugby on the principle of selection, adaptation, and careful manipulation. He was sending away every boy not likely to do good to himself or to the school. Contenting himself with a general oversight of the rest, he chiefly devoted himself to the twenty boys most qualified to benefit by his instruction. He also innovated considerably on the old routine of books and studies. It is impossible to imagine a greater innovation than to occupy lads of sixteen and under in the unfathomable problems of Niebuhr's ' Roman History.'

Some years before this, when at Charterhouse, beaten as I was out of the construing by the quickness of the pace, I amused myself with drawing up a genealogical table illustrating the absurdities of Livy's chronology. I handed it to Russell, who looked over it and returned it with a smile, as much as to say it was a matter one need not trouble about.

The position Arnold made for himself was that of

a private tutor, with the pick of a large public school, itself purged by frequent dismissals, and in the hands of colleagues of his own choosing. It is hardly to be supposed that he would have advised his friend the Provost of Oriel to inflict on the three tutors an invariable routine, without any choice in the selection or the arrangement of the young men admitted into the college, not invariably by the rule of selection, some indeed chiefly on the recommendation of wealth or rank It is true the example of a public school does not apply in all respects to a college ; for in a public school the head master is the teacher, while the head of a college is not. But Arnold's practice pointed to the necessity of careful selection, manipulation of classes, and adaptation of studies, to be placed in the hands of the actual teachers, that is the tutors.

Both the statutes of the university, and the practice ancient and still existent, left the studies very much in the hands of the tutors and at their discretion— indeed, during last century to an extreme degree. The Provost had to confess to this by altering the usage, and virtually violating the statutes, for thenceforward he had to enter undergraduates no longer under respective tutors, but under one common name for form sake. By accepting the tuition on this footing, Hampden lent himself to alter the custom of the college, to deprive the undergraduates of real tuition, and to oust the real tutors, whom he was invited to supersede.

Hampden was the man of all others to appreciate the advantage of real tuition. It must have been ever present to his mind that the practical interest taken in him by his own tutor, Davison, from the day he entered Oriel, had been, as they say, the making of him. Davison himself was very strong on this point. The 'Edinburgh Review' had charged the University of Oxford with the scantiness and weakness of its public examinations. To this Davison replied that the reviewer had forgotten that at Oxford the colleges did the work of the university ; and that every undergraduate was under examination sufficiently public every day, finishing with a solemn examination by the Provost and tutors at the end of the term. This would not be thought a sufficient answer in these days, but its very insufficiency shows the immense reliance which Davison placed on the then existing system of handing the undergraduate over to the tutors, and expecting them to do everything for him. Of course Hampden must be assumed to have thought himself right, under the present circumstances, but he was not quite in a position to complain of persecution, carried on, he said, not merely in controversy, where he gave as much as he took, but in the more painful form of social affronts, which he imagined himself to be continually receiving.

More than a year elapsed between the introduction of Hampden and Newman's final release from the tuition. He held on till he found himself alone, when he felt his position no longer tenable. Meantime there had arisen an awkward question. The college, not the Provost alone, had the appointment to the college offices, dean, treasurer, junior treasurer, and librarian. They had generally been held by tutors. Froude and Wilberforce thought it important that the Fellows should assert the right of independent choice, as otherwise a precedent would be set up for allowing the offices to be as much at the disposal of the Provost as he claimed the tuition to be. There were certain names which it was understood the Provost desired. A counter-programme was suggested, containing Newman's name. On these occasions it was the custom of the Fellows to form themselves in the order of seniority, and for the youngest Fellow to be called on first to name the man for the office. I happened to be youngest Fellow. Every name of the opposition programme in my hand was carried. I found it too much for my nerve. Passing the night without sleep, all next morning's chapel I was in tears. However, I met with nothing but kindness, and between the Fellows themselves there was no sore on this point.

Late in 1835 or early in 1836, the Provost walked across the Quad in his academicals, and asked me whether I was willing to take a part in the tuition. I was much surprised at the question. I can now hardly say why. From the beginning of the controversy I had taken the part of the three tutors, and had given up all thought of the tuition. I did not take into account that the Provost had no call to recognise this, even if he suspected it, and that he was justified, indeed necessitated, to do whatever he could to carry on the tuition as much as possible in the old lines, that is by resident Fellows. But I had to reply. I did not wish to argue the question between him and Newman ; indeed, it would have been ridiculous for

me to make the attempt.   So I replied that I did not
feel myself equal to the tuition.

A thousand times have I asked myself the question
whether I lied or not in that statement.   I had unbounded confidence in myself. I had all my life learnt
more by teaching than by solitary study.   I could
certainly keep ahead of my pupils, which was all that
many tutors ever did.   I could come round my class
by questions they were not prepared for.   I was sure
always to hear mistakes which it would be easy to
correct.   In matter of fact a tutor often did no more
than half of the class could have done quite as well.
Though the method of instruction was very effectual,
yet it was easy sailing.   Moreover, I had not quite
given up my classics, for I had been tutorising a
younger brother, and had just taken a Winchester lad
at a hand gallop through the Odyssey, my instructions—very unnecessary—being not to make him too
much of a scholar.   I had also had nightly village
classes in the New Testament.

The Provost made matters easier for my conscience by the next question, which was to the effect
that he was to understand I had not kept up my
books.   As for 'my books,' those that I had taken up
for my examinations were a beggarly account indeed,
but the phrase was usually employed to denote the
'sciences,' that is the chief philosophical works of
Aristotle, and other books of special difficulty.   It
was quite true that I had not once looked into the
Rhetoric, or the Ethics, or the Politics, or the Greek
Plays, or Pindar, or even Herodotus.   So it was true
I had not kept up my books.   But though that was

true, it was not the whole truth; for I had purposely not kept them up, as having no thought of the tuition, and this I did not tell the Provost. As far as I am concerned I hope I have now made a clean breast.

But why did the Provost make the proposal, and with such solemnity? I think I see it. On his view of the case I was bound to take part in the usual college duties. Nay, I had taken the office of junior treasurer, and also that of Censor Theologicus. As it was my duty to take part in the tuition, it was his duty to propose it. He had also laid down, as Coplestone had before him, that a Fellow ought not to take rooms in college unless he were tutor, and there I was in college, and not a tutor.

CHAPTER XXXVII.

NEWMAN AT ST. MARY'S.

NEWMAN was now one of the preachers of the day. Oxford, it must be remembered, receives twelve hundred young men from all parts of these isles, three times a year, sending them back again after a few weeks, to stand a fire of questions, to tell their fresh experiences, to cheer solitudes with bright images, and to enliven monotony with novel characters and utterances. Every undergraduate visits alternately the centre and the extremity of his system a dozen times, and is every time more and more looked for and welcomed. By the year 1831 undergraduates from the Lakes, from Ireland, even from Scotland, from houses long addicted to Cambridge, or sat upon, from all time, by the metropolis ; from parsonages occupied by the same family and the same traditional opinions time out of mind ; were all coming up and securing the next Sunday afternoon a good place at St. Mary's.

Many of them, perhaps most of them, being of other colleges, were never in the same room with Newman, and never exchanged a word with him. Frederick Faber came up in the summer of 1832, and at once attached himself to the St. Mary's congregation. He was a singularly attractive and popular person, making friends all around, but was not personally acquainted with Newman till three or four years after. He missed at St. Mary's the continual introspection, the experiences, the emotions, and the assurances in which he had been bred up.

No wonder that Newman now found himself regarded with deep though indefinite suspicion by the party which had hitherto claimed the monopoly of gospel truth. That undergraduates should flock to a parish service, to hear a man with whom they had no university or college relations, was a serious incident and must have its meaning. It brought, however, no accession to the weekly tea-meetings at St. Edmund Hall, and there was evidently a distance between the two circles. The Evangelical parents of the man who came home talking about nobody but Newman, and about nothing but his sermons, were sorely perturbed and seized every opportunity for penetrating the mystery.

Visiting such a household, many miles from Oxford, in the summer of 1831, I was urged, besought, and invoked a dozen times over in one evening, to say truly and outright, with no faltering or speciality of tone, but in the orthodox accents of unflinching certainty, whether Newman was a 'good man.' On the right ring of the response depended the happiness of a poor lady who had recently dismissed, after many years of faithful service, a housekeeper whose only crime was escorting a visitor across a single field in her master's grounds on a Sunday afternoon.

An Oxford clergyman of the same school gave a remarkable, though unintended testimony, to this oft-challenged 'goodness.' There was cholera in Oxford, and he had to take his usual holiday. There might be some visiting necessary, and funerals involving danger. Clergymen under no obligation to incur the risk might hold it their duty to avoid it. So he carefully drew up a long list of clergymen to be applied to in the order stated, and gave it to his clerk in case of need. One of the clergy applied to took the list out of the clerk's hand, and found it headed with Newman's name, followed by those of his known friends in the order of their reputed devotion to him. After this came the clergymen of this gentleman's own school. It was never known whether he made this arrangement as thinking the clergymen first in his list more likely to attend the summons, or as deeming their lives less precious than those of his own friends.

Whether acting in defence or not, Newman had resigned the secretaryship of the local Church Missionary Society, on the ground that it dispensed with the necessity of bishops, as he explained at length in a pamphlet. The step much simplified his relations with some former coadjutors. This pamphlet I read at the time—indeed, I think Newman gave me a copy. I remember my impression, superficial as it might be. It was that Newman had found it necessary to make a stand against a general decay of faith and authority. He would not be swept down in a current overpowering in its bulk, though composed of inferior material. He must cling to something, and it must be a Divine ordinance, and this he found in the Bishops, or in what shortly became a watchword, and then a byword, 'Apostolical Succession.'

CHAPTER XXXVIII.

ST. EDMUND HALL.

In a back lane, buried between the splendid buildings of Queen's, the Norman tower of St. Peter's, and the tall limes of New College garden, is the very ancient Hall of St. Edmund, so named after an Archbishop of Canterbury, canonised by Innocent III. It had not been true to the *religio loci*; in fact Henry VIII. had stept in the way. When I came to Oxford, it was soon pointed out to me as the headquarters, the cave, the den of the 'Evangelical party.' It was entirely in the hands of the Vice-Principal, Mr. Hill, who ran a long, a consistent, and an honourable career, but, so far as the Hall was concerned, singularly unsuccessful—indeed, doomed to disappointment. Mr. Hill was a good scholar. He did his duty to his men as a tutor and as a shepherd of souls, and the Hall had, I believe, a good character in the schools. But it was expected to do and be more. It was to be a burning and shining light in the surrounding darkness, and that it entirely failed to be.

The society was formed by selection. It consisted of young men who had shown early ability, and some interesting form of goodness ; who made a profession and aspired to the ministry, but whose immediate relatives were too poor to send them to an ordinary college. A benevolent friend, a good uncle, or a society, had taken compassion on them, and sent them to St. Edmund Hall, where spirituality and economy were said to be combined. Thus all the circumstances and signs of failure were here concentrated in one focus. All were poor, struggling men, starting with the fixed idea that they were out of society, which, it was a comfort to think, was too worldly and wicked a thing to be coveted, or envied.

There were men of reading and of learning there, but they did not find themselves at home, and they made their escape to another college at the first opportunity—Jacobson to wit. Matters must have been even worse at the beginning of the century. An old family friend of mine, Mr. Wayland, together with his friend Mr. Joyce, who became a popular private tutor, and used to help Lord Grenville to write Elegiacs on his departed dogs, and another literary gentleman, found themselves thrown together by misdirected kindness in St. Edmund Hall. I cannot say that they blessed the friends who had so ordered their career. They were French and Italian scholars, and had seen a little of the world. Mr. Wayland's favourite author was Horace, and one of my saddest experiences was the death of his only son Horace, when I was on a visit to his parsonage. These three gentlemen, who must have been at the Hall in the first years of the century, declared there was then nobody there they could associate with.

These Edmund Hall men could be known any-where. They were either very shabby or very toppish They all had the look of dirt, which perhaps was not their fault, for they had dirty complexions. How is it that goodness, poverty, and a certain amount of literary or religious ambition, produce an unpleasant effect on the skin? There must have been something in the air of the spot, which certainly was a dark hole. In those days the university sermons were occasion-ally preached at St. Peter's, adjoining St. Edmund Hall. The undergraduates of the Hall felt it their own ground, and took early possession of the front rows of the gallery. I shall not say who it was—but he became a very distinguished Prelate—proposed that before the opening of the church door, there should be arranged a row of basins of water, with soap and towels, on the book ledge before the front row, with the admonition to wash and be clean.

Having no secular literature, no great matters to talk about, and very little indeed of what is now called Biblical literature, these men gossiped, gossiped, gossiped, from morning to night, running about from room to room in quest of somebody to talk with and something to talk about. An acquaintance of mine with friends there related that an undergraduate, finding himself obliged to disappoint some regular callers, chalked on his ' oak ' 'I shall be out till two, after that I shall be in.' Wit was not altogether extinct in St. Edmund Hall, for a friend chalked ' st ' before ' out,' and ' th ' before ' in.'

As the St. Edmund Hall men divided their time between self-contemplation, mutual amusement, and the reading of emotional works ; studying no history, not even critically studying the Scriptures, and knowing no more of the world than sufficed to condemn it, they naturally, and perforce, were driven into a very dangerous corner. This was invention. Their knowledge was imaginary. So too was their introspection, their future, sometimes even their past. All precocity is apt to take this form. The quick ripening mind, for lack of other matter, feeds upon itself. These young men had been reared on unsubstantial and stimulating food ; on pious tales, on high-wrought deathbeds, on conversations as they ought to have been, on one-sided biographies. Truth of opinion, they had always been told, was incomparably moie important than truth of fact. Henry Wilberforce used to relate the rather unguarded speech of a well-known Archdeacon, friend of Sumner, Bishop of Winchester. 'It's remarkable that all the most spiritually-minded men I have known were in their youth extraordinary liars.'

Golightly was shy of the St. Edmund Hall men. He could not but be shy, for they would have expected introductions which he could not have given them Nor did he much like them. However, one of them, by his insinuating manners and glibness of tongue, managed to break through social defences, and Golightly became much interested in him. He had already won all hearts in his own Hall. His name I remember, but when I have finished my say the reader will see why I do not state it. When this man had been at Oxford so long as to be about to take his degree, there was a sad exposure. He had been going on for years showing every now and then most interesting love-letters from various ladies competing for his hand, while he could still say he was free. He showed also copies of his own replies, and there would sometimes be a muster of his friends to hear the next news from this or that distracted adorer.

All at once it was discovered that the man had written all the letters, those of the ladies as well as his own. He had to humble himself before the Hall, and Golightly came in afterwards to administer a tremendous verbal castigation. In a year or so Golightly heard that the man was about to be ordained with a title to an important town curacy in one of the home counties. He immediately drew up a full statement of the man's delinquencies and sent it to Sumner. By the very showing of the case it was now a bygone affair. The man had repented ; he had made public amends, and he had been absolved by Mr.

Hill, whose testimonials he presented to the Bishop. Sumner could do nothing.   But Golightly was far from satisfied.   He, shrewdest of men, with a special insight into character, had opened his house and his heart to a liar and an impostor.   Unless I am mistaken in the identity, the man achieved a long, useful, and honourable career.   No doubt, in other spheres as well as in the Church, many a youthful liar has become an honest man, though finding honesty the less easy for his early bias the other way.

CHAPTER XXXIX.

THE 'THEOLOGICAL LIBRARY.'

In the year 1831, in a Vacation, when Newman and Blanco White had the college very much to themselves, the same post brought them invitations from Mr. Hugh James Rose to contribute to the 'Theological Library,' about to be published by Mr. Rivington. The first number, containing the 'Life of Wiclif,' by Mr. Le Bas, came out the following year, and the annexed programme announced that there were already in preparation—the 'Consistency of Revelation,' by Dr. Shuttleworth ; the 'History of the Inquisition,' by Joseph Blanco White ; the 'History of the Principal Councils,' by J. H. Newman ; and the 'Life of Martin Luther,' by H. J. Rose.   They were to be handy little volumes, uniform, and with appropriate embellishments.

Both the Oriel men were well pleased. It would be Newman's introduction to the literary and theological world, for he had not yet achieved any considerable publication. Blanco White was at the time very much out of humour with *littérateurs* and publishers, and was becoming rather tedious in his gossip about people little known at Oxford. So this was a turn of fortune in his favour. The two colleagues, as they were now to be, compared notes, and immediately made inquiries about the books it would be necessary to read and the time they would have to do it in. As they met frequently, and could not but ask one another questions, there was a growing sense of difficulty and something like reserve on both sides. Up to this time there had been no reserve beyond that arising from difference of occupations and studies, and from each having his own more intimate friends.

Both were violinists, but with different instruments. Blanco White's was a very small instrument whatever its technical name. Poor gentleman ! Night after night anyone walking in the silence of Merton Lane might hear his continual attempts to surmount some little difficulty, returning to it again and again, like Philomel to her vain regrets. With Reinagle and an amateur, Newman and Blanco White had frequent quartettes at the latter's lodgings, where I was all the audience. I have long been unable to recall the figure or the performance of the nameless amateur, and have latterly suspected him to be a shade of my own raising, and that these were trios. Most interesting was it to contrast Blanco White's excited and indeed agitated countenance with Newman's sphinxlike immobility, as the latter drew long rich notes with a steady hand.

Neither of the above undertakings was fruitless, but in neither case did the results appear in the 'Theological Library,' or in the intended form, or upon the matter that Hugh J. Rose had indicated. In July, 1833, Newman's labours revealed themselves in the 'History of the Arians,' completed the previous year, in writing which he saw what he calls the 'ghost,' which eventually drove him to the Church of Rome ; and in June, 1835, Blanco White gave to the world, from Liverpool, his 'Observations on Heresy and Orthodoxy,' announcing his rejection of the whole patristic theology, and his profession of Christianity as a Unitarian. That Hugh J. Rose should have conceived it possible that either Newman or Blanco White would be able to contain himself within the form and dimensions of an entertaining manual, shows how little even great men can estimate the volcanic working of free and independent thought.

Before these two friends finally parted in their opposite directions, they could confer pleasantly upon the restraints they were respectively suffering. One Council Newman soon found to be more than enough for his limits, and Blanco White soon made the discovery that a true history of the Inquisition would properly include every act of man which put the professors of a different creed at a disadvantage, or made them uncomfortable. This he deemed the special

vice of religious establishments, indeed of all definite
creeds, and very naturally expected all good people
to agree with him.

As the two contributors to Mr. Rivington's series
warmed up to their labours, they saw less and less of one
another. One Sunday evening, in the common room,
Newman roused himself and exclaimed 'Who's seen
anything of Blanco White lately? Let's go and take
tea with him.' Some three or four of us went off to
his lodgings, and found the poor gentleman at home.
After an hour's forced hilarity and agreeableness, we
all felt it a relief to say 'good-night,' and part for
our own rooms. It was about the last incident of a
long residence, which had been a picturesque and
pleasant element in college society, but had latterly
taxed the forbearance of both the college and its
guest.

Blanco White enjoyed conversation, even with
much younger men, from whom he could learn but
little; but it frequently occurred that he brought a
topic suddenly to a close, gently intimating that he
did not think it fair to say all he had to say when the
hearer might not be duly prepared for weighing it.
Nevertheless his topics were apt to be suggestive.
Indeed, they could not fail of it, for out of the
abundance of the heart every man speaks. One of
his topics was false enumeration, that is the number-
ing of things not in the same category. It is a folly
to be found sometimes in our ordinary school books.
For example : ' Write down a man ; his hands, his arms
and legs, his fingers and toes, his nose, eyes and ears,
his heart and his brains. How many are they alto-

gether ?' Such an enumeration and such an addition imply misapprehension at every step, and a complete abeyance of the reasoning faculties. The bearing of Blanco White's special dislike of this practice is of course obvious.

Then, what did people mean when they talked of the Church? What was it? Who was it? Where was it to be found? Did it signify more than certain persons agreed to act together, and to make the same profession? But Blanco White was not the only man then asking this question, for it would be hard to say who were not asking it, if not openly, not the less anxiously in their own minds. Though there were men with a cut and dried answer, and very positive, yet it might be found that no two agreed. It was Keble who began at Oriel what some think the worship of the Church as the mother of us all. For my own part I will confess that I had to use great force in regarding the Church as a mother, though there was no gainsaying the fact that I was born in her.

In the latter days of the movement proper, when Newman felt his moorings to the old shore looser and looser day by day, a singular incident compelled him to recognise openly his changed position. Isaac Williams published a volume of poetry, called the 'Baptistry,' upon a series of very curious and beautiful engravings, by Boetius a Bolswert, in an old Latin work, entitled *Via Vitæ Æternæ*. In these pictures, besides other things peculiar to the Roman Church, there frequently occurs the figure of the Virgin Mother, crowned and in glory; the object of worship, and distributing the gifts of Heaven. For this figure

Williams substituted the Church, and thereby incurred a protest from Newman, for adopting a Roman
Catholic work just so far as suited his own purpose,
without caring for the further responsibilities. Blanco
White would certainly have objected to the substitution quite as much as the original, probably still
more.

As to the subject of false enumeration I have
mentioned above, the Provost used to approach it
from the opposite quarter, urging the convenience of
keeping in the head the number of persons, or things,
or duties, or engagements, each separately liable to
slip out of recollection, but easily retained by the
bond of a number. Frequently recurring to the
point, he instilled the convenience of number, and so
justified the wisdom of antiquity in arranging all
things in numerical groups ; twelve of this, nine of
that, seven of something else, and three in some cases.

This, however, was comprised in a general and
very important instruction, often given by the Provost to young writers. It was, to pay such attention
to the arrangement of paragraphs and clauses, to the
due prominence of names and important words, that
upon returning to the MS. the writer would immediately find himself as much at home with it as
when he left it, instead of having to waste precious
time and strength in recovering his lost relations with
his own handiwork. A MS. thus written has some
chance of impressing itself on the memory, and enabling the writer to recall what he has written, without
having the trouble of going to the MS., and perhaps
having to look for it.

CHAPTER XL.

THE REFORM BILL.

WE were nearly all Tories at Oxford. The comparatively few Liberals had indefinite yearnings in the other direction, but no plans that we heard of. Bonamy Price used to tell us, with bated breath, on the authority of Arnold, that at Paris it was a settled thing the Duke of Orleans was to succeed Charles X. Price may not remember this. I do. I was a Bourbonist, knowing next to nothing of the Bourbons.

I did not know, for example, that not only Charles X., but even Louis XVIII., always had ready for the emergency the programme of a war with England. Fortunately they were like the old lady who will keep her ace of trumps so long in hand that it has at last to be played in vain. Louis Philippe and Guizot thought to profit by the mistake, and accordingly kept the little quarrel with England always simmering, apologising privately all the time, on the ground of political necessity. So whether it was for the elder or for the younger branch, English sympathy was equally unrequited. When the July Revolution was coming on, I was exceedingly moved by Prince Polignac's manifesto against the Orleanist machinations. I thought it a document for all ages. All Oxford, indeed, was for the 'elder branch,' and was greatly scandalised when Harington of Brasenose, then Denison's close ally, hoisted the tricolor in his sailing boat.

We seemed very soon to be following in the wake
of France, excepting that here it was the King himself that led the way.   During the progress of the
Reform Debates, Oxford men gave their characteristic
contributions to the controversy.   Keble circulated a
most moving appeal to the British electors.   Pusey
left the matter to his brother Philip.   Newman neither
did nor said anything that I can remember.   His
particular aversion was oligarchy.   A monarch may
be ' a fell monster of iniquity,' or he may be a church
founder, or even the converter of a race.   Democracies
may be wielded.   They acknowledge the tongue and
the pen.   Aristocracies have their divine tradition and
their natural gifts.   But an oligarchy is powerful for
evil only, never for good.   There are always bad elements in it, and the bad elements always prevail.
These, however, are abstract opinions.   Newman had
plenty to say on this or that utterance, but I cannot
recall that he had formed any estimate of the working
of the Reform Bill.   When the Reformed Parliament
began to show its animus towards the Church of
England he became outspoken, but not, that I can
remember, till then.   For my own part, not speaking
much, I took in all the more.   While at Oxford that
year one heard every day dreadful accounts of what
was done, said, threatened, and designed in all quarters.   Much of this has been since actually done ;
and yet I live to tell the tale, nay more, to have helped
in doing some of it ; for I have to confess that some
things I thought very bad then, I have since thought
better of.

At Derby, such Tories as there were or had been,

were in despair. For many years the True Blue
Club, of which I was not a member, had annually
testified to Church and State with jovial and exulting
celebrations. County and town then met together,
and the *élite* of the town received with open arms
some of the queerest personages to be found in it.
But the Reform Bill came like a simoom on this gay
and motley company. Our strenuous friend James
Dean, my brother James's private tutor, all backbone,
but all fire nevertheless, was quite ready to take a
part in a counter-demonstration. So after he had
consulted some old Tory colleagues, we set to work.
I was to write the petitions, to both Houses of Parliament I think, though that to the Commons would
not be of much use.

I drew up a monster indictment of some fifty
counts against the Bill ; the policy, the party, Radicals,
dissenters, and the rabble generally. I think I pretty
well succeeded in enumerating, as the inevitable consequences of the measure, almost everything that has
actually come to pass during the last fifty years —not
quite everything, indeed, for the present state of things
in Ireland and in the House of Commons was beyond
my most dismal forecast. A meeting, summoned
by circular, was held in a room used for committee
meetings, over a bookseller's shop in the market-
place, kept by a good sort of man whom my father
had brought to Derby in 1815. The leading 'Church
and State' banker was in the chair ; and my pretty
petition was, as I then thought, mauled a little, and I
daresay pruned of some extravagances. There had
been a magnificent display of moderation in the

original, but my friends. now deemed it expedient to make still further admissions. They were all now desirous of a judicious and well-considered Reform.

We must have had wonderful faith to stand up for the existing Parliamentary system, with such a state of things as we saw even immediately around us. Derby, Nottingham, and Leicester kept common political accounts in the Whig interest. Any man who could be perfectly trusted was made burgess of all three boroughs, and these threefold burgesses were a large if not preponderating part of the three constituencies. In Derby every burgess who chose to ask for it had his regular fee of two guineas for his vote, as young William Strutt, afterwards Lord Belper, found to his sorrow. Though a man might have large property in the town, live in one of its best houses, and employ scores of men, he had now no chance of the freedom, unless he were a known Whig.

The Reformers had the run of the Town Hall, opposite our committee room. Poor ' Charley Hope,' the leading spirit of the True Blue Club, was now near the close of his fifth mayoralty, and they insisted that he was bound to summon a meeting to take the sense of the town. He consented, distinctly stipulating that as soon as he had opened the meeting he should be at liberty to vacate the chair, leaving the meeting to fill it with some one more to their mind. He did as he said he would do, but I, who was present, saw it struck a damp into the people, and they did not like to see his back as he left the room. He ought to have retired facing the foe, and covering his retreat with a blessing. But this is more easily said than done.

His withdrawal left the coast clear, and full advantage was taken of it. The enemy immediately denounced ours as a ' hole and corner meeting,' and the petition itself as a hole and corner petition.

It lay at the shop for signature, just opposite the Town Hall, with due notice in the window that there it lay within ; and my colleague and I went about night and day rallying the scattered forces of the old cause. Most declined on the ground of the uselessness of the movement and the probable dangers to themselves. But there were more than a hundred names, many of them of good and brave men. A better hundred I believe there never were.

I sent it up, so it had been indicated to me as the proper course, to the Marquis of Londonderry, forgotten now, but then a respected though vehement politician. Together with it I sent a private letter, describing, in what I thought proper terms, the character of the meeting in the Town Hall, the language of the speakers there, and the intentions everywhere avowed, and extending far beyond Parliamentary Reform. The Marquis presented the petition, and I think read some of it, though that would be a long business. He also read my letter, or the greater part of it. I called one good man a ' democrat.' I mentioned that Edward Strutt, now the young leader of the Liberal party, did not himself altogether approve of the Bill, which was probably true, if only because it retained the freemen. But what was most needless and most foolish, I mentioned the withdrawal of the clerical Mayor from the chair, after formally opening the meeting in the Town Hall. The

Marquis gave their lordships, and consequently the people of Derby, the benefit of these communications. The Duke of Devonshire, finding his manor poached upon, demanded the name of the writer, which the Marquis gave. The Duke had only heard of one of the name in Derby, and he was not likely to write such a letter. He was quite right there. The gentleman, whose name was pronounced, though not spelt, like mine, was an eminent solicitor who had the care of several large county estates, and with whom the Duke had business relations.

This was on Tuesday. The Bill was thrown out after sunrise on Saturday, and the news, by a great effort, arrived at Derby soon after sunset the same day. Immediately very strong placards appeared in the hostile shops, and wherever bills were usually posted. The Reformers got at the late Mayor's own church tower and rang a muffled peal. The placards and the bellmen summoned the population to the market-place. The streets were, however, already thronged with the men who had just received their week's wages. Speakers were soon forthcoming in the market-place. Some one proposed they should wreck the shop, then right before their eyes, where the 'hole and corner' petition had lain for signature. So they set to work, gutted the shop, and broke the windows.

Amongst other drunken men there were some from the iron and lead works. One of them conceived the happy thought of fetching a sledge-hammer and breaking the slight iron pillar supporting the front of the building. He and his comrades struck at the pillar for some time, with no result happily

for, had they succeeded, the whole building would
have come down upon them. The mob waited to see
the expected downfall, amusing themselves meanwhile with a bonfire of the books and stationery.

As the iron pillar refused to yield, something else
must be done. A voice suggested our house, and a
friend in the crowd ran to give us warning. We all
rushed to close the front gates and the shutters.
While we were so engaged the mob made its appearance, and as the road contractors had left some
heaps of broken stone handy, the stones soon began
to fly in. Every pane in the forty front and side
windows was broken, but somehow the mob were
afraid of being caught in a trap by getting behind the
house. Of course the shutters, as well as much of the
stone work, were injured. It was a still night, and the
breaking of the glass was heard a mile out of the town,
and mistaken for a discharge of musketry.

Another body of Reformers went from the market-
place to the house of a Mr. Eaton, a surgeon, and a
rather noisy member of the True Blue Club. This
gentleman was great-grandson of Alderman Eaton,
who attended on the Duke of Perth in 1745, and over-
heard the council of war in which the young Pre-
tender declared he would rather be buried alive
where he was than give up his march to London ;
but, after a long and hot discussion, had to consent
to a retreat northward. The Reformers gutted the
poor man's house and drove him into the Derwent,
that flowed by the foot of his garden.

Attacking many houses as they passed, they
gathered strong and took a stand in St. Alkmund's

churchyard, at the vicarage of the late Mayor, who had offended them by vacating the chair at the Town Hall. Here they broke every pane of glass, besides other damage, and kept up such volleys of stones that the inmates, including several ladies, were driven from one corner to another, and even into cupboards, to escape them. One division went to Chaddesden, and broke every window in Sir Robert Wilmot's house, back as well as front. Another went to Markeaton Hall, the seat of the Mundys, and did the same. It was the poachers probably who directed the mob to these two houses. They were at this work most of the night. A good gentleman, still living, whom I had described as a democrat in my letter to the Marquis, sent to offer us the use of his house for the night. We managed to do without it. He had not been quite hitting it off with his own workpeople ; indeed, one of the charges I brought against the leading Reformers was that they were trying to turn against the political state of things the discontent they were suffering from at home. Of the wisdom or the justice of this charge I say nothing. It must have been many mobs who did the work of that night, several of them probably directed by merely personal malice, since no other reason could be found. Plunder there was, too, but it was just the accident of a fellow fancying some article and rescuing it from the wreck.

I and a brother got up early and visited the scenes of devastation. The town was placarded with notices put out by the new Mayor, inviting all well-disposed citizens to a meeting in the Town Hall to take measures for the restoration of order. The previous evening, at the approach of the mob, my brother had been sent off to the Mayor to ask for assistance, though what assistance he could render it was not easy to see. So the poor man thought himself, for as soon as he heard of the mob in the market-place, and the work going on there, he went to bed. However, he presented himself to my brother in his nightcap, and told him he didn't know what he could do. In the course of the night he issued the notice I have mentioned. The bellmen who the evening before had been calling the population to a meeting in the market-place, were now calling the citizens to a meeting in the Town Hall. The Mayor's notion was that the friends of order would be in the majority.

At nine, the appointed hour, the Town Hall was full. By a side door I got to a seat a place or two from the Mayor. Some one came up to me and warned me of the danger of exposing myself, but my face was not much known in the town ; nor did I think anybody would harm me. In a few minutes a man got up and proposed that they should proceed to the town and county gaols, and let out all the prisoners. It was carried by acclamation. Upon this I went home to breakfast, expecting the mob to pass on its errand very soon. Some long-winded fellow must have kept them, for they did not come, and I began to think they had thought better of this move.

Soon after breakfast we started for the half-past ten service. On passing out of our gates we saw the mob coming up the street. Common instinct took us all, nine or ten, into the middle of the road, so that we met the mob face to face. It divided for us, and we passed through without hearing a word; indeed, some touched their hats to us. During prayers we heard distant tumult, and before prayers were over we heard shots. The mob had gone first to the old county gaol, now used as the town gaol. Taking up an iron lamp-post, they applied it as a battering-ram against the door. When that began to give, the governor surrendered at discretion, having already opened the doors of the cells and mustered the prisoners. There were about a score of them, some debtors and some small offenders; who now walked out of gaol to gratify their deliverers, and returned that evening or the next morning.

Thence the mob went a couple of hundred yards to the newly-built county gaol, standing on an octagonal area surrounded by a high wall, and with a deeply recessed Doric entrance. The assailants could not be touched from the walls, and a hundred of them could have worked for an hour at the door without molestation from within. The governor and his turnkeys scrambled to the top of some ornamental stone work over the entrance, pointed guns, gave due warning, and then fired as much downwards as they could, killing one young man and wounding another —mere lookers-on, of course. I might just as well have been shot myself as I stood in the crowd that was breaking the windows of the 'New Times' office, on the withdrawal of the Bill of Pains and Penalties in 1820. The siege of the county gaol was raised quickly, but the mob had entire possession of town and neighbourhood till the middle of Tuesday.

The wonder is they did not do worse than they did.

A troop of Yeomanry came into the town on Monday, but as they were all neighbouring farmers and well-known faces, it was judged best that they should do nothing. This might be right, but one may yet ask what Yeomanry are for, if they are to do nothing in the only case in which they can be wanted. The question has also an important bearing on the scheme of military centres, and regiments raised and kept within given localities. The magistrates sent to Nottingham, where there were two troops of cavalry; but these were wanted in the market-place to protect the shops, while the mob were gutting and burning the Castle, situated in another hundred, and belonging to the Duke of Newcastle. On Monday morning the authorities sent the bellmen around again with a general invitation to a meeting in the Town Hall to address the King, praying him to persevere in Reform, but the populace paid no attention to it; indeed, most of them were now too drunk to do anything but break windows and commit petty acts of destruction.

On Tuesday there arrived a troop of Hussars, which drew up and formed in the market-place, waiting for orders. The mob assembled opposite them, and the pavement all round was crowded with spectators. Some fellows came out of the mob, made speeches, and defied the soldiers to do anything. The Riot Act was read, and the soldiers were ordered to charge the mob, which they did slowly. One orator held his ground till the horse's head was almost over him, when the hussar fired his piece over the man's head, and so killed a poor fellow as he was carrying a tankard of ale across a street near two hundred yards off. The hussars quickened their pace; the mob fled in all directions up lanes and courts, pursued by the hussars, one of whom charged up a high flight of stone steps, reared his horse against the door, burst it open, and presented himself in the midst of the terrified foe, returning however in peace.

The town was quiet immediately, except that the rioters were too drunk to return to work, and lounged about the streets. The well-disposed inhabitants were formed into patrolling parties, marching about night and day for a fortnight, and were hospitably invited to supper by those who could afford it. Some rode about in pairs, with directions to give immediate information of any gathering. I visited most of these pickets, and was told I had better take care of myself.

The casualties were not many, but were very sad. Henry Haden, eldest son of an eminent surgeon, and uncle of Mr. Seymour Haden, the distinguished etcher, was a favourite with the town and a musical amateur. While watching the progress of the mob in the heart of the town, he heard some fellows say they meant to go next to Kedleston Hall, the magnificent seat of the Curzons, containing a fine gallery of paintings. He was their medical attendant. Trying to force his way through the mob to send a messenger to Kedleston, he fainted, was brought home, and died before morning. It could never be known whether he had been exerting himself too much, or had had some rough usage.

Poor Mr. Hope, whom I have introduced in a former chapter as one of two clergymen of the period, received such a shock to his system, and felt so deeply his undeserved usage at the hands of old neighbours and acquaintances as it were, that he soon dwindled into the shadow of his once portly figure. Mr. Eaton, the surgeon, who was driven into the river, died of vexation and the chill. The poor youth who was shot from the county gaol had shortly before told his mother he would go out and see what was going on, and was brought home dying.

When all was over people began to inquire into the composition of the mob that had held possession of the town so long. Derby was not then so populous but that everybody could be traced. The active members of the mob were a handful—two or three dozen perhaps ; except that boys will always throw stones when they can do so with impunity. There were many operatives then off work, or on half time. The men who made the apparently senseless proposal to break open the gaols were poachers, who seized the opportunity to release some of their friends in prison just at the beginning of the pheasant season. The fellow who harangued the dragoons in the market-place had been for many years in the habit of coming to the benevolent ladies of Derby with long stories of distress, want of work, and the inhumanity of his employers.

My father and the rest of the sufferers demanded compensation from the borough. The demand was resisted on the ground that the mob had not tried to pull the houses down, which was necessary by the Act. The sufferers were also told it was their own fault. They made a common cause, and put forward first the case of the shop in the market-place where the obnoxious petition had been agreed on and had lain for signature. It was proved that the mob had done its best to demolish the house by hammering away a long time at the pillar supporting the front. This decided the case against the corporation. No such case of intended demolition could have been made out for the other sufferers, but they proceeded to prosecute their claims, and the corporation were so disgusted by the length of their lawyer's bill that they gave in, seeing that submission would cost much less than victory.

The county, finding their new gaol ill adapted for defence—in fact, utterly unable to point a gun at any assailant who could get close enough to the wall, built eight lofty round towers at the corners of the octagon, so pierced as to rake the walls outside. They sadly jar with the very severe Doric entrance. County magistrates are a race beyond the reach of ordinary comprehension. Only a few years since, having to provide a depository for the arms of the Militia, the Derbyshire magistrates bought a deserted brick-field commanded on all sides by ground varying from ten to twenty feet above the site, and there they planted their arsenal and barracks, which anyone could look down into from all sides. Some said it was a job, but as these were honourable men, the probability is they did not know better.

It was about three weeks after the above disturbances that the populace of Bristol took advantage

of Sir Charles Wetherell's public entrance into the
city as Recorder, to burn down a square, several
streets, and the bishop's palace. James Dean, my
colleague at Derby, had the luck to engage the very
last thoughts of the unreformed House of Commons.   Upon the occasion of a Fast Day early in
1832, two fellows went about Derby putting up
blasphemous placards and making speeches upon
them.   Dean tore the placards down, and was accordingly assaulted by the men.   He had them up
and they were sent to prison for two months.   Four
thousand men in London petitioned for their release,
on the ground that they were in the right and Dean
in the wrong.   There was a debate on this petition
which had gone some way when the House was
counted out on the very eve of the dissolution.

CHAPTER XLI.

WHATELY, ARCHBISHOP OF DUBLIN.

IT was just about this time, that is the rejection of
the first Reform Bill by the House of Lords, that
Whately was made Archbishop of Dublin, to the
great delight and encouragement of his friends and
admirers in and out of the Anglican communion. The
appointment took most people very much by surprise,
probably because they had not thought about it.   I

had not thought at all about it, but even if I had, I am sure I should never have guessed Whately for a bishopric anywhere, least of all in Ireland.

I had always supposed Whately so disgusted with the whole state of affairs in this country, temporal and spiritual, and so dissatisfied with the creeds, the rites and ceremonies, and the Orders of the Church, that he would be prepared any day for any violent change, a reformation of the Church on thoroughly liberal principles, or a separation of Church and State. Whately had been some time credited with an anonymous pamphlet, pointing to the latter of these alternatives, for no other reason that I am myself acquainted with than that it agreed with his usual utterances, and there was nobody else in Oxford likely to have written it.

Cardinal Newman has something more to say as to this question of authorship. He has a recollection of having assumed the pamphlet to be Whately's in a conversation with the Provost, who could hardly fail to know whether it was his or not ; and of having been left by the Provost to understand that the assumption was right. But he has told me the Provost does not remember this. So I leave it in the Cardinal's hands.

Whately's whole life had been a continual protest against pomp and formality, and this was all the more noticeable inasmuch as nobody ever found him wanting in good manners, or, at Oxford, in social kindness. I remember, indeed, a story which might be interpreted as showing him not quite equal to a not very uncommon difficulty. He had asked some neighbours to dinner at his country parsonage, and after dinner their conversation became so disagreeable that Whately threw the window open, jumped out, and disappeared till late in the evening, when the coast was clear. One cannot help thinking he might have played the triton easily among such very small and dirty minnows.

Shortly after the news of Whately's appointment, I came up to Oxford from Derby. I do not think I was excited, though perhaps more than usually wanting in circumspection. My head must have been running a good deal on the scenes I had left, and one cannot look forward and backward at the same time. The Provost greeted me with the remark that he supposed I had made Derby too hot to hold me, which, as a fact, was by no means the case.

Immediately on my arrival I made straight for Christie's rooms. There I found in conversation with him a rather common looking man, of no particular significance or expression. I delivered at once the fulness of my soul about the new Archbishop of Dublin. 'What an appointment! Could there be a worse one? Was he sent to Ireland to destroy the Church and faith altogether?' Christie became unusually excited. He stamped about the room; looked daggers, as they say, bit his lips, all in vain, for I went on, thinking it possible the dull stranger might be the cause of all this fidgeting. The dull stranger left the room. It was Christie's old friend Pope, Whately's brother-in-law. He was saying good-bye, as he had to accompany Whately to Ireland. It was painfully evident in after years that

Whately did not carry away pleasant impressions of Oriel, or of the university.

When Christie was in the last of his many and serious illnesses, his sufferings were increased, and his recovery rendered hopeless, by his circumstances. He had a numerous family, and he was leaving very scant provision for them, having been open-handed like the rest of us. He persisted in doing the duty of his church and his parish, for he could not afford to pay a curate, still less to find another temporary home. A kind cousin, who had come to see him, was shocked to see him struggling on in this deplorable state. He knew Christie had had many and good friends, and that at one time he had seen much of Dr. and Mrs. Whately. He drew up a circular, stating these lamentable circumstances, and proposing a subscription to pay a curate, and so give Christie the rest essential to his recovery. I received the circular and responded to it. The cousin sent one to the Archbishop, and received an exceedingly rough reply. A few days after that he would see Christie's death in the papers.

That Whately should think the case possibly exaggerated, and that he should find himself under the painful necessity of drawing strong lines in the distribution of his bounty, is so likely that any applicant might have to take the risk of that. But the reply received indicated a resolution to efface the memory of Oxford, and of his Oxford friends generally, from his mind, and to be as if he had never been at that university. This was, to say the least, very ungrateful, for Whately owed a good deal to Oxford.

It certainly was more than half the making of him, whatever that making might be worth.

Whately had a strange idea that his acceptance of the see was a service of danger, and that there were many Irishmen fanatical enough to be ready to assassinate so known and so powerful a foe to super-stition.   Blanco White may have contributed to this belief, for he had himself a firm conviction that the first day he showed himself in Dublin would be his last.   Accordingly, besides Pope, who was a very robust person, a still more stout and muscular cousin, named Willis, was to form part of the escort.   This gentleman prepared for the worst, for he carried an armoury of pistols.   On the arrival of the whole party at Holyhead, Willis was despatched to the post office. It was dark, and he fell into an ill-protected cellar, breaking several bones badly.   He had to be nursed many weeks at Holyhead, and was then found un-necessary at Dublin.

It was not long before there came from Dublin some rather absurd stories.   At the Viceroy's table the Archbishop was airing his Liberalism gaily.   After a rapid succession of magnanimous surrenders, he suddenly felt he must make a stand somewhere. There was at least one thing he could not and would not abide.   His Excellency smiled so graciously that Whately went on stronger than ever.   By and by he felt various toes approaching his feet and shins under the table, some right across.   He broke out indignantly, 'What are you kicking me for?'   This final stand happened to be the very point on which the Viceroy was most open to censure.   The young *aides-de-camp* tried to sharpen their wit upon the strange arrival, and it was said had been worsted.

An Archbishop, like everybody else, has to beware of the prophetic force his own words may one day be found to bear. The Viceroy wrote to ask whether he had any objection to meet Dr. Murray, the very gentle and amiable Roman Catholic Archbishop. Of course he did not object, and need not have said more than that. Privately, however, he said to his friends that he would not object to meet anybody, no, not even the Devil himself. Many years afterwards this was remembered when Whately had to meet Cullen, and did not get the best of it.

Whately took his Vice-Principal, Hinds, with him, to act as Examining Chaplain. At Oxford they had been almost inseparable ; the white bear and the black bear, as they were called. As I remember, Newman had a certain tenderness for Hinds, even when the divergence from Whately had been considerable. He would speak of 'poor Hinds.' But I think there was just a suspicion of craziness. I was myself very much startled one morning by finding all the corners of the streets posted with 'The Three Temples, by the Rev. Samuel Hinds,' as if the writer had made some grand discovery, or was suddenly throwing out a challenge to the Christian world. I did not, however, take the trouble to see whether it was so.

It spoke well for Whately's affection, but not for his perception of character or general forethought, that he should take with him as his best man one so unfit for business, and so different in all respects from any kind of Irishman. Whately very soon found others on the spot more serviceable than Hinds, more popular, and perhaps also more agreeable to himself. Hinds had not the magnanimity to accept what really was a matter of course, and he became jealous and querulous. Whately, however, could not send him into outer darkness. He would appear to have borne long the discontents and caprices of his old friend, and to have done what he could for him. At last it became a State difficulty, and the knot had to be cut, since there was no untying it. Whately and Lord Clarendon, so it was said, recommended Hinds to Lord J. Russell as a fit subject for high English promotion, and Hinds became accordingly Bishop of Norwich, a post which perhaps he had better not have accepted, and which his characteristic sensitiveness on a delicate matter induced him to resign.

Whately had a very good saying about the majority of preachers. ' They aim at nothing, and they hit it.' Is it possible to describe better his own episcopate ?

CHAPTER XLII.

UNIVERSAL MOVEMENT OF 1831–1832.

PEOPLE who talk about the Oxford movement seldom say anything about the universal movement which immediately preceded it. In the year 1831 the whole fabric of English, and indeed of European society, was trembling to the foundations. Every party, every interest, political or religious, in this country, was pushing its claims to universal acceptance, with the single exception of the Church of England, which was folding its robes to die with what dignity it could.

There is a singular feature of that period, almost unnoticed, which must be described by a reference to Plato's saying, that Truth is so beautiful that were she seen really as she is, all men would love her. Every clique, every sect, almost every middle-class family, believed itself that Truth, and felt no doubt that if any one of its members were to have the management of public affairs but for a very short period, it could and would entirely regenerate the world. The belief, monstrous as we may deem it, was not quite unnatural. At that time all who held office in the State, in the Church, in our county and municipal institutions, and in the management of the army, the navy, the colonies, and the other dependencies — in a word, the entire administration of the country, had long been under a load of depreciation amounting to the bitterness and weight of an anathema.

The people who contemned, denounced, and anathematised, regarded it all as a matter simply of right and wrong, and believed that every question could be solved instantly and for ever by the triumph of the right—that is, of themselves. In the story books of that date, and even long after that date, the good man, the right man, and the true man, has only to show himself and to say a few words, and he carries all with him.

Indeed for a long period before this the assumption of ' good books ' had been that all the world was wrong except a few of the author's own mind, and that this privileged few only wanted the opportunity to set everything right. Every ambition found its stimulus in the doctrine that everything was wrong, yet capable of being effectually, and almost instantly rectified. Popular writers urged the rising generation to choose their lines of reformation at once, and pursue them obstinately to the assured end.

In all these matters, and in the census thus taken of human affairs, people looked generally, so to speak, over the hedge. One class took its measure of another ; one trade of another ; one Christian body of another. The towns had but the most outside knowledge of the county families, and by what they saw passed judgment upon them. The Church was pursuing an exclusive line. It made little appearance in the good works of the day, and was condemned by default. But nobody wished to be better informed about the Church, for egotism was now the great virtue, and nobody wished to go out of himself to be another's friend and adviser, except to destroy him, or tie him to his own chariot wheels.

Thus there prevailed universally, in one form or another, the idea of a great enterprise, in which one man was to save his country, not to say the whole world, the achievement to be all the greater because done against the wishes and opinions of those that were to be saved, and by the discomfiture and humiliation of all existing powers and influences.

At such a time, when a thousand projectors were screaming from a thousand platforms, when all England was dinned with philanthropy and revolution, spirituality and reform, when the scissors and paste-pot were everywhere at work on the Prayer Book, when Whately was preparing to walk quietly over two Churches in Ireland, and Arnold was confidently hoping to surpass Bunsen's scheme of universal comprehension in England, Newman was laboriously working his way into the hitherto unvisited region of patristic theology, and closing his work almost before he had begun it, in order to accompany a sick friend to the Mediterranean, and there pass the winter and spring, far from home, beyond the very tidings of the demolition to be any day begun.

CHAPTER XLIII.

ST. NICHOLAS AND ST. RUNWALD.

THE year 1832 was to me a very broken one, as indeed it was to many of us, for the vast locomotive of 'Church and State' was that year being shunted from one line to another. I had just been ordained to Deacon's Orders by Bagot, Bishop of Oxford. To his very recent death, I never heard or saw the name of Archdeacon Clerke, Bagot's chaplain, without a fresh twinge of conscience at the remembrance of the very

indifferent figure I must have made in the examination. I had no occasion to be jealous of the reader
of the Gospel.

Early in January, Whitaker Churton, whom I
had admired as a sweet little child at Charterhouse,
and whom I should have liked if only for his brother
Edward's sake, drove me to take his brother-in-law
Loveday's Sunday's services at East Ilsley, a village
in which the principal thoroughfares are divided into
pens for the periodical sheep fairs, the pens being the
best property in the place. A new parsonage was
rising from the ground. Loveday occupied it thirty-
four years, and died, or resigned, fifteen years ago.
My first initiation into the secular responsibilities
attached to the pastoral office was when the clerk,
after service, requested me to sign a certificate that a
man I had never seen or heard of was the proper
recipient of a pension. I requested to see the man,
and I did see him, but of course I was not much the
wiser for that, unless it were that I thought the man
looked like a pensioner. However, I signed the
document.

I wished for regular clerical duty. Newman and
Ogilvie of Baliol soon planned it for me, Ogilvie
taking me several times round the 'Parks' to satisfy
himself as to my seriousness and to give good advice.
His chief recommendation was excellent, but unfortunately too late, and I pass it on to those whom it
may concern. It was that I should start with a good
stock of written sermons. The only sermons I had
were those I had written for East Ilsley. I can
never say that I have wanted the opportunity of

ministerial usefulness, for the opening now offered was a most exceptionally good one. James Round, father of the present member for East Essex, but then unmarried, had been Proctor the previous year. There had been a visitation of Cambridge men, who had come with the set purpose of making disturbances. Round had taken vigorous measures, shutting some of them up in the Castle. Their Oxford friends had retaliated in various offensive ways, particularly at Commemoration. He had taken it to heart, and was suffering neuralgia.

I undertook his whole duty at Colchester—two parishes, one of them populous ; two churches, daily service, two full services on Sunday, two sermons to write every week, and what was more than all, not a minute's repose in the day. I lived with Round, and had to be with him as much as I could. He was a most agreeable and most instructive companion, while his habitual seriousness was specially adapted to supply my own lamentable want of it. The house itself was charming to my tastes. It contained the very large and interesting library of Mr. Morant, an eminent antiquary, in a grand room built for it ; and the gardens surrounded what was left of Colchester Castle, stoutly but vainly defended by the Royalists against the Parliamentary forces. Time out of mind there had been a family of wood-pigeons in the garden. The ruins of a grand Norman church were a few steps off.

But I had never five minutes of that absolute rest which my poor nature required, and which less scrupulous or more courageous people obtain by the use of tobacco. Had I gone there provided with a few dozen sermons, or with some speaking power, I might have remained at Colchester to this day. But the necessity of writing two sermons a week interfered with everything; with the occasional rest I required, with exercise, and with my night's sleep. They were always on my mind, and, becoming drudgery, I was conscious of their being ineffective. My visiting, though there were some twelve or thirteen hundred people in the two parishes, was not such a burden; indeed Round seemed to think me rather an enthusiast in that way. Yet my first visit was a nervous one. On returning to 'Holly Place,' after my first afternoon service, I found waiting for me a summons to a deathbed. I went to the 'Barracks,' as the place was called, a large quaint old pile, let in tenements; a warren of poverty. Groping about and winding about, I found myself at last in a wretched bedroom, where two men, one evidently a minister, stood by the sick man's bedside. They immediately made way for me, and asked, as it appeared to me simply and unaffectedly, that they might join in my prayers, for they saw I had a Prayer Book in my hand. How I acquitted myself, and what good I did, I cannot say, but if I was not prepared for the pulpit, neither was I for the bedside.

One little matter of housekeeping I will mention, not because it affected me, but because it affected my Rector very much, and illustrates what people were doing in those days, before the appearance of the 'Tracts for the Times.' Round, though a thorough invalid, very nervous, and full of aches and pains,

fasted all Lent, and particularly on a great fast, I think
for the cholera. He would scarcely touch animal
food, or any other pleasant food that had passed
through a cook's hand. But his friends had put him
under the care of an old family servant, who did not
like to see him fast, and who tried to circumvent the
Church by a constant profusion of very heavy plum-
cakes, plum-bread, honey, jams, and other sweet things.
I used to wonder how a man of sense could allow
himself to be duped by such a distinction. On the
great Fast Day he ate a scrap of hard dry salt fish, and
would not look at the egg sauce. I had had one full
service, and had another before me, so I brazened my
front, and helped myself largely to the contents of
the tureen. It was not fasting, for I did not fast, but
work without rest that was too much for me, and I
soon broke down utterly. The tone of Holly Place,
it will be seen, was High Church. There was a Low
church at Colchester, and a Low Church clergyman ;
a very good man I used to hear, for I never saw him.
Round would drop hints about making approaches to
him, and so bringing him round a little. Some time
after this episode, Round married a lady of a family
certainly not High Church, and I believe it ended in
the Low Church clergyman neutralising Round. My
Rector made Bishop Ken his ideal, and Ken, I suppose, now occupies a neutral position in the Church
of England.

When nearly as ill as I could be, I went to Oxford to vote for Dr. Mills in the contest for the newly-
founded Boden Professorship, as I had promised
before leaving Oxford. My friends told me I must

see a doctor, so I saw Dr. Wootten, and no doubt he went by the Pharmacopœia. He gave me a prescription, which on my return I took to a good London chemist. What he gave me I know not ; but it must have come from Medea's own medicine-chest. I took the proper quantum and went to bed, for I had been directed to break my return journey by a night or two. I immediately passed into another state of existence, which next morning I resolved never to return to if I could help. It was chaos rather than life.

My Rector had given me a note to Blomfield, then Bishop of London. It was the Bishop's rule that newly ordained deacons must be examined with his own candidates before they could be admitted to curacies in his diocese. So I had to receive instructions. I was also to ask whether my license was to be for one of the two livings, or for both. This I did. The Bishop seemed exceedingly put out, and exclaimed 'What can it possibly signify ? ' I quite agreed with him, but I had done as I had been bid. Nor could I be expected to know the technicalities of the business.

I was so ill at the time, that on leaving the house, which I did instantly, seeing it was expected of me, I staggered across the street, and held for a quarter of an hour to the garden rails. This was the only time I ever saw or heard Blomfield, except when I heard him preach upon an occasion, the same sermon, I need not say a very good one, at the Chapel Royal, St. James's, and at St. Paul's ; much better, of course, in the morning than in the evening.

On my return to Colchester my friends there were

all as kind as they could be, but when, in another
month or so, the doctor told them confidentially I
was dying, they were rejoiced at my receiving an invitation to join our family circle at Teignmouth. I
went in one long day, from London to Exeter, feeling
better every mile of the road. A lady who chanced
to see me stepping down from the coach next morning at Teignmouth, exclaimed, 'What is the use of
that young man coming to lay his bones here?' In
three weeks I was wandering over Dartmoor, losing
my way at nightfall, and passing the night in a poor
cottage at Manston. With my friends I took a very
pretty tour, much enlivened by the political situation,
for it was the conclusion of the long Reform debates.
Totnes looked dilapidated, the Reformers having
smashed every Tory window in the town the previous evening. We were rowed down to Dartmouth,
and received with discharges of artillery from the
quay by Colonel Seale's supporters, to the sad discomfiture of a nervous lady and her invalid daughter. We
took shelter in the first hotel we came to, and in ten
minutes saw under the window the principal Tory of
the town, brought to bay by a triumphant Liberal
mob, thrown on the ground, and deprived of a pistol
he had been foolishly pointing at everybody. As
there was no quiet to be expected on shore, we took
to the water, and were immediately surrounded by
the most impudent shoal of porpoises I ever knew,
staring at us, switching their tails, and squirting water
all about us. After catching a sight of Start Point,
we returned through a sea of brilliant phosphoric
effects. It was a *dies mirabilis*, pleasant to recall.

CHAPTER XLIV.

BUCKLAND.

A FEW weeks more and I was back at Oxford. Moreton Pinckney, in Northamptonshire, just then fell vacant. It was about thirty miles from Oxford, and had been served many years by a dual arrangement. Tyler and Dornford had successively held the living, with curates in charge, occasionally taking their place, and frequently riding down even in term time. They had found it an agreeable relief from their college duties. Froude, whether spontaneously or not, suggested that I should take the living and he should share the duties. I agreed at once, and for a week or two supposed that to be the arrangement. But Froude had by this time begun to show the approach of that disease which always seemed imminent, but which he had defied rather than guarded against. His father put his veto on the plan. I have to confess that I felt a little relieved, for I knew that a moiety of the work on high ecclesiastical principles would prove to me a heavier burden than the whole on my own lines. My Derby friends hardly knew what to say to my taking the living. My father consulted Pickford. He must have studied the college patronage, dividing it into prime, secondary, and inferior joints, for he told my father Moreton Pinckney was an 'offal' place. It had the recommendation of lying between Oxford and Derby. The curate in charge wished to remain till Michaelmas, but meanwhile John Marriott had accepted as a title for orders the curacy of Buckland, a pleasant ride from Oxford, and he wanted a *locum tenens* for four months.

The arrangements made for a population not far from a thousand illustrate the kind and comfortable practice of those days. The Vicar having died, leaving two young children, the Roman Catholic patron, or his trustees, gave the living to old Mr. Stevens, Rector of Bradfield, to hold with his own, on the understanding that, after providing for the duty, he would hand the proceeds to his sister-in-law, the late Vicar's widow, for herself and her children. Bishop Burgess was an old friend of the Rector of Bradfield, and paid him occasional visits ; so he could be sure the arrangements would be properly carried out. Indeed there was no doubt it would. Marriott had taken an empty cottage with four rooms and two garrets, and he gave me 50*l.* to furnish it. Mrs. Newman said it could be done, and she would do it for me. She went with me from shop to shop ; and we completely furnished the cottage, parlour, kitchen, two bedrooms, and two garrets, for the money, not a shilling over. When Marriott came into the cottage he was quite satisfied with the use we had made of his money, excepting that the ' sofa,' or settee, besides being large and ugly, was very hard and knotty.

Newman rode in from Oxford, more than once I think. It was about that time he wrote to me a long and earnest letter, calling me to greater devotion of life, more regularity in duty and study, and more consideration of the end of my being. Already his name was great, and through him the name of Oxford was greater than it had been. The widow at the parsonage—poor lady, who sang one song, and that was ' The Last Rose of Summer '—was most anxious to see him, for her son was going to Oriel, where her brother Tinney, the Chancery barrister, had been Fellow.

Even more desirous to see him was her daughter Cecilia, a very lively, talkative, clever girl of thirteen, as honest, good, and true as her wretched brother was the contrary. She charged herself with a store of questions about the great Oxford world, and all that was doing there and everywhere, and when Newman came she kept up an incessant battery, which, as she was very nice looking, and had a sweet voice and a charming manner, was not disagreeable. Newman answered so fully and pleasantly that time only failed for more. He relapsed into a musing mood ; perhaps he was thinking of John Marriott. ' I suppose Cecilia will marry the curate some day,' he said. *Heu vatum ignaræ mentes !* Her mother was a sad wilful woman. When I had carefully prepared two of her servants for Confirmation, she sent word at the last moment that she could not spare them, as she had asked a friend to dinner that day. This from the widow of the Vicar and the occupant of the parsonage ! When she left Buckland she took up her residence at Bath. Cecilia had had an epidemic, and was not quite sufficiently recovered to go to a ball. But she must go, and she must be set up. The doctor gave a prescription that was to fortify her. It was taken to the druggist. The shopboy made some horrible blunder, and Cecilia died in agonies the next day.

Yet since I wrote these very lines memory has brought together what had laid separate in my mind for half a century. Newman's forecast was fulfilled in some secondary sense or form. The coming curate, that is John Marriott, married Cecilia's cousin, Tom Stevens' sister, who thus took her place in the prophecy.

Even for so little as four months Buckland would be a long story to tell. Some of the incidents, however, are of the period. I took forty candidates to be confirmed by Bishop Burgess at Abingdon, but I had to reject a good many. Farmer Church way-laid me at a stile and begged hard for four grown-up daughters. I had tried them; they could not say the Catechism or learn it. The father said he had never heard of a man or woman who could say the Cate-chism. It was very hard. ' But,' said I, ' they cannot even say the Belief or the Commandments.' ' Nor can I,' he said, 'and I'm not the worse for it.' I heard a few months after that when he was about to introduce a step-mother into the house, the four un-confirmed daughters made him break off the engage-ment, with the threat that if the lady came they would throw her into the horse-pond.

As I am confessing the faults of others rather freely, aye, of poor souls long gone to their account, I ought not to be chary of myself. I had had four baptisms one Sunday afternoon during service. A few days after a good woman, begging many pardons, said she wished to tell me something that didn't much signify, but it made people smile. Why did I put my finger into the font before signing the baptised child with the sign of the cross? They had never seen it done before. It was a fact that I had been doing this, and must have done it scores of times at Colchester. Of course it was inadvertency, nay, downright stupidity on my part. Before I administered myself I don't know that I had ever seen a baptism, so as to have my eye on the performance of the act. I had certainly never seen a Roman Catholic baptism, which might have suggested some such idea. I had never seen anyone using 'holy water,' as is done upon entering and leaving a Roman Catholic church. Of course there is not the slightest warrant, or excuse, or even palliation of my little piece of hyper-ritualism. A very little thought would have put me right. This present confession will cause a few smiles, not all of them as kind as could be wished, or as respectful; but I think it just possible that there are other clergymen doing the same thing, with nobody to tell them they are wrong.

I was kept well informed of those who were backward in bringing their children to baptism. There was a well-to-do couple, the husband a shoemaker, who had a fine child two years old, not yet baptised. It was the usual story. None of their friends were good enough to stand for a child. My sister Anne, who was with me all my stay at Buckland, undertook to be godmother, and the little girl was baptised the next Sunday.

I had a warm controversy with one of the very few Unitarian survivors of a Presbyterian congregation, that the first Lord Barrington, his friend Locke, and, in his earlier days, Shute Barrington, afterwards Bishop of Durham, had occasionally joined. There were more than a hundred Roman Catholics, and a resident priest, whom I only once caught a sight of. There was a village raven that walked backwards and forwards before the blacksmith's shop, ready to pick a quarrel with anybody that came that way. I had accepted a quarrel, and was gently teasing him, when suddenly the 'priest' appeared on the scene. 'So there are three of us,' I said to myself, and walked away.

Just before I went to Buckland some village miscreants had stolen a number of silver pheasants on which Mr. Robert Throckmorton set great store. So he resolved to make a clean sweep of the bad subjects. To as many men as, with their families, amounted to more than a hundred, he offered the choice between the workhouse and emigration. They chose the latter, and were soon put on board a ship at Southampton bound for the United States. Coming on deck the next morning they saw the Isle of Wight, and shouted for joy at having so soon arrived at a beautiful new home. They would have at least six weeks' tossing before they reached it.

The parsonage was a house divided against itself, for a sister and a gentleman parishioner living there while Carswell House was building, were Low Church and strongly anti-papist. They gave me warning of several dangers ahead. One was that I was not unlikely to be asked some day to let the son of the late Vicar read the lessons in service.   This came to pass, as did another warning.   In due time a man came to me, asking me to add my signature to that of six householders, backing his petition for a public-house license.   As advised, I refused.   There were too many public-houses already, and one of them was only a few steps from the house for which application was now made.   I had to refuse again and again, but before long I heard the license had been granted, and that my signature had not been found necessary. My parsonage friends—that is the coterie in the Ultra-Protestant parlour—affirmed that Mr. Throckmorton held a mortgage on the property, and would never have got either capital or interest unless he could manage to get it made a public-house.   Is not this a case of permissive legislation, and is that compatible with a squirearchy ?

The Throckmortons were very civil to me, asking me to dinner and so forth.   They always had foreign visitors, among them a very handsome young German Baroness, rather on the look-out for amusement.   Nicholas Throckmorton, the wicked wit of the family, had taught her all the slang he could think of, making her believe that it was ordinaiy and fashionable phraseology.   The result was she sometimes surprised even a fast partner at a county ball.   As taught by the said Nicholas, upon some appeal to her finer intelligence, she replied to her partner, not at all prepared for it, by putting up her forefinger to the side of her nose and saying, ' I smoke.'   I still tingle with shame at the recollection that, having promised to take her up to the top of my church tower, I thought better, or worse, of it and absconded.

Another young friend of ours at Buckland was a girl just from a boarding-school, and almost as lively as the Baroness. This was Miss Pusey, afterwards Mrs. Cotton. The widow at the parsonage found Philip Pusey a man of the world, and a very agreeable neighbour at a dinner table, but somehow could never feel much at home with Edward, who had nothing to say to her that she cared for. My own brief experience was the other way.

When I had been at Buckland about two months, to my great surprise I heard the church bell ringing at a very early hour—four o'clock I think it was. This was that all the gleaners, or leasers as they were called, should start fair. The women and children assembled at certain points just out of the village, and when the bell went down, made the best of their way to the fields. The farmers complained that they could get no women to assist the reapers or to rake the corn. It was so much more worth their while to pick it up for themselves.

No doubt many things are much improved since then, there as everywhere else. Yet in these days of universal reading, writing, and arithmetic, people may be little aware how much could be once done without them. I was giving some commissions to the Oxford carrier, a plain, elderly man, and, finding he took no notes, asked if he was sure he could remember them, for there were not only shops and articles, but quantities and qualities in my orders. He answered that he could not read or write, that he carried his

accounts in his head, that he had sixty-three different
orders for his next day's journey, and often had many
more.   The people at the parsonage told me that he
never was known to make a mistake.

In the neighbourhood I met Archdeacon Berens,
an old Oriel Fellow, and a very pleasant man.   He
amused us all with his stories of country life, then
new to me.   In those days wills were occasionally
proved before the Archdeacon after the other work of
a visitation.   A farmer's will was presented and duly
spread out.   'What's this?' exclaimed Berens.
'Here's a name scratched out.   Explain it, please.'
The widow stepped forward.   ' I tells you how he be,
sir.   When we comes to look into the will, we sees
50*l*. left to John Wheeler.   What's he to do with
master's money? says I.   So I gets a knife, and us
scratches he out ; and that's just how he be, sir.'
The Archdeacon replaced the name, and warned the
family party of the consequences of another meddling
with a will.

It was the year of the cholera.   The widow at the
parsonage walked into the vestry as I was preparing
for the morning service, entreating me to take care
of myself, for Mr. New, a very fine young gentleman,
had died of cholera the day before in the next parish.
Only on Thursday he was eating currants from a
garden wall.   I had the exclusive use of a very fine
fig-tree at the parsonage, as Charles I. had had during
his captivity at Buckland House.   Nobody else cared
for figs that year.

I was here in the thick of the excitement conse-
quent upon the first general election after the Reform

Act. The Puseys were very grave indeed about it. Philip had written rather violent political tracts for distribution. William had found himself charged with the payment of the shillings which the farmers, on principle, would not pay for registration. Mr. Throckmorton could only laugh about it, especially when the other Liberal candidate was named. I chanced to mention this many years after to the other Liberal candidate. ' He had a right to laugh at me, for he left me to pay his expenses as well as my own.'

CHAPTER XLV.

NEWMAN AND FROUDE ON THE MEDITERRANEAN.

IN July 1832 the ' History of the Arians ' was ready for the press, and as Newman was now relieved of his college duties, he was more a man of leisure than he had ever been, and was also in more need of rest. Hurrell Froude, as Richard was always called, though there was another Hurrell in the family, had now to submit to be ruled by his anxious relatives. He must spend the winter on the Mediterranean and its shores, friends were taking him, and Newman was easily persuaded to go with them. In these days it requires little persuasion to induce ordinary people, who happen to be free from pressing engagements, to accept the offer of a continental trip, especially southward, in the winter

But this did rather take Newman's friends by surprise, and the only reason they could suppose was his great anxiety for Hurrell Froude.

The new circle of which Oriel was the centre had no sympathy, or even charity, for the common run of tourists going a round of cathedrals and mountains simply to amuse themselves, and bringing home a sorry stock of hotel gossip, road adventures, and old tales.   Sacrifice and self-denial were the new fashion, and there were those who were giving yearly to new churches and other religious objects what would have taken them pleasantly half through the Continent, and might have done them much good.

It had been a busy year with Newman, and he was full of work to the day of his departure.   The tour he was about to make was in those days more of an epoch in a man's life than it now is, and it might itself be a turning point in his career, as many have since felt that it really came to be in Newman's. But he was now just over thirty.   A man had made up his mind at thirty, if he ever made it up, he used to say.   This very year he had been writing earnest letters to us all, urging a more definite plan and more devotion of life, with reasons addressed to our respective characters, powers, and circumstances. Early in the year he had put together and circulated among his friends his birthday poems and other fugitive pieces, of all dates from 1818 to 1831, with the title of 'Memorials of the Past,' and a motto which showed that a change was passing over him, and he was entering upon a future.   This very month, as he said long after, a 'ghost' was pursuing him.

He had already vowed to give his heart to no earthly
surroundings, however sweet or beautiful. But the
crisis was a stirring one. The Reform Bill had
passed, after a long struggle, and more reform was
coming.

At Oxford, Mr. W. Palmer, of Worcester College,
but a frequent guest at Oriel, had now, with much
assistance from Bishop Lloyd's papers, completed
and brought out his 'Antiquities of the English
Ritual.' Palmer was so quiet a man, so unimpas-
sioned and so unambitious, that he really hid his
light in a bushel. Yet when this work came out it
made a great sensation. Its simple statement of
facts and documentary evidence took with people
who were wearied with logic and jaded with style.
If Newman was to disappear from the scene for half
a year, this seemed to come opportunely to supply
his place.

Once on the road, with his plans laid out for him,
Newman found his spirit taking wings. Among the
things of the past is the old corner inn at Whit-
church, where the road from Oxford to Winchester
crosses that from London to Exeter. Many a weari-
some hour can old Oxford men of the south-western
counties remember to have spent at that dull spot,
the interior of the inn, and the town, being equally
unattractive. I have seen a respectable representation of the university there, forming groups on the
road side. The landlord's only chance was a good
shower of rain, when the men, even if they would not
eat or drink, must find shelter, and had to pay a
shilling a head for it. It was here, while waiting for

the mail to Falmouth, that Newman wrote the verses
on his Guardian Angel, beginning, 'Are these the
tracks of some unearthly Friend?' and going on to
speak of the vision that haunted him.   On such occasions as this he composed whatever appears with his
name in the 'Lyra Apostolica,' published at first in
the 'British Magazine.'

In his 'Apologia' Newman gives a very brief
sketch of this remarkable tour.   The materials for a
full account must exist in the very interesting letters
he found time to write to all his friends, but their
place has been supplied so far by large extracts from
the correspondence of his humorous and brilliant
companion R. H. Froude, published in his 'Remains.'
Even with much time lost in quarantine, storms,
calms, and slow steamers, they saw more of the
Mediterranean ports, cities, churches, and peoples,
than is usually done in little more than half a year,
and whatever they saw or heard came upon highly
sensitive minds and concentrated attentions.   They
had not the time, the opportunity, or the desire to see
the interior of either the political or the religious
systems they came upon.

Most tourists leave their own religion behind
them, and amuse themselves by gazing at the externals of other religions.   The two voyagers and their
kind friends were at one in this matter, for the
yacht was their church, and they kept up their daily
devotions, as good Church of England men.   All kept
their eye on the compass, as it lay on the cabin table,
to be sure they addressed their prayers towards the
east, that is to Jerusalem and not to Rome.   Arriving

at Rome, they had interesting conversations with Dr. Wiseman and Mr. Bunsen, but no more approximation to one than to the other, at least no more that they were then conscious of. They seem to have found things abroad very much as they had left them at home. The people had a religion of their own sort ; the cities had that show of religion which consists in churches, services, and bell-ringing, and so reminded them of Oxford ; the clergy were everywhere trimming and knocking under to the State, which was generally irreligious as well as rapacious. In Rome they saw the magnificence of all the world collected by a Pagan power to be converted into the monuments of Christian saints and martyrs.

A single word dropped by Newman at Rome, soon forgotten, and indeed variously related, reached Arnold, and fell on him with the weight of a papal excommunication—taken off some years afterwards.

The only service they attended at Rome, or anywhere else, was the Tenebræ, at the Sistine Chapel, for the sake of the Miserere. Newman says his general feeling was, 'All save the spirit of man is divine.' The Bill for the suppression of Irish Sees was in progress and filled his mind. In a fit of indignation with the course taken by the Bishop of London, he wrote from on board a steamer to decline that Prelate's offer of one of the Whitehall chaplainships, just put on a new footing. He had 'fierce thoughts against the Liberals.' Perhaps even when he long after recorded these feelings, he little anticipated that Mr. Gladstone would one day supplement the obnoxious half measure with a whole one.

Newman left his companions and returned alone to
Sicily, for which he seemed to have a strange longing.   Sicily, besides its extreme natural beauties, is
the common ground of Greek and Roman history and
poetry, and has always been the abode of an op-
pressed and comparatively simple people.   Palermo
the traveller had thought more beautiful than Naples,
and the temple of Egesta grander than those of Pæs-
tum.   Cicero's picture of Enna, now Castro Giovanni,
described by other ancient as well as modern writers
as the most beautiful spot on the face of the earth,
had always dwelt on Newman's memory.   He went
there, and being now alone, and moving about more
freely, had conversations and adventures.

Some days before he was aware of it, he was in
the gripe of a dangerous fever, in which priests and
others nursed him for several weeks.   In his long
delirium he said things which he knew not, but which
they brought to his remembrance.   For a long time
after his return to Oxford there arrived frequent
letters elaborately addressed to the Reverend John
Henry, brother of the college *Stæ. Mariæ Virginis* at
Oxford.   The burden of a work to be done was too
much for one no longer cheered by company, and
encountering fatigues ; he was really sick unto death,
but he felt he should not die, so he said in his delirium, for he had not sinned against knowledge.

Returning homewards in an orange boat bound
for Marseilles, he was becalmed a whole week in the
Straits of Bonifacio, and there, within sight of Ca-
prera, since known as Garibaldi's home, he wrote,
'Lead, kindly light,' now sung in all our churches,

with a various, but we will hope a convergent, significance.

All this time there was raging at home a controversy on the whole matter of the Church of England,
if controversy that could be called which was almost
wholly on one side. Every table was covered with
pamphlets, many of bulky dimensions, and generally
embracing all the topics comprised in the idea of
Church Reform. Writers not wanting in learning or
conscientiousness gave their views under thirty or
forty heads on the Liturgy, the Creeds, the Bible, the
revenues, the government, the basis and composition
of the Church. Pamphlets were quickly followed by
postscripts and second parts. Industrious men were
already publishing *Collectanea* of the views of all the
reformers in the field—a legion of them. The one
idea pervading all these divers utterances was to sur-
render everything which the old school of churchmen
had thought essential to the Church, for the sake of
the Church, that is for the sake of the name.

Newman, hardly yet recovered from his Sicilian
fever, and travelling too rapidly for his strength,
reached England and his mother's house on July 9,
his brother Frank having arrived there from Persia a
few hours before. This was on Tuesday. The following Sunday, July 14, Keble preached the Assize
Sermon in the University Pulpit, published under the
title of ' National Apostasy.' ' I have ever considered
and kept the day,' says the writer of the ' Apologia,'
' as the start of the religious movement of 1833.

CHAPTER XLVI.

FROUDE'S COMMENTS ON THE PANTHEON.

IT must have been soon after Froude's return from the Mediterranean that I had with him one of our old talks about architecture. He was as devoted to science and as loyal to it as any materialist could be. But architecture and science are very apt to be at variance, and Froude was always disposed to side with the latter. As for Greek architecture there is no science in it except the mystery of proportion and a certain preternatural and overpowering conception of beauty. The temple of Egesta, which won the hearts of our travellers, has no more science in its construction than Stonehenge. But Roman architecture was for all the world, for its gods as well as for its mortals. The arch, and still more the vault, were mighty bounds into the time to come.

Always leaning on tradition where possible, Froude wished to believe the pointed arch the natural suggestion of a row of round arches seen in perspective. Of course a deep round arch in a thick wall only shows its roundness when you stand directly before it, but seems pointed from any other direction. I remember ventilating this idea to Sir Richard Westmacott and Turner, the great painter, at the former's table, and I remember also the great contempt with which the latter dismissed such mechanical ideas from the realm of the picturesque.

But it was the dome that chiefly exercised Froude's mind. It was a positive pain to him that so grand a building as the Pantheon should have been constructed, as he believed, in such ignorance of science. His notion was that if Agrippa had known the qualities of the catenary curve he would have used it instead of the semicircular curve—that is, in this instance, the spherical vault. A spherical vault requires one of two things ; either an immense load upon the haunches, indeed on all the lower part of the vault, or a great quantity of metal ties passed round the vault.

The Romans adopted the former plan. With any quantity of rough material at their command, and any quantity of slaves trained to march in procession up zigzag inclines, they very quickly filled up the space between the vault and the parapet walls, and made it all one mass of hard concrete. As it stands, the Pantheon is a huge grotto cut out of a solid mountain. This required walls of proportionate solidity. With a catenary curve the masonry of the vault need not have been more than two feet thick, that of the walls not more than four.

Had any common utilitarian made such a suggestion I should not have thought it worth notice. I only mention it as showing the scientific character of Froude's tastes. The objections are obvious and overwhelming. In the first place beauty must lead in architecture, and construction must obey. Like poetry and music, it is an art that lives to please. The catenary curve, familiar as we are with it in a chain, is a very ungraceful one, and would utterly fail to satisfy the eye in a vault or a dome. There is no want of examples sufficiently near the catenary curve to test the question of beauty. The Italian domes of the age before St. Peter's, the Saracenic domes, such as at Cairo, and the two domes of the International Exhibition of 1861, at South Kensington— lemon-shaped, or melon shaped, they are called—are very distasteful to the English eye. Their plan is the catenary curve slightly modified and disguised. It is a sound principle of construction, whereas the semicircular dome is an impostor.

Yet nature and education combine to make the sphere the most beautiful of forms, whether concave or convex. The heavens expand overhead, and do not converge rapidly to a point or form a hollow cone. Neither do they start abruptly inwards from the horizon. The eye requires that a dome shall not leave the upright walls too abruptly, that it shall not rapidly incline from the upright, that it shall afford a large space overhead nearly horizontal, and that it shall be roomy and recessed midway. These conditions are fulfilled in a spherical dome, and they are not fulfilled in any other form of dome, not at least nearly so well. Even the most graceful elliptical dome seems flat and unnatural.

If anybody will take the trouble to draw a semicircle, and then hang a chain by the two ends so that the two curves may hang from the same points and fall down to the same depth, he will see that the space included in the catenary curve is not nearly so large as that in the semicircle ; that the catenary curve starts at a palpable incline from the upright, and that the greater part of the catenary curve would form not so much a vault as a cone, that is a common kiln. It is needless to speak of the exterior effect, which would be quite as unpleasant. So much for the effect.

Then for the construction. The catenary curve would stand strong enough and long enough, if secured at the base, that is at the spring of the arch. This could only be done by a metal tie like that imbedded by Wren round the cone of St. Paul's, or by an adequate abutment, which would have to be provided by raising the walls, as Wren has done also.

Spherical domes are the crux and the pitfall of architecture. They involve false construction and positive deception. Froude appears to have remained under the impression that the dome of St. Peter's was a piece of simple masonry, for he notices with surprise the fact, if such it be, that the courses are laid horizontally. There are, I believe, a hundred and twenty iron or bronze bands round that dome, which would not stand for a second without them. It is therefore substantially a metallic construction. One of the finest domes in the world is in this metropolis, viz. that of the Reading Room in the British Museum. But it is an iron structure, filled in with the lightest possible brickwork.

A cupola, both for the structure and for the effect, is not compatible with an exactly spherical dome. But a dome without a cupola does not please the eye. All London would be in a fury if the dome of the Reading Room at the British Museum were to show itself over the roof of the portico. I well remember the indignation of the British public at the big pudding, as they called it, on the top of Buckingham Palace as it came out of the builder's hands. It had to be hidden immediately.

Froude had a soul for beauty ; but he did not like shams. He did not like a thing to seem what it was not. Few buildings are prepared to stand such a test. Amiens Cathedral, for example, the first love of the English tourist, is nothing more than an iron cage filled in with stone.

The dome, that is the hollow hemisphere, is always regarded as the grandest of Roman additions to Greek forms. It proved too much even for its Epicurean poet, who complained of the Roman millionaire, *mutat quadrata rotundis.* To raise the Pantheon over the grand vaulted basilica of Constantine was the proud boast fulfilled in St. Peter's. The Pantheon, whatever its first destination, represents the universe. It is a globe, 145 feet every way, placed on the ground, with the substitution of a cylinder for the lower half. In one respect it has a strange resemblance to that vast temple of Nature into which one can enter day and night. It disguises its own immensity. I have entered it scores of times under every condition of light, and I have seen it from an inner balcony under water, in which the pillars seemed to double their length, but I never could realise or even quite believe its enormous dimensions. It is half as high again as the nave of Westminster Abbey, the highest in England. It is twice as high as Westminster Hall, and more than twice as wide.

CHAPTER XLVII.

AFTER THE MEDITERRANEAN VOYAGE.

IT was now deep in Long Vacation, but no period in
the annals of Oxford was ever more pregnant with
consequences than the next two months. The returning travellers had lost time. The world had got
the start of them, and they had to make up for it.

Froude's imagination teemed with new ideas, new
projects, topics likely to tell or worth trying ; to be
tried indeed and found variously successful. They
came from him like a shower of meteors, bursting
out of a single spot in a clear sky, for they had
been pent up. Every post had brought the travellers
some account of fresh 'atrocities.' The 'Examiner'
was the only paper that talked sense. Conservative
churchism Froude now utterly abhorred. In passing
through France he had listened with hopefulness to the
dream that a deeper descent into republicanism than
that represented by Louis Philippe, would land that
country in High Churchism. How could the Church
of England now be saved ? By working out the oath
of canonical obedience ? By a lay synod, pending
the apostasy of Parliament ? By a race of clergy
living less like country gentlemen ? By dealing in
some way or other with the appointment of bishops ?
By a systematic revival of religion in large towns ;
in particular, by colleges of unmarried priests ? By
excommunication ? By working upon the *pauperes*

Christi? By writing up the early Puritans who had so much to say for themselves against the tyranny of Elizabeth ? By preaching apostolic succession ? By the high sacramental doctrine ? By attacking State interference in matters spiritual ? By an apostolic vocabulary giving everything its right name ? By recalling the memory of the Gregorian age ?

It was perhaps a happy diversion of his thoughts that he had so much to say on other topics, such as architecture, and the construction of ships and dock-gates. It was now plain that he had brought home with him not only his own fervid temperament, but some of the heat of sunny climes, where indeed he had not taken proper care of his health, or any care at all. Like most other Englishmen, he would not be indoors by sunset, or put on warmer clothing when the thermometer dropped twenty or thirty degrees. It happened to be an exceptionally cold winter in the Mediterranean. As far as regards health, the experiment had been a failure.

One thing, however, is quite clear from his letters and other remains ; and, as he was all this time somewhat in advance of Newman, it has a bearing on his mental history. Froude came home even more utterly set against Roman Catholics than he had been before. His conclusion was that they held the truth in unrighteousness ; that they were wretched Tridentines everywhere and of course ever since the Reformation ; that the conduct and behaviour of the clergy was such that it was impossible they could believe what they professed, that they were idolaters in the sense of substituting easy and good-

natured divinities for the God of Truth and Holiness.

Froude stayed in England just long enough to
take a present part in the great movement, and to
contribute to it, and then, as he sorrowfully said of
himself, like the man 'who fled full soon on the first
of June, but bade the rest keep fighting,' he found
himself compelled by his friends to leave England
for the West Indies.

All these vivid expressions, delivered with the
sincerity of a noble child or a newly-converted
savage, chimed in with Newman's state of feeling,
and struck deep into his very being, to bring forth
fruit. Yet in neither Froude nor Newman could
now be discovered the least suspicion of what these
outbursts might lead to, for at every point they found
Rome irreconcilable and impossible.

Newman, as we have seen, did not return to
England till July 9, 1833, and it was exactly two
months after, on September 9, that the first four, or
rather in regard to the subjcets, the first eight 'Tracts
for the Times' suddenly appeared, beginning with the
famous words, 'I am but one of yourselves, and a
Presbyter.' The 'movement' then, in the very form
in which it actually began, had but a short incubation
and a very perturbed and unpromising one. Newman
was scanning earth and sky, and casting his arms
about wildly for some one to help him, and for some
form of action more practical than those which had
hitherto been found ineffective.

Strange to say, the alternative for the 'Tracts for
the Times,' perhaps one may say their first form, was

a series of letters to the ' Record.' Five years before
this, in 1828, Newman had contributed a small sum to
the starting of that paper, and had become a sub-
scriber and constant reader. So he now wrote several
letters on Church Reform, beginning with Church
discipline in its various aspects. The letters, besides
being long, could not be very palatable to the habitual
readers of the ' Record,' and by and by came to a
point of absolute divergence. The editor cut short
the correspondence, explaining his reasons in a cour-
teous letter to the writer.

It must be considered that Newman had now
been seven months away, in another world, at sea, or
seriously ill, or in strange scenes and among new
faces. For a long period before that he had been
engrossed in his ' History of the Arians.' He had
found that a very laborious, difficult, and, his critics
discover, an ungenial work, for he had laboured to
throw himself into those times, and had not succeeded, so they say. Instead of comprehending all
the principal Councils, he had not seriously treated of
more than one, that of Nicæa, and had only given it
twenty pages out of four hundred. Newman, these
critics observe, had evidently not got into the spirit of
the Church of those times when he wrote this book.
That is not only true, but confessed by the very fact
of it costing the writer so great an effort to introduce
the reader and himself to the period. The book
represents the operation of sinking a shaft for water,
or for precious ore.

An incident of the two months that intervened
between Newman's return from the South and the

appearance of the 'Tracts for the Times,' rather relieved the stern character of the crisis, though Newman did not seem to think it quite in keeping. Clerical celibacy used to be either a vulgar necessity or a heroic devotion at Oxford, where the great majority were Fellows waiting for livings. In its more exalted form it was one of the favourite ideas of the new school, which, however, had by and by to suffer a long list of cruel disappointments as one Benedick after another proved faithless to his early professions.

Newman was full of something for a day or two which he hardly knew how to tell. At last it came out. He was afraid Keble was about to make a 'humdrum marriage.' It was for the best of reasons, that is in order to discourage young men from aiming at a standard above the age, and possibly also above their own power to attain. It was like Keble, the humble, lowly, retired walk, and there was much of the sort in his poetry. I was fairly taken in by this account of the matter. I had known what I might have called humdrum marriages that one could hardly account for. I might indeed have remembered how I had been taken in by Froude's explanation of Bulteel's unexpected marriage, and how the flesh-chastising 'housekeeper' in that case had turned out to be a lady not wanting in either youth, looks, wit, money, or accomplishments. The stupid, however, are always deceived, and only recover from one mistake to fall into another.

Keble was over fifty. The intended was the sister of his younger brother's wife. Of course it must be the elder sister, and that would make the union 'suitable.' For the younger brother to marry the younger sister, and the elder brother to marry the elder, is quite proper and even humdrum. But it was no such thing in this case. The lady was the younger sister of Mrs. Thomas Keble, and was a rather strikingly handsome, pleasing, and dignified woman. Not only was Keble quite justified on the most ordinary grounds in marrying her if she would have him, but he had already shown the bent of his inclination, having, long before this, 'loved and lost,' on the lines of youth and beauty.

CHAPTER XLVIII.

MEETING AT HADLEIGH.

IN a very few days after his return home, Newman was in communication with Hugh J. Rose, who besides being one of the two editors of the 'Theological Library,' and the editor of the 'British Magazine,' was the one commanding figure, and very loveable man, that the frightened and discomfited Church-people were now rallying round. Few people have left so distinct an impression of themselves as this gentleman. For many years after, when he was no more, and Newman had left Rose's standpoint far behind, he could never speak of him or think of him without renewed tenderness.

There ensued much correspondence, and, to bring

matters to some point, there was a meeting of Rose's friends at Hadleigh. They were rallying round the Church of England, its Prayer Book, its faith, its ordinances, its constitution, its Catholic and Apostolic character; all more or less assailed by foes and in abeyance even with friends. The suppression of Irish Sees gave immediate prominence to the doctrine of Apostolic succession, which it was said to set at nought. This of course would not be the aspect in which Apostolic succession is generally regarded, which is that certain special gifts of the Spirit are, ordinarily, only communicated by officers appointed for that purpose by the Apostles, and by successors occupying their place in the Church. The aspect now regarded was that insisted on by some of the Nonjuring Bishops, not by all. It was that each see, and each local succession, must be perpetual. The Roman Church, it is well known, makes a point of preserving every episcopal succession, even though the see has long ceased to possess any visible existence; and there have been bishops *in partibus* who could not even say where their sees lay, or had ever lain.

Dr. Morris, Bishop of Troy, was for many years one of the best known names in this metropolis, being always at hand when a bishop was wanted. All the world credited him with the city founded by Rome in the Troas, at or about the site of Homer's Troy, and so he did himself. Having to preach at the Oratory in behalf of the sick and wounded in the Crimean War, he introduced with much propriety and feeling the neighbourhood and relation of his own diocese to a war which was not without points of resemblance to that which had made ancient Troy memorable. In the vestry Frederick Faber thanked his lordship, but pointed out that he appeared to be under some misapprehension as to the locality of his see, which lay in Magna Græcia, rot Asia Minor. During the Saracen occupation of that part of Italy, Troy had disappeared like its Asiatic sister, and a more convenient town had risen in its neighbourhood. But Rome would not allow the title to pass away. The perpetuity of the see was the pledge of the perpetuity of the Church, and must thus therefore be contended for as a vital question.

It was Newman's way to accept the suggestion of times, circumstances, and persons, and so to allow people to believe themselves the original movers, if it were at all possible. This sometimes gave an undue appearance of originality and finality to a proceeding, or to a mere concurrence. If he always left as it were a nest egg for something beyond, that he did not heed, for though it might not be in the programme, it was not beyond the scope of the occasion.

From the first he insisted on what may be called a loose formation. He would neither bind or be bound. He had seen enough of societies. He did not like committees. He suspected everything metropolitan. Great cities were great evils, he used to say. Yet there must be a centre. Universities he said were, in this country, the centres of intellect and of religion. So they that chose to write on the lines of the Church of England might send him what they had to say, and he would see to have it printed and circulated. Of course there must have been also

some distribution of subjects.   But several writers, in
particular Mr. Perceval, conceived a most extraordinary idea of the ' Hadleigh Conference,' as if it were
at once a great beginning and a grand finality. They
who heard of it as one of the many incidents of the
day can only be surprised that any man of sense
should think it possible Newman, or even Froude,
could be comprised and shut up by a few strokes of
the pen, and henceforth warranted to keep pace with
so very casual an acquaintance as Mr. Perceval.

CHAPTER XLIX.

THE ' TRACTS FOR THE TIMES.'

IN two or three weeks accordingly appeared that
portentous birth of time, the ' Tracts for the Times.'
Tracts had long been the most familiar form of religious propagandism, and there were many thousands
of ladies and gentlemen who made it their business
to deliver tracts by the house row, by the post, or to
anybody they chanced to meet.   Yet this was a
startling novelty.   The distributors of tracts, that is
the clergy and educated classes, had hitherto enjoyed
themselves an exemption from tracts.   So this was
to turn their own battery against them.   There were,
too, great practical difficulties.   The booksellers did
not like tracts.   They are litter ; they occupy space,

they encumber accounts; they don't pay. Messrs.
Rivington, however, undertook the London publication, it must be presumed for conscience sake. For
the convenience of the publishers they were to come
out with the monthlies. They were to be anonymous
and by different hands, each writer singly responsible.
If such an arrangement be not simply impossible, it
could at least only work upon an occasion and for a
brief movement. In a series or in a periodical either
the editor is responsible or the writer, and in the
latter case the name must be given. The plan
worked because the writers were soon known; indeed proud to be known, and so were responsible.

But now came the great difficulty. The only one
who could write a tract, possibly because the greatest
reader of tracts, was Newman himself. He urged
all his friends to contribute, and if any one of his
acquaintance did not contribute, it was because he
was idle or was not in heart. The contributors wrote
sermons and treatises, but not tracts. They discharged the contents of their commonplace books, or
they compiled from indexes, and thought it impossible to give too much of a good thing. Compared with Newman's, their 'tracts' were stuffing
and makeweights, learned, wise, and good, but not
calculated to take hearts by storm. They were
useful because it is an ascertained fact that bulk is
necessary, as they say it is in food, and that it helps
the real essence of a publication to keep its place on
the table, or on the shelves. There are, too, people
who really think more of an opinion when they see
that a great deal is to be said for it.

The tracts had to be circulated by post, by hand, or anyhow, and many a young clergyman spent days in riding about with a pocketful, surprising his neighbours at breakfast, lunch, dinner, and tea. The correspondence that ensued was immense. Nobody was too humble in intellect or in clerical position not to be invited, and enrolled as an ally. Men survive, or have but lately passed away, who can never have known what it was to share a glory and a greatness except at that happy time. The world would now wonder to see a list of the great Cardinal's friends. He had a remarkable quality which presents a strange contrast to the common habit of vulgar depreciators. Like Walter Scott, he could only see the best and highest parts of the human character, hoping ever against hope. He expected rivers out of the dry ground, and found poetic beauty in the quaintest and most rugged writers. Wise and experienced Oxford observers smiled at the confidence he reposed in men who were at best broken reeds and bulrushes, if not stocks and stones. He could appreciate writers whom nobody else could, seeing sense in their obscurity and life in their dulness.

But it is proper to say that this excessive appreciation was not confined to the crisis when the zeal of propagandism, or of partisanship, might seem to account for it. When Newman was tutor the college wiseacres often commented on his misplaced confidence, and lost labour upon the most barren and ungracious material. He would often have to his rooms for private talk and instruction men who went away and called it a bore. There were some men of high rank and expectations in Oriel at that time who had come to Oxford, they conceived, to learn how to enjoy this world, to take their place in its society, and to win its prizes. Newman tried to reach their hearts and understandings. It was not without effects, which revealed themselves many years after, but which did not show themselves at that time. There were other examples and advisers in the college too potent for Newman, and these he could not reach or eliminate. The most courageous law-makers and founders have declared it to be impossible to lay down rules for the young nobility of this country, insomuch that they must be treated as exceptional and foreign. But they have hearts, and a time arrives when they are no longer young. A bitter experience has then reduced them to the level of a common humanity.

The heir of an ancient and much-loved name, who lived to take a high part in the government of the country, and to be anxious to retrieve by magnificent Church work the errors of his youth, found that he must choose between Newman and associates more of his quality and more to his taste. He closed with the latter. He studiously adopted the tone and the conduct most likely to repel interference. When Newman finally gave up the tuition, his pupils subscribed near two hundred pounds to purchase a set of the Fathers for him, and the movers of the subscription would gladly have done without this man's money. He heard of the subscription and sent ten guineas, which it was impossible then to refuse. But George Ryder and the other members of the committee had good reason to suspect that Newman would refuse the testimonial if he knew this name was in the list of subscribers, and, notwithstanding his frequent entreaties, they would never let him know the names. Had Newman been less hopeful he might have been more forgiving, for it is the most generous and confiding who most feel ingratitude.

At the time now under consideration Newman seemed to have had hope of everybody. Whoever was not against him might be for him. For months he kept his friends daily informed of the reception which the tracts and the views contained in them received in many and unexpected quarters. The great world, indeed, whether of politics or of religion, was but slowly moved, and this new mode of assault had to be carried on for two or three years before it encountered an opposition worthy of its own audacity. The tracts indeed were for some time as seed cast on the waters. It must be said that some were heavy reading, and the series presented even greater varieties of style than are commonly found within the same covers.

Meanwhile it was not without a certain degree of impatience that Newman found himself only one strand in the weighty and multifarious coil of the ' Tracts for the Times.' While he was anonymous the crowd of other writers deadened, if they did not drown, his own intense individuality. So, with a great effort, he got over his old scruple against divulging to the world at large what had passed between him and his congregation, and published in 1834 a volume of ' Parochial Sermons.'

It was as if a trumpet had sounded through the land. All read and all admired, even if they dissented or criticised. The publishers said that the volume put all other sermons out of the market, just as 'Waverley' and 'Guy Mannering' put all other novels. Sermons to force their way without solicitation, canvassing, subscription, or high-sounding recommendation, were unknown in those days, and these flew over the land. They rapidly proceeded to successive editions, and were followed by 'University Sermons,' and 'Sermons on Holy Days.'

The title of 'Parochial Sermons' represents the fact, but not fully. The parish contains a score or two shopkeepers, their servants, and some college servants also. Strangers used to wonder to hear sermons which might tax the highest intellect delivered to housemaids. But long before the publication of his sermons Newman had gathered round him the best part of his own college and of some others— men to whom the sermons were the treat of the week, and who would often recall to one another the passages that had most struck them.

Newman and his friends had for some time been contributors to the 'British Magazine,' in Hugh J. Rose's hands. Much of the 'Lyra Apostolica,' whether by him or the other six contributors, appeared first in this magazine. This now famous collection was the growth of many minds, and many places, and many occasions. It has been abundantly criticised on the score of poetry, Christianity, and common sense. But it holds its ground and seems to address itself to a great variety of readers, for the very reason perhaps that it actually represents that variety of origin and suggestion which poets are often obliged to affect and to invent for the occasion.

/

CHAPTER L.

ROUTH, PRESIDENT OF MAGDALENE, AND PALMER, OF WORCESTER.

SINCE the movement became historical the question how it began, and who began it, has been continually asked, and answered in very different ways. Fashion has put its form on a fact which it could not easily accept or conceive in any other form. For a long time past it has been a fashion to ascribe causes, revivals, and human changes generally either to individuals possessed with extraordinary qualities and a distinct forecast of the future, or to some very exceptional origin. The fact is, as far as the bystanders could see, there was no such idea of origination of a cause or a party in Newman's mind, even though Froude, and possibly one or two others, might play upon the thought. He stirred up everybody to act for the best on his own lines. He had a wonderful faith in men and in the call of circumstances. He much desired to impress upon everybody the great power he possessed for good, though generally content to leave the work and the manner of it to the man

himself. He put into the hands of his young friends
the books that had done his own soul good. He
saw substantial merits and recognised services in all
quarters, and never encouraged the tone of disparage-
ment too common in young people full of themselves
and new to persons and things.

Long before the earliest date that could be assigned for a ' movement,' Bishop Webb, Mr. Forster,
author of ' Mahomedanism Unveiled,' Canon David-
son, the Oriel writer on Prophecy, and John Miller,
of Worcester College, were great names in the circle
of friends ; indeed a sort of foundation for such
work as there was to be done. Newman held Van
Mildert in much esteem, and quoted his Bampton
Lectures. Old-fashioned clergy of those days talked
much of Norris of Bemerton, of Tucker's ' Light of
Nature,' and of Jones of Nayland, as a kind of esoteric
school leading to better things, but like many other
authors these had been crowded out of Oriel.
Froude early established Law as the prophet of
the last century. Resigning assigned specialities to
other hands, Newman devoted himself to the great
questions immediately before him. This could not
but limit the range of his studies. He had now
begun a life of action, and even reading must be subordinate.

The greatest name in patristic theology at Oxford
—indeed a name in Europe, which is a rare thing to
be said of any English scholar—was Routh, the aged
President of Magdalene. Newman was sometimes
asked why he did not enlist the old gentleman more
directly in his cause by dedicating to him one of his

works. The reason of this he gave in confidence to
a few friends. It was a painful one. The President
had been for a very long time notoriously negligent
of the discipline of his college. In his excessive care
of himself and his almost morbid craving for longevity—the longevity of Tithonus—he made a rule
of caring for no other person or thing, and of letting
the college go its own way, as it did. He could
even derive amusement from the scandals which the
seniors of the college would have prevented if he had
given them the requisite authority and support.

It was long after this, when Routh must have
been ninety, that Faber, the chief college officer
in the matter of discipline, called upon him one
morning, evidently preparing to break some sad
news. 'Stop, I know what you're going to tell me,'
he said. 'One of the Fellows has died drunk in the
night.' 'It is indeed so,' said Faber. But before he
could give the name the President exclaimed, 'Stay,
let me guess.' He guessed right. 'There, you see I
knew the men well. He's just the sort of fellow to
die drunk.' As longevity is justly regarded as a
blessing, it may be well to remember that it is
possible to survive, not the physical powers, or the
mental, but such heart as one may have. It may
be possible to attain length of years without becoming
at all better for it.

Newman's early scruples as to the enlistment of
Routh's honoured name was one of the delicacies
which, like his hesitation to publish his 'Parochial
Sermons,' he lived to abandon. The 'Lectures on
Romanism and Popular Protestantism,' referred to

above, and published in 1837, are dedicated to Routh
in terms which the writer no doubt hoped might
suggest to him 'the day of account,' in which he
would want 'support and protection.' There was no
help for it. All the work of life has its roughness.
There is some defilement in all labour. *Hinc mihi
sordes.* If a man will save every scruple he will have
to sit still and do nothing. Yet it seemed to those
about Newman as if a little of his bloom was rubbed
off when he addressed what to vulgar eyes seemed a
glowing panegyric to the faithless guardian of a great
Christian college. But what they grieved was the
necessity forced upon him.

William Palmer, of Worcester, had the English
Liturgy and the Constitution of the English Church
for his work, and Newman was almost alone in
recognising his great services. Palmer's extreme
sedateness, shyness, and seeming coldness of manner, stood much in the way of his general acceptance.

Among the many and great scandals of the
Church of England there is hardly a greater than its
gross and stupid neglect of this able and excellent
man. He came from Trinity College, Dublin, to
pursue inquiries for which Oxford was a more congenial as well as convenient place. In his own preparation for Holy Orders he had had to study the
Prayer Book, and for this purpose he found abundance
of commentaries of a doctrinal and practical character.
But he desired to learn the origin and history of our
formularies, and for this he could find little or no
help. So he came to Oxford. Fate, or the kindness

of a friend, directed him to Worcester College; choice took him often to Oriel. He had at once placed in his hands Bishop Lloyd's annotated folio Prayer Book, and an older document of the same kind in the Bodleian, besides other MSS. there.

It should be said there had been a sort of revival of these studies a few years before. Shepherd, a promising young clergyman, had announced a Prayer Book with historical illustrations ; and had set about it with industry, when he died. The very fragmentary work done was published by his sister, and several thousand guinea subscriptions testified to the interest felt even then in the antiquities of our ritual.

Mr. Palmer brought out his ' *Origines Liturgicæ*,' as stated above, in 1832, the year before the appearance of the ' Tracts for the Times.' There is not a more interesting work to a scholar and divine, and hardly a more useful one to an ordinary clergyman. It was a great addition to our national literature. To most Oxford men it was like an incident of continental travel before railways—the sudden view of a vast plain full of picturesque objects and historical associations.

Mr. Palmer was always ready to talk on the subject and to exchange information. He could impart his knowledge clearly and succinctly, in good and incisive language. There could be no suspicion of party, or bigotry of any kind about him. The work was in the straightest lines of the Church of England, without a shadow of deflection.

Henry Wilberforce thought he had detected a

latent humour in Palmer's defence of the introduction of the Ten Commandments into the Communion Service. The gist of that defence was that all Churches had read some portion of the Scriptures, generally of the Law and the Prophets, in this place. Some had varied the passages, some had not. The old Irish Church, and the Malabar Church, had used the same passages always. Comparing one passage with another, the Ten Commandments were as useful as any. All this, however, is put with so much gravity and solemnity, that if there were humour, there is great virtue in its effectual concealment.

His ' Treatise on the Church of Christ,' published six years after, in 1838, is a defence of the Church of England, full of careful statement and valuable information, though the writer's Irish birth and education come out with unexpected force in the history and denunciation of the 'Irish schism,' that is the Roman Catholic Church in that island.

After residing some years at Oxford, taking the tenderest care of an aged mother, long the sole companion of his walks, Palmer left for a remote country living, and died, it may be said, in obscurity. Reward he wanted not, but he had not even recognition.

CHAPTER LI.

BISHOP MARSH.

MOST people have some information, and consequently some rational grounds for their own opinions upon the working of the 'Oxford movement.' Such opinions will vary according to predisposition and circumstances, but there will always be something to be said for them. It is far otherwise with regard to the times before the movement, and its antecedents so to speak. The popular ignorance with regard to that period is amazing. People have taken up a book, generally a biography, and upon finding it chiming in with their own ideas, they have accepted it for authentic history, and given it even a wider application perhaps than the writer intended. My own belief is that the history of no period in our Church is to be written, or judged, in that way. In particular, I feel sure, as the result of much observation and inquiry, that people are under a very great error in their depreciation of the last century. The clergy lived and worked under the greatest difficulties. Their net receipts from their livings were little more than two-thirds what they now are, or about 70 per cent. The country roads were very bad, and in many months of the year almost impassable. There were but scanty means of enlivening the rural solitude with newspapers and periodicals. Few clergymen could afford a horse, or a man-

servant, and if they could, both horse and man must
have been of the roughest.

I believe that, as a rule, the clergy did their best
under these circumstances, and were often shining
lights in dark neighbourhoods. I can attach no credit
whatever to the stories of clergymen frequently
marrying the lady's maid, or lower still, picked up by
Macaulay from satirical novels, farces, lampoons, and
caricatures. These were generally written by men
who had forfeited their character with all respectable people, and who accordingly revenged themselves
on the gentry, the clergy, and Christians generally by
their pictures of extraordinary characters whom they
represented as typical of the class. Macaulay wished
to believe the worst of the gentry and the clergy,
and he would not be at a loss for evidence, nor would
he care to sift it.

In my time at Oxford, and I suspect long before
my time, the expression ' three-bottle orthodox,' was
often used to denote some class supposed to exist in
the last century and reaching down into this. The
phrase is one to fix itself in the memory, like many
other foolish phrases, but it will not bear a minute's
examination. Putting aside the question of physical
possibility, which would involve an inquiry into the
question whether port in those days was a beverage,
like claret, or a liqueur as it now is, the cost of the
feat would prevent its performance, except by very
few persons, and on very rare occasions. If it could be
supposed a daily practice, the great majority of
livings would not pay the wine bill.

But the whole clergy, one used to hear it said,

frequented the public-house, and drank beer with their parishioners. That they sat and talked with their parishioners was so much to the good, and it could not be worse to drink beer with their parishioners than to drink wine with their neighbours. If there be any moral difference between drinking a pint of wine with the squire and a pint of beer with the labourer, the latter has the advantage in economy and health, and opens a wider scope of usefulness. The squire both can and will educate himself, but the labourer has to be taught both the will and the power. In the course of long walks, pedestrian tours, and cross-country travelling, I may safely say I have never found such disgusting conversation as I have heard at gentlemen's tables, or anything to censure, except now and then a piece of ignorance to smile at. Every clergyman sincerely desirous to have talks with his poor parishioners finds it difficult. He must not interrupt them at their work, and it is very seldom that he can find them at home. Why should he not join them when they are taking a rest, and talking with one another? With the Bible in our hands, it will not do to throw the public-house out of the pale of the Church.

When I went to live in Salisbury Plain, I saw at Netheravon an elderly, grave-looking clergyman, a very spare figure, living alone at the dull roadside parsonage. ' He's a queer fellow,' people said ; ' he goes to the public-house, and drinks with his parishioners.' I did not hear anything worse about him. This was the parish, and the parsonage, where Sydney Smith had been once for two years, dining generally at the great house, but very much put out, and giving bad names to the locality, because, when he sat down to some roast veal, he found he could not get a lemon without sending to Amesbury, five miles off.

Netheravon is just two miles from the humbler village where Addison spent the first fifteen years of his life. He went daily to Amesbury School, and it was in his walks to and fro, in the very track the servant would have to go for a lemon, that he gathered the touching imagery for his translation of the 23rd Psalm. Here, too, it was that he found the original of his Sir Roger de Coverley in Richard Duke, of Bulford House, which he daily passed. The Pakingtons claim Sir Roger de Coverley, but Addison is more likely to have taken his ideal from an acquaintance of his youth than from a gentleman who survived him many years.

Samuel Rickards, of whom I hope to say more, told me that his uncle, a Leicester incumbent, used to take a seat every day before a public-house in the market-place, ready to have a talk with anybody who wanted it. He was never without a companion, and sometimes had a circle of listeners.

I took charge of my Northamptonshire living about Michaelmas, and was ordained Priest at Christmas, at Oxford, by Murray, Bishop of Rochester, Bagot being then unwell. I was to go to Peterborough, to be licensed, not instituted, for it was a Perpetual Curacy. This name has been abolished, young incumbents not liking a designation which seemed to imply perpetual subalternship, but it may be doubted whether they have gained much by being called Vicar or Rector, as if they had received their final preferment and had nothing better to expect.

I went to Peterborough from Derby. The palace struck me as a dull solitude. Marsh, who, if my memory is not at fault, wore a Welsh wig, sat at a small reading-desk in the middle of a scantily furnished room, looked a homely old gentleman, and made kind inquiries about my parish and my predecessors. 'Mr. Mozley,' he then said, 'how do you propose to go to your living?' 'That is just what I am in a difficulty about,' I replied. He went on: 'I have always found that my best way from one end of my diocese to the other is through London.' It was quite true, as I found, that this would be the best, the cheapest, and the most expeditious route. I wished, however, to see Northamptonshire, and therefore traversed that long county.

The Bishop added: 'Mrs. Hinchcliffe, widow of Bishop Hinchcliffe, told me that her husband used to go about in his visitations and confirmations on a pillion behind the churchwarden, and that this was the only possible way he could travel in Northamptonshire.' I thought of this when I saw many years after a beautiful picture of Mrs. Hinchcliffe and her sister, by Sir Joshua Reynolds.

As I walked away from the palace with Mr. Gates, the secretary, he seemed to think it necessary to make some apology. The Bishop's palace was out of the way, and there was no society, but the Bishop was in years, and it was an advantage that he had not the trouble of entertaining.

The Cathedral, as I remember, holds its own for grace, solemnity, and cheerfulness. Catherine of Arragon lies there, and when Henry VIII. was reminded that she wanted a monument, he used to say she had the finest monument in England—the Cathedral itself.

I met the Bishop and Mrs. Marsh, who always took charge of him, on two occasions afterwards—a visitation and a confirmation ; and being the youngest incumbent on both occasions had to take out Mrs. Marsh to the lunch. I think there was rather more under-play going on than I expected or liked, but the clergy had come from long distances and were glad to see one another. At Brackley there must have been near four hundred young people, most of them coming in waggons, as mine did. Old women occupied all the approaches to the church with large baskets of black cherries ; the day was hot, the roads dusty, and the young people soon blackened their lips, faces, and hands, much to the spoiling of their pretty looks. One clergyman, singularly wanting in self-management and with a remarkably large mouth, fell into the snare, and made himself a terrible object. Head, in his 'Bubbles from the Brunnens of Nassau,' relates an incident of the same kind.

Not long before I went to Moreton Pinckney, Bishop Marsh had attempted to stop the use of a hymn-book at a church near mine, and after an expenditure of 4,000*l.* had been foiled or worn out. His opponent had been a good-looking shopman at a linen-draper's, who attracted the notice of a young woman left with a large fortune, and became her husband. She took him to a university. He was ordained, and in due time she presented him to a good living. Though he beat the Bishop, he avenged the Bishop himself, for he became a scandal to the Church. He had to hide himself, his living was sequestered, and he only reappeared to make a disgraceful figure in the courts.

CHAPTER LII.

DISTRIBUTION OF THE TRACTS AMONG THE OLD CLERGY.

WHEN the 'Tracts for the Times' made their appearance I had been a twelvemonth at Moreton Pinckney, but while that put me right into Northamptonshire, it did not take me far from Oxford, and the distance was nothing to me. Upon going to the place I had felt under an obligation to do whatever work Newman might think me capable of. I was now to put the tracts in circulation, and to inform people of the movement generally. Names were given to me. The most distinguished churchmen in Northamptonshire, not to speak of a political agitator mentioned elsewhere, were Mr. Sikes, of Guils-

borough, Mr. Crawley, of Stowe Nine Churches, and
his son Lloyd Crawley.

Stowe Nine Churches lay the nearest, and perhaps
the name was something in the scale. Putting on a
great-coat and mounting a shaggy pony at the dawn
of a winter's day, I rode there with a bundle of
tracts. I passed close to the window of a room where
a considerable party were still at breakfast, and I was
conscious of fluttering the Volsci. The front door
was promptly opened by a wonderfully handsome
man, much over ninety, asking shortly what I wanted,
and looking askance at the hoof-marks of my pony
on his smooth gravel. I explained, and instantly had
a most welcome invitation to come in and have some
breakfast. He seemed puzzled by the tracts themselves, but had that eager thought of a better time
coming that would accept anything. He gave me
names and directions, and advice, but above all, I
was to see his son Lloyd.

The old gentleman was himself a martyr, or at
least a confessor, to the good old cause of——
what shall I say ? But it really was not so small a
matter as some of my readers might imagine. When
he first came to Stowe Nine Churches—it must have
been before the Declaration of American Independence—the village was singular for its beauty, its
seclusion, its simplicity, and its virtues. The world
had not found its way to Stowe Nine Churches. But
the Birmingham people wanted a straight way to
London, and didn't care what they did for it. They
got an Act for a road right through his parish, and
so let both London and Birmingham loose upon him ;

besides mauling his sweet hill sides, choking up some valleys, and spoiling some pretty lanes.

He had scarcely recovered from this blow when the Birmingham people found they could not do without something else—a canal, of all things in the world. This he would fight against, and he did, but to no purpose. They got their canal, and from that time it was impossible to have fowls, ducks or geese, or anything worth carrying off, within half a mile of the canal. It certainly was the fact that the boatmen laid their hands on all the poultry they could get at, spent the night in plucking them, sold them in London or Birmingham, and the next time they had a furniture removal ripped open the featherbeds, took out the costly down, and replaced it with the dirty and blood-stained feathers of their other booty.

Mr. Crawley now thought he had suffered all that human cupidity or malignity could inflict on him. But no ; at an age when he might justly expect to be left gliding peacefully to the grave, they were making, almost by the side of the turnpike road and the canal, a railway cutting his hills right in two, stopping up his streams, and transforming his parish almost beyond recognition. But, thank Heaven, he did not believe they would ever complete it. The traffic could never pay ; the poor rates alone would ruin it ; the damages for setting fire to crops and farm-buildings would be overwhelming. As far as I remember the old gentleman had most of the talk. But he inquired much about my Oxford friends.

Soon I rode to his son, Lloyd Crawley. I found him a very spare, active little man, near seventy,

with a great deal to say. His living had been given
to him when he was still young, on the understanding
that he was to vindicate some disputed rights of tithe.
He did it and succeeded, for the case was clear, but he
had never had a day's rest since, or, to judge from his
large wakeful eyes, a night's rest either. The beaten
tithepayers had built a meeting-house, and he could
have no dealings with them. He and his people
were most interested in the Oxford doings, but he
kept returning to the London world, and the work of
the Societies, as the true scene of action. I must see
Mr. Sikes, he said. It was too far, I replied ; twenty
miles or more from Moreton Pinckney. I gave it up.
My pony was a borrowed beast.

However, I made my appearance there again,
just in time to see Lloyd Crawley mounting for a
ride. 'What a pity!' he said ; 'I must go and see
Sikes. They say he's not well. We can't afford to
lose him. But stay, I'll mount you. It's nothing of
a ride ; only ten miles.' I accepted the offer gladly.
Another horse was brought out, which Crawley
mounted, giving me that I had found him on. The
new horse looked, for a horse, just what his rider
looked for a man—all wire and fire. When a little
way on the road Crawley observed, 'I've ridden this
horse twenty years. But he tires me. He pulls too
much. He will take his own pace, which is rather
too much for me now. I come home with a strained
arm, fatigued rather than refreshed.' It was just as he
said. Do what the rider could, his horse would keep
ahead of mine.

In three quarters of an hour or less we were at

Sikes' gate, and were received in a charming library, light, airy, and full of well-bound books, ornamental as well as useful. Sikes was a fine-looking, elderly man, with a dignified bearing and a very kind expression, ready to talk about everything, but with a certain languor and sadness which might or might not be more than his wont. We must join him at his early dinner. I remember it was a boiled leg of lamb and spinach. I had never seen a boiled leg of lamb before. Sikes made the kindest inquiries about the Oxford people.

But all his talk was against pushing Church principles too hard, and making breaches never to be healed. There were zealots in Northamptonshire, he said, who would bring Church teaching to a point that would necessarily exclude dissenters. As things were there was inconsistency on both sides, on the side of the Church managers as well as the dissenters. But he had always urged privately that these inconsistencies should be endured. If the dissenters will bear it, surely we may. Their children are often the best in our schools. They do us good, and we may do some good to them. The Northamptonshire schools, he said, stood high, and he believed it was owing to a quiet, conciliatory policy. Avoid disturbance if you possibly can.

I may seem to claim a too distinct memory of a conversation so far back as 1833 or 1834, but it impressed itself upon me much, and has recurred a thousand times, especially when I chanced to read any of G. A. D.'s effusions. I have often asked myself what gave the conversation this turn. I suppose that

Sikes regarded me as another firebrand, nay as one of a whole pack of firebrands, and he then was longing for peace. Yet he spoke with much respect of my Oxford friends. At parting he was very kind, and indeed tender. There was a great work to be done. He was not to have a part in it. He could only give his prayers. A fortnight after I was shocked to hear of his death. Had I put things together I should have been better prepared for it.

I could not but think of his words in connection with my own village school. The best boy in it was the only son of a small Baptist farmer, and had not been baptised. The chief book in my school, as I found it, and kept it, was Crossman's Catechism. I always shudder as I write the name, as I should shudder at the mention of the rack, the boot, or the wheel. My schoolmaster was a machine, and drove his plough and his harrow fast and straight over the ground. I spoke to him occasionally, asking special consideration for the poor lad, who might well have been allowed to leave Crossman alone, for he could repeat every answer in the book without a single mistake, and did so. But the master must go his own pace. Like the omnibus horse, he could only do his day's work on the condition of not having to think. Once or twice have I had the opportunity of inquiring about the poor lad taught after the straitest manner of Crossman. The only conclusion I have come to is that in such cases there ought to be a distinct and friendly understanding with the parents, and some special and private instruction given to the child necessarily placed in an ambiguous and dangerous position. Carpenter, for that was his name, did not much credit to his school, to Crossman, to his master, or to me.

By the time we got back to Lloyd Crawley's parsonage, it was too late for me to continue my journey to mine. So he gave me a bed. At seven next morning he tapped at my door and asked if I would like some warm water. I had never used warm water in my life for washing or for shaving. Well, I said to myself, here my good host has got up early to take the trouble to offer me hot water; it's only a proper acknowledgment of his kindness to accept it. In the course of the morning he mentioned that he always used cold water himself.

CHAPTER LIII.

NORRIS, OF HACKNEY.

THAT year, or early the next, I had an urgent summons from Lloyd Crawley to attend a meeting of the Christian Knowledge Society, at which a great issue was at stake; nothing less than the future of the Society and of the Church of England. The question lay between an existing committee and a new one altogether. But what committee was it? Was it a committee for the choice or preparation of books of useful or entertaining knowledge, or a committee for the selection of all the new books to be put on the list ? Whatever it was, the difference between the committee, past and to come, was said to compromise the principles of the Society.

I seem to remember that Tyler and Cunningham of Harrow were names in the new committee proposed. To me the question was one only of principle, or of party, if the reader thinks that the truer way of putting it. I had never been able to read or to use the Society's books. If I couldn't, I could scarcely expect my poor parishioners.

However, I went up to town, met Crawley, and with him proceeded to Bartlett's Buildings. A very large room was already crammed. By-and-by the landings and staircases were crammed too. Most of these people had come great distances, and had started with a strong impression that they were likely to be outjockeyed in some way or other by the people on the spot. So now they were desperate. There arose a wild cry for space, which became louder when it was known that Howley had taken the chair. Angry voices came up as from an abyss, and imputations of foul dealing were freely made. Some one proposed an adjournment to Freemasons' Hall, a couple of hundred yards off, then often used for like purposes. It was seconded by a thousand voices.

The Primate mildly and effectively remonstrated. What would the world say if it heard of a long procession of excited clergymen, perhaps in warm discussion, passing along a public thoroughfare ? It would put the worst construction on such a scene. At present we kept our differences very much to ourselves, and so got over them. The outsiders were therefore sent to another room, with a suitable chairman, and they were to be kept well acquainted with the proceedings of the larger assemblage.

It was soon plain how things would go. The Archbishop said it was quite gratuitous to suppose that the new committee would represent a different theology than that of the old one, and so make a substantial change in the Society. The names in the proposed committee were a sufficient guarantee for that. It would undertake to make no such change, but to work on the old lines. The members of the Society themselves would watch, and they would have the remedy in their own hands. He could not say that he wished often to see a meeting beyond the capacity of these premises, but he would take from the present occasion an assurance that their future meetings would not be so ill attended as they had frequently been. If the gentlemen before him would be so good as to come, some at a time, they would be of the greatest benefit to the Society's deliberations. All together, they were too many for counsel.

My good friends had committed the usual error of impulsive natures. They had had no definite programme, or common forecast, and they had not borne in mind that the moment the Primate opened his mouth, he would be master of the situation. That would be pretty sure of any Primate ; it would be a dead certainty in Howley's case. With my then boyish ideas of eloquence, I was much struck by his perfectly simple and conversational way of speaking. But there was no answer to it, for when the Primate

had pronounced the new committee all good and true
men, who could say otherwise?

But this day really was the day of doom to the old
High Church party. The chief clergyman in the committee to be superseded, or supplied with new blood
in a preponderating quantity, was Norris, of Hackney,
commonly called the Bishop-maker. During all
Lord Liverpool's long premiership, it was said that
every see was offered to him, with the request that if
he could not take it himself, he would be so good as
to recommend some one else. Now for seven years
he had been relieved of this unenviable responsibility.
But he was still everything at the S.P.C.K., and the
country members looked to him to represent them.
So this day his reign was over, and Norris was a
dethroned potentate.

Crawley, who was to be Norris's guest at Hackney,
introduced me, and I was asked to accompany him to
dinner. Norris took us in his carriage. We arrived
at a large and comfortable house—parsonage or not I
do not remember. It seemed quite in the country,
standing in the midst of thirty-five acres of green
fields, plantations, and full-grown hedge-rows. One
could hardly see a roof or a chimney to remind one
of the metropolis. There was something like a farmyard, with a large haystack, near the house. We
walked out and looked around. Norris was thankful he had been the means of reserving all this open
space so long from the invasion of builders. He
said nothing of its future. Looking up I saw some
strange objects far overhead. Crawley, who lived
near Lord Spencer's, said at once they were herons.

Norris said he often saw them. They were on their
way from a heronry down the Thames to one far up, I
think near Cliefden, and they made a point of skirting
the metropolis to avoid its smoke and smell.

But I have not given my recollections of Norris.
With his very well-formed and well-chiselled features, he seemed to me an ideal of Cardinal Wolsey,
finer, though not so powerful. At dinner the talk
ran on people. There was not a word about the
business of the day. Not very long after Mrs. Norris
and another lady or two had left the room, Norris
fell into a very deep sleep. Crawley was embarrassed.
What was he to do? The butler came in and told
us what was the regular thing. We were to steal out
into the drawing-room, separated by a door. The
door would be left just ajar. In due time, when Mrs.
Norris gave the word, the butler would step in and
tell his master tea was waiting. This was the course
every evening. But here was the deposed monarch
of a mighty spiritual empire, sleeping the sleep of a
child, the day of his fall from that high estate.

Hackney had long been regarded as a sort of
High Church rival and counterpoise to Clapham.
But Norris must have found himself sadly destitute
of resources. He lacked the men, the measures,
and the literature. Edward Churton had a pro-
prietary school there for some time, but what he
did out of his school, or could have done, I never
heard. Norris was so ready to close with anybody
who was not an 'Evangelical,' that he had strange
mishaps. He had Hampden, Bad Powell, and I
think Hinds among his curates.

Late in the evening I returned to the city, as it seemed to me through several miles of tillage, by very scantily lighted roads. The next time I heard the name of Crawley, it was, I think, in connection with Littlemore.

CHAPTER LIV.

OUTCOMES OF THE MOVEMENT.

NEWMAN took little or no part in those special outcomes of the movement in which it is most presented to modern eyes. He left to others hymnology, though himself a writer of hymns; church music, though a devotee and a performer; and even church ritual, which has latterly given a name to the Anglican section of his followers. Church architecture and church decoration he even more easily resigned to those who might care much for them. In all these matters he acted not as an author, or as prime mover, but as a sympathetic bystander, hailing the heaven-sent gifts of genius and grace.

The year 1834, in respect of events, was as the calm which precedes the storm, but it was one of vast preparation and incessant labour. Nine or ten men were now doing their best to out-talk, and out-write, and out-manoeuvre the world, and so heartily did they set about it that there ensued a certain degree of competition. There were writers who could write nothing short ; writers who could write a good sonnet or an ode, but nothing in prose under a volume ; and all disclosed a life of incubation. If one of them saw that his colleague had ventured on thirty pages, he would take sixty, and soon found himself exceeded by the same rule. The tracts took time to write, and perhaps more time to read. Sermons were preached everywhere, even in the Chapel Royal, but mostly in country places, and published with long introductions and copious appendices. High and Low Church stood by amazed, and very doubtful what it would come to ; but meanwhile equally pleased to see life in the Church, which the House of Commons seemed to think incapable of thought, will, or action. The correspondence grew. Oxford resumed its historic place as the centre of religious activity. This was the golden age of the movement, and men talked rather gaily. Some readily accepted the charge of conspiracy, and were far from prompt to disavow that there was more in the background.

As the vastness of the work to be done now loomed before the hardy projectors, it became evident that a school of divinity had to be founded. There was no provision either for students or for teachers in divinity at Oxford. A university that could make Doctors of Divinity as easily as Birmingham can make brass tokens, had no occasion for teachers or examiners. Oxford was too conscious of its want of discipline to encourage residence, except for the twenty months necessary for a B.A. degree. It was then the merest chance whether a man got a

Fellowship, and even that did nothing for him in the way of divinity, except board and lodging, and a society more or less disposed to think theology worth a sensible man's attention. I remember a conversation with a newly-elected probationer at Oriel, a 'first class' man, when something was said as to the choice of a profession. He had made up his mind against Orders. There was nothing more to be learnt in theology. There was no progress in it. This gentleman eventually took Orders, and became a rather popular preacher.

So Newman and Pusey took a house nearly opposite the west front of Christchurch, fitted it up in simple fashion, and supplied housekeeping for young graduates willing to study divinity. Some will set this down as a device for ensnaring, training, and chaining young minds to some narrow circle of ideas. It might be the very danger that drove the Provost of Oriel to extreme measures. The experiment had a fair trial. My brother James had recently taken his degree ; as also a young relative of Pusey's. There were one or two others. After a couple of years, the 'Hall,' for such it was, was found not to attract inmates even on gratuitous terms, and Pusey very generously took the surviving members under his own roof. This might be construed into the device of the fisherman for drawing his fish into a smaller and still smaller enclosure. But whatever had been proposed, Heaven disposed otherwise. My brother James, who was his inmate till his election to a Magdalene Fellowship, became the very distinguished Regius Professor, and the author of works in which agreement with Newman, or with Pusey, was apparently the last thing desired.

What was the rest of the university doing? What especially the old Oriel school? If work is to be estimated by events, they must be credited with marvellous sagacity and prescience. Towards the end of 1834, Dr. Hampden, who was now, thanks to his loyal and steady friend the Provost of Oriel, Principal of St. Mary's Hall, and Professor of Moral Philosophy, produced an able but startling pamphlet, entitled 'Observations on Religious Dissent, with particular reference to the use of Religious Tests in the University.' Without referring to the 'Tracts for the Times,' or other publications of the day, he struck at the root of the movement; for he stated that the Creeds were but opinions, for which a man could not be answerable, and that they were expressed in obsolete phraseology. In this pamphlet and in other forms, there was now before the university a distinct proposal to abolish subscription to the Thirty-nine Articles.

A Bachelor of Divinity, writing with the pen of a master, commented on the proposal, and on the pamphlet, in a circular laid on the common room tables; and early next year, 1835, a 'Clerical Member of the University' (Henry Wilberforce), addressed a very powerful letter to the Primate, entitled 'The Foundation of the Faith Assailed in Oxford.' Beyond a certain degree of irritation betrayed by Hampden, nothing came of these anonymous attacks, for the object of them was not a man to waste his shot on

344 OUTCOMES OF THE MOVEMENT.

an unseen foe. He knew too that the issue would be decided in London, not at Oxford.

A local work, small, but charged with consequences, now began to cost time and money, and some anxiety also. Attached to the vicarage of St. Mary's was the hamlet of Littlemore, three miles off, without even a place of worship. Newman often walked over, generally with a companion. His mother and sisters had taken charge of the school and the poor. The names of the families and of the most interesting characters had become familiar to Newman's friends. There must be a church some day there, but there was no prospect of endowment ; the vicarage of St. Mary's was but a poor one, and when Newman, no longer tutor, continued to occupy his rooms in college, it was because the vicar of the parish attached to the University Church had no other residence.

Not a few must still remember the lower London road as associated with the Newman family, and perhaps with some slight incident. Here is one, pleasant and suggestive. As Mrs. Newman, her daughters, and myself were walking on the road between Littlemore and Iffley, we passed some labourers digging a large rotten stump out of a bank. One of them ran after us, exhibiting a portion of the stump, with several enormous grubs or caterpillars eating their way through it. I brought it home to Oriel, showed it to George Anthony Denison, and asked him to take it to his brother Edward, at Merton College. He immediately brought it back, with the box neatly inscribed in handwriting long afterwards presenting itself from time to time in the midst of more anxious matters: 'Cossus ligniperda, or Great Goat Moth. For its anatomy, see Lyonnet, who has written an octavo volume upon it. It is figured in Donovan.'

It is easy to understand how a church became every year more regarded as a necessity at Littlemore. The want of it was even a scandal, for there had once been a chapel there; nor was this the only place where a chapel had been disused on Oriel property. There was the perfect, but desecrated, chapel of St. Bartholomew's, in a farmyard not a mile out of Oxford, in the same direction as Littlemore.

Newman's own ideas of a village church were simple, almost utilitarian. So little part had he in the great ecclesiological and ritual revival, which has changed not only the inside of our churches but the face of the land, that from first to last he performed the service after the fashion of the last century. At his own church of St. Mary's was retained the custom, said to be from Puritan times, of handing the sacred elements to the communicants at their places down the long chancel, the desks of which, covered with white linen for the occasion, looked much like tables. All he wanted at Littlemore was capacity and moderate cost.

He consulted me, but I was equally at a loss for an original idea. A happy thought occurred to me. My Northamptonshire church had a simple Early English chancel with lancet windows; a triplet filling the east end. I had much admired it. A London cousin of mine, an amateur in watercolours, had made a beautiful picture of the interior. Taking drawings of this, adapting them, and enlarging the scale, I produced something like a design, which was at once approved and handed to an Oxford architect to put in working form. The material was to be rough stone, dug on the spot, the corners and windows in Headington stone. There was to be no chancel, or vestry, or tower, or porch. The work became an object of much interest, and long before it was completed, it was evident that much more might have been done ; but one of Newman's rules was to owe no man anything, not even on a church account.

As soon as the building showed what it was likely to be, it was perceived that a mistake had been committed in supposing that a design good on a small scale would be equally good on a much larger one. However, it became the model of many churches and chapels, and Pugin himself, after expressing high approval of it, reproduced it in the Norman style next year at Reading.

The first stone was laid in July 1835, when Newman noticed the discovery of four skeletons lying east and west, showing that this was holy ground, and that the dust of saints was under their feet, with the moral that ' the ancient truth alone endures ; as it was in the beginning, so now and for ever.'

Froude, who had now bidden farewell to Toryism, much in the same key as he had written of old Tyre and the Cities of the Plain, was contributing to the tracts from Barbadoes, and also freely criticising them when they seemed to him to temporise or to fall into modern conventionalisms. In fact he was keeping Newman, nothing loth, up to the mark.

In May 1835 he returned from Barbadoes. On landing he found a letter from Newman calling him to Oxford, where there were several friends soon to part for the Long Vacation. His brother Anthony was summoned from his private tutor, Mr. Hubert Cornish. Froude came full of energy and fire, sunburnt, but a shadow. The tale of his health was soon told. He had a 'button in his throat' which he could not get rid of, but he talked incessantly. With a positive hunger for intellectual difficulties, he had been studying Babbage's calculating machine, and he explained, at a pace which seemed to accelerate itself, its construction, its performances, its failures, and its certain limits. Few, if any, could follow him, still less could they find an opening for aught they had to say, or to beg a minute's law. He never could realise the laggard pace of duller intelligences. I have not the least doubt he did his best to explain Babbage's machine to his black Euclid class at Codrington College, and that without ever ascertaining the result in their minds.

The third or fourth day Anthony returned to his tutor at Merton, a few miles from Oxford, availing himself of a 'lift' I offered him in that direction. Within sight of Merton he suddenly woke from a reverie and exclaimed, ' Lor', what a goose I am ! I haven't told Hurrell Bessie's going to be married.'

Hurrell Froude went home a dying man, though it was not till the following January that the end was seen to be near.

A remarkable illustration of the state of the Oriel society at this time, and of Newman's relations to it,

occurs in a published letter of the late Bishop of
Winchester.   It is dated November 10, 1835.   ' By
the way, Newman is just publishing a third volume
of sermons.   I spent a day very pleasantly at Oxford.
Newman was very kind indeed—stayed at our inn
till eleven o'clock with us.   I dined in common room,
where the sights and sounds were curious : the cantankerous conceit of ——— ;   ———'s pettishness ;   the
vulgar priggishness of ———'s jokes ;   the loud un-
gentlemanliness of ———'s cutlip arguments ;   the dis-
interred liveliness of ——— and the silence of Newman,
were all *surprenant*, nay *épouvantable.*'

Samuel Wilberforce, it should be borne in mind,
had tried for a Balliol Fellowship and had not been
elected ; his brother Henry had tried without success
at Oriel.   He might now be excused for even an
over-anxiety to prove to himself that a wise Providence had ordered better things for him than an
academic career.

But perhaps he did not consider sufficiently that
these men, thus disposed of with a dash of the pen,
had had few or none of his own immense advantages.
Few men, certainly few college Fellows, have such a
father, or such friends, or the choice of all the best
households, whether in the Church or in the State, to
comprise in a round of visits recurring not unfrequently.
A college Fellow, that is, in an open college, becomes
such by force of character more than by force of circumstances.   He has generally had to make his way through
a mass of opposing difficulties, and among such friends
as he could make or chanced to find.   With great force
of character there mostly goes some peculiarity, if not

eccentricity. The open colleges, inviting candidates from all quarters, were bound to be true to their profession, and to elect men by worth and merit, without favour or prejudice, that is, whether they liked a man or not, or whether they expected to find him a pleasant companion or not ; and it has happened that a man has been twice rejected for his rough manners, and finally elected for his solid recommendations, which it was felt could no longer be disregarded without positive injustice.

Samuel Wilberforce was not the first who found himself out of his element and his plumage a little ruffled among Oriel men. There is a remarkable passage in one of Lord Dudley's letters to Dr. Coplestone which makes a very good pendant. 'I saw Davison the other day in town,' he says ; 'it is quite astonishing how with such an understanding and such acquirements, his manners should be entirely odious and detestable. How you could live with him without hating him, I do not understand. Clever as he is, there must be some great defect in his mind, or he would try to make himself a little more sufferable.' The man who stunk in Lord Dudley's nostrils, and from whom he recoiled with detestation, was one of the best men and the greatest minds that ever came into Oriel College. So true is it of manners, as it is of raiment, 'They that wear soft clothing are in kings' houses.'

There can be no difficulty in identifying the characters touched off by Samuel Wilberforce's too ready pen. The portraits are highly exaggerated, and they also afford some explanation of the Bishop's patronage in after times. He showed a decided preference for men of good family, good figure, and good social qualities, but he was sometimes deceived ; and on the other hand he neglected men who were not in his eyes sufficiently men of the world.

CHAPTER LV.

HAMPDEN REGIUS PROFESSOR.

THE year 1836 was eventful. Richard Hurrell Froude died, working and writing with his usual spirit almost to the long foreseen end. He had just time to specu-late on the results of Dr. Burton's death, for the chair of the Regius Professor of Divinity was thereby vacant. To look at Burton's large bony frame, and to hear his strong voice, few would have thought he was to die before Froude. He seemed destined to a long episcopate in some see requiring a man of work. But his reply to Bulteel showed him excitable, and not always able to command himself. Feeling not quite well, he went down to Ewelme for a few days' rest, took a walk in the fields, met a dissenting farmer who told him he did not preach the gospel and so forth, had a warm argument with him—the farmer getting very violent—came home in a fever, and died in a few days.

Lord Melbourne had designed to nominate Ed-ward Denison, who, besides his strong personal claims, had one of a political character, his eldest

brother having carried his election at Liverpool at a
critical time, before the passing of the Reform Bill,
after a long and expensive contest. It was represented, however, to Lord Melbourne, that Hampden
was suffering much tribulation, particularly for his
pamphlet advocating the abolition of university
tests, and that he ought therefore to be supported.
George Anthony used to say that Newman and his
friends had to thank themselves for the appointment,
as they had forced it on Lord Melbourne, who would
much have preferred Edward Denison.

As soon as it became known that Hampden had
been recommended to the King, his Bampton Lectures, delivered in 1832, when Newman was preparing
to accompany Froude to the Mediterranean, emerged
into notice.

It has been stated by writers who no doubt
believed what they said, that these lectures were attended by large and deeply interested congregations,
as if Hampden had really been the Abelard his antagonists would make him. As generally happens, a
considerable number went to hear the first lecture,
because something startling was expected ; but when
they were not startled, but very much puzzled, and
when indeed they found it difficult to understand the
lecturer at all, they ceased to attend, and left the
preacher to the empty benches which are often the
only audience of a Bampton lecturer. If the lectures
were not heard, neither were they read, and no one
who knows what the mass of Oxford men are, and
who will also take the trouble to read a few sentences
in these lectures, can think it at all likely that they

were either listened to or read. Perhaps they ought
to have been listened to, and perhaps they ought to
have been read, but the question is one of fact, and
they were neither.

Their history was no secret at Oriel, and it had
been several times asked why nobody called attention to them? Why indeed? when there were not
more than half a dozen people in the world who
could have recalled a single passage. Not very long
after the publication, some one—Hugh J. Rose, I
think it was—wrote to Newman, 'You must notice
Hampden's Lectures, and if possible move the university to condemn them, for they say he is to be made
a bishop, and then what shall we do?' Newman
replied that he could do nothing in the matter, for
there was necessarily a personal question between
him and Hampden, the latter having been employed
by the Provost to oust him and the other tutors.
Under the circumstances he wished to keep at peace
with Hampden, whom he was coming across daily.
He was, however, at that time, telling everything to
Henry Wilberforce, who would do something. He
fagoted Hampden's pamphlet on 'Religious Dissent'
with several other scandals, as he deemed them, in
the 'Foundations of the Faith Assailed,' already referred to.

At the time the Lectures were written, there was
only one man in Oxford who knew anything about
the scholastic philosophy, and that was Blanco White.
Hampden, an intimate friend of that gentleman from
his first appearance in Oxford, was now thrown a
good deal into his society, and was qualified as well

as disposed to enter into Blanco White's favourite subject of comment and denunciation. They saw one
another almost daily, and Blanco White's spirits rose
as the time approached for the doom of orthodoxy.
Most feelingly did he express his disappointment
when he heard that the lecturer had stopped short of
that decisive blow which he held to be the legitimate
conclusion. The difference between the two men was
great, for Blanco White was singularly destitute of
judgment, decision, and self-control, whereas Hampden, while ready to make a plunge, yet knew where
to land himself.

Hampden recognised, as he believed, the en-
croachments of a rash and presumptuous human
element in the domain of revelation, which he could
both describe and arrest. It was reasonable and legitimate that he should avail himself of the only
guide through this intricate region to be found in
Oxford, even though he knew there must be a point
where he must take his stand, and say ' Thus far and
no farther.'

Blanco White is so little to be regarded as a
perfectly reasonable being, that it really was small
blame to Hampden that Blanco White held himself
aggrieved, and to a certain extent duped. He felt it
very severely, indeed it was the deathblow of a long-
cherished hope. He now saw that his work, whatever it was, could not be in the Church of England,
and must therefore be pursued out of it, as Archbishop Whately before long had to impress upon
him.

CHAPTER LVI.

BLANCO WHITE'S PART IN THE PREPARATION OF HAMPDEN'S BAMPTON LECTURES.

THE above particulars as to the relations of Blanco White and Hampden have been disputed with much warmth, and some very rough language which it is not necessary to recall. It is, however, a question of testimony. I am certainly a competent witness as far as opportunity goes, for I had frequent talks with Blanco White at the time Hampden was also frequently at that gentleman's lodgings, and that was while Hampden was preparing these lectures.

It is rather ignominious for any one to be called upon, in very unpleasant language, to corroborate that which he has stated as a matter of actual knowledge. This, however, I must do to the extent of disposing of the argument against it. My statement is that in the latter part of 1831 and the early part of 1832, these two gentleman saw a good deal of one another, and that one of them derived from the other material assistance in the way of information, authors to be read, and general insight into the subject, in view of the lectures he was about to deliver on the 'Scholastic Philosophy considered in its relation to Christian Theology.'

The main objection made to this statement is that the 'germs' of these lectures are to be found in Hampden's previous writings; in particular in an

essay on the ' Philosophical Evidence of Christianity,'
published in 1827, written with the view of carrying
out and applying the principles of Butler's ' Analogy ' ;
in two articles contributed about 1831 to the ' Encyclopædia Britannica ' on ' Aristotle and Aristotle's
Philosophy ; ' and in another article contributed to the
same work on ' Thomas Aquinas and the Scholastic
Philosophy.' These articles, Hampden's biographer
states, were written partly in London, where he still
retained his house in Seymour Street, and partly in
Oxford ; and of that last article, viz. that on 'Thomas
Aquinas and the Scholastic Philosophy,' the biographer specially adds : ' This article appears to have
excited much interest. It opened up a branch of
inquiry that had been much neglected, and the subject (which might seem a dull one) is made of interest
to the reader by the deep interest with which the
author evidently enters into the research, and by the
power and vigour of the writing.'

By other writers it is added that there is such a
unity of thought and of style in the whole series of
Hampden's writings, as to forbid the idea of a certain
intrusion of foreign elements. A very excitable dig-
nitary thought it necessary to his purpose to speak
rather contemptuously of the ' Spanish Gamaliel,' or
the ' refugee from Seville,' and, since everything that
grows must come of a parent stock, he declared that
Hampden's works generally were the legitimate off-
spring of the old Oriel school, so much so as to
repel the suspicion of a foreign graft.

Now, in the first place, whatever may be said about
the ' germs ' or the original stock and the parent stock of

the lectures, ' Scholastic philosophy,' to the extent to which Hampden treated it, was a decided novelty. So is it said with much emphasis and proper pride by Hampden's biographer. There was a remarkable ignorance of the subject at Oxford. Before Hampden's reappearance at Oxford, Newman used to say that Whately, and his master Coplestone, had missed Aristotle's logic, and certainly without having caught that logic no one can understand the schoolmen. The old Oriel school would not have blundered as it did in its desultory attempts to mend the Athanasian theology, had it possessed even a moderate acquaintance with the ' Scholastic philosophy.' The classics were everything in those days, and the great scholars would then rather enlarge the circle of the classics than leave an opening for early Christian theology. Gaisford induced the Clarendon Press to spend 2,000*l.* in an edition of ' Plotinus,' by a German he brought over. Showing Christchurch library to a visitor, he walked rapidly past all the Fathers. Waving his hand, he said ' sad rubbish,' and that was all he had to say. Hampden's biographer was proud to cite a high authority as to the singular originality of his design. In a letter from Lord Melbourne to the professor, he says : ' I see Hallam in his new publication, 1837, says you are the first Englishman who has ever known anything about Scholastic theology. People who will tread into new and untrodden ground cannot expect to do so with impunity, as you have found.'

Blanco White brought this ' Scholastic theology ' with him from Seville ; he was ready to produce it on every occasion, and he had been one of Hampden's friends many years before the date of these conversations, which were in 1831 and 1832. Blanco White began a year's residence in the city of Oxford, under the auspices of Shuttleworth, whom he had met at Holland House, in October 1814. His most intimate and most valued friends at Oxford at that time were the two Bishops, of whom William was already Fellow of Oriel. At the previous Easter, 1814, Hampden had been elected Fellow of Oriel. Shuttleworth, who had brought Blanco White to Oxford, was among Hampden's 'most valued friends,' though in after years there arose differences between them. William Bishop was also his very attached friend. Here, then, were the two Bishops, Shuttleworth, Blanco White, and Hampden, all in a bond of close intimacy in 1814.

After a long interval, passed chiefly in London, and the neighbourhood, and in frequent communication with his old friends, Blanco White returned to Oxford in August 1826, and after the Long Vacation became a member of the university and of Oriel College and common room. In 1829 Hampden returned to Oxford, and resided there in frequent communication with the older members of the Oriel circle, including Blanco White, till the delivery of the Bampton Lectures.

Let it be observed that all the matter in question, including the 'germs' and what not, was written and published in the period between 1829 and 1832, while Hampden and Blanco White were residing at Oxford and seeing much of one another. The articles on Aristotle and Thomas Aquinas were written in the years immediately preceding the delivery of the Bampton Lectures, and may be considered as preparatory to them. The single ' germ ' mentioned as to be found in any previous work, that is before Hampden's return to Oxford, is in the preface to the essay on the ' Philosophical Evidence of Christianity,' where the author says : ' It will readily be acknowledged there is a strong *primâ facie* objection to the assertion of a philosophical theology,' &c. But there was nothing here conflicting with the statement that in 1831 Hampden opened what at Oxford was entirely a new subject, with Blanco White, a most competent, well-informed, and willing adviser at hand.

But instead of treating the alleged part of that gentleman in the history of these lectures as a gross affront to the lecturer, and something like a charge of dishonesty, which certainly was never intended, it would have been quite competent to ask what that allegation really amounted to. Is it wrong for a man charged with an important public duty, and undertaking a new and difficult task, full of peril, to avail himself of the only informant, the only man at all familiar with the subject, within reach, that informant being also an old and intimate friend ? Would it have befitted the lecturer himself, his position, or the interests of the university, to neglect an opportunity ready at hand, and of a very exceptional character ? There is no such folly, no such cause of utter breakdown and disgrace, as the silly pride of doing things quite by oneself, without assistance. Hampden never claimed that originality, which as often as not is the

A FRIEND IN NEED.

parent of error. He was a laborious and conscientious reader and thinker, whose chief anxiety seems
to have been to work on a recognised foundation, and
to use all the means at hand for doing his work as
well as he could.

What, then, are universities made for, if not to
bring students together, and to enable them to compare notions and render mutual services? Nor does
a statesman or an orator demean himself, and practise a fraud, because he avails himself of professionals
and experts.

Blanco White was a very pleasant talker, only
wanting somebody to draw him out, and perhaps also
to keep him to a subject. He only desired to be
drawn out by any one with whom he could feel on
equal intellectual terms. Newman and the other
Fellows at this time were no longer caring to hear
much what he had to say. They did not want to
be engaged in a controversy which would only end in
nothing; and to be brought to agony point, only to
recoil. It was no longer as it had been four years
before, when Blanco White entered in his journal:
'February 18, 1827. Taken ill and confined to the
house the whole day. Newman drank tea with me.
March 11. A walk with Newman and Whately. October 31. Called on Pusey, who walked with me.
Pusey, Wilberforce, and Froude came in the evening
to learn the order of the Roman Catholic Service of
the Breviary.'

There is a very remarkable passage in a letter of
Hampden's, written October 31, 1835, in reply to
some remarks in the nature of friendly warning from

Archbishop Whately. 'I have certainly tried to think for myself, and have had a fondness for taking up subjects of discussion which appeared to me not to have been fully treated before, because they coincided with my turn of mind, or stimulated my curiosity more than some others. At the same time I have not pursued the study with the *vanity* of an independent thinker. I have always sought every information that I could obtain, whether from books or conversation, and have taken care, where I remembered it, distinctly to refer to the source of my information—not with the view simply of avoiding the imputation of plagiarism, but often for the purpose of leading those who might be so disposed to examine the points referred to in the authorities themselves.'

And now what is the account of these lectures strenuously and angrily maintained by persons who can have no pretence whatever to a present and contemporary acquaintance with the circumstances, such as I have? It is that this extraordinary revelation came and went of itself in a day, so to speak, beginning in 1831 and ending in 1832. Excepting the above 'germ,' which had shown itself a year or two before, there was nothing in Hampden's publications before 1831 to prepare for his Bampton Lectures, nothing in his after publications in keeping with them. The 'Observations on Religious Dissent,' published two years after, admit of being described as the practical application of the Bampton Lectures, but they are, in fact, simply a summing up of the Latitudinarian plea, with arguments long familiar to the politico-religious world. Hampden assumed his position in regard to Scholastic philosophy in 1832, and immediately abandoned it. Not that he renounced it; not that he would budge an inch, or explain away, or meet objections in any way damaging to his own writings, but simply that he laid the matter down. He dropped it, for he had now something else to do.

But he could not have dropped it had it been a part of his ·mind in a developed and habitual form. It must have stuck to him and come out in all he said. The subject, for a time so important and engrossing, was discarded, and thenceforth was nothing to him. Hampden acted for the best, from his own point of view. But it would have been impossible for a man to be so filled with a great theme, and so utterly discharged of it, to all appearance, had it not been substantially the work of a day, done upon a concurrence of favourable circumstances, including a very opportune informant and sufficient aid.

To my apprehension the tone of the Bampton Lectures is that of a man almost carried off his legs by the sudden sense of a great discovery and a delightful emancipation. It has often reminded me of the well-fed horse that Homer describes as breaking loose from his stall, and galloping, with loud neighings, to join the wild herd in the open plain. Without the thought of a comparison, I felt much the same of the 'Essays and Reviews,' chiefly of Wilson's, I believe. 'Why, this fellow's a cow in a clover field,' I said, almost unconsciously. Hampden, I must allow, deserves the nobler comparison of the two.

CHAPTER LVII.

CONDEMNATION OF THE BAMPTON LECTURES.

THE Bampton Lectures, however, unread as they were, and unreadable as they might be to ordinary readers, had now the authority of a Regius Professor of Divinity. The majority of the residents only wanted some one to move and to lead the way. First there must be definite grounds to proceed upon. The 'Elucidations' were drawn up by Newman for this purpose in one night—at a sitting, so to say. The pamphlet became the text of the controversy, to the shame, it must be said, of many who could have turned to the original lectures, and, as self-constituted judges, ought to have done so.

A now famous meeting was held in the common room of Corpus Christi College, under the presidency of Mr. Vaughan Thomas, a much respected, though rather grotesque, specimen of Oxford orthodoxy. There is a singular absence of authentic history as to what was done ; and they who were in the thick of it, and lent a hand at every stage, will differ as to the many proposals made, accepted, and acted upon. It was soon seen that it would be useless to ask that the appointment might not be made. The university had no choice but to submit to the appointment. So it was proposed and carried that the Convocation should be summoned to suspend, so far as Dr. Hampden was concerned, the provisions of the statute for the nomination of Select Preachers, constituting the Regius Professor of Divinity one of the Board of Nomination ; and also to deprive him of his place as one of the judges on any complaint of heretical teaching made to the university. The alleged ground of the double deprivation was that the university had no confidence in Hampden. This was vote of deprivation to the utmost extent possible. It would still rest with each Bishop whether he would require, or even accept, as a qualification for Orders, a certificate of attendance on Dr. Hampden's lectures ; but this was really a very small affair, and very much a matter of form.

A mythical account of these proceedings describes the meeting of forty Fellows from all the colleges in Oxford in a common room as a conspiracy, and adds that the conspirators adjourned from Corpus common room to Baxter's printing office. I have no recollection of any such adjournment, nor can I see what occasion there could be for it.

One ridiculous incident I do remember, which shows the slack and open character of our operations. After helping to fold and direct some hundred copies of a circular—I forget which—I undertook to post them. Stuffing as many as I could into my pockets, I set out with unusual gravity for the Post Office. Near Carfax I made the discovery that my pockets were lighter than I expected, and, turning round, I saw that the pavement all the way from St. Mary's was strewn with circulars. The passengers, seeing that there were many of them, concluded that they were not worth picking up, and I believe I recovered the whole, though it is quite possible one or two may have fallen into strange hands.

A Convocation was summoned, and the clergy came up from all England. A shower of pamphlets in every form, every tone, and every variety of title, descended from Oxford over the land, covering counters and tables, more easily written than read. The vote of exclusion from the choice of Select Preachers and from judicial functions had a majority of the Doctors and of the Masters, but was vetoed by the Proctors, as had indeed been anticipated. A few weeks afterwards there were new Proctors, and, another Convocation being convened, the vote was carried.

If any one will think quietly upon the nature of this audacious act, he will be led to the conclusion that the clergy, and probably the people in general, had a less defined and less exalted idea of the Royal Supremacy, and indeed the whole Royal Prerogative, in 1836, than they have now. Whether the lawyers maintained it or not, it would now be generally understood and felt that whenever the Queen appoints to an office, she appoints to that office with its full existing complement of powers and privileges. To say to the Sovereign, ' You may take the hard letter of your right, but we will shear it and prune it till nothing is left but the name,' certainly would have cost a few heads in Tudor times, and historians would have accepted that result as a matter of course.

Any reasonable person, too, may doubt the validity of an act depriving the Regius Professor of Divinity of privileges appertaining to the very essence of the

office. If he is not to have a voice in the selection
of university preachers, or upon a charge of heresy,
where is he ? The delivery of lectures to candidates for Orders—a few young men twice a year—
is but a small part of his office. Some account
has to be given of the facility with which many
hundred well-educated gentlemen defied and insulted
the Crown. That account is to be found, perhaps, in
the continual decline of loyalty from the days of the
Regency to the end of William IV.'s reign. The
language employed about all the royal personages
during that period—the vituperation, insinuation,
and ridicule, not only in the lower organs of the
press, but in journals taking a side in religious
controversy, and laid on the tables of the wealthy,
the educated, and the good—would be incredible in
these days. To judge by the simple facts, the Crown
is indebted to the present wearer for the recovery of
its old prestige and its inherent dignity.

One other feature in this act of deprivation the
triumphant majority could hardly fail to be aware of,
though resolved to encounter it. There would inevitably ensue a war of retaliation, for if one side
ostracised Hampden to the extent of their power,
Hampden's friends would assuredly ostracise every
one in the opposing ranks; and if they thought the
law had been stretched or even broken against themselves, they would have the less scruple to stretch
or break the law in their turn.

By this time, Dr. Hampden's inaugural lecture
was eagerly waited for ; but he had now to defend
an ecclesiastical as well as a philosophical position.

He contented himself with a series of doctrinal statements which it would have taken a great deal of learning and ingenuity to prove quite incompatible with his lectures, and which so far saved his orthodoxy. Neither of the belligerent parties liked a result which seemed to show that it had been wasting a good deal of power, not to say character; and it spoke well for Dr. Hampden's private virtues, that he still had the sympathy and admiration of many friends.

CHAPTER LVIII.

UNREADABLENESS OF THE BAMPTON LECTURES.

THE whole proceeding has received from the beginning a great variety of comments, and time has continually thrown new lights upon it. A great university, the most important theological university in the world—for Oxford was now the only rival of the Vatican—pronounced the strongest possible condemnation of a book and of its author, inflicting upon him an injurious and penal deprivation. He was now to have no voice in selecting the preachers of that theology of which he was himself the chief professor and teacher, or in protecting it from error. The great mass of the multitude that inflicted this penalty were very, if not entirely, ignorant of the book which was the *corpus delicti*. They might have seen it on a counter, or on a table ; they might have opened it, turned over a leaf or two, and might even have had their attention directed to a few passages. The very great hurry in which the thing was done, and the fact that the book was and is comparatively rare, forbid the supposition that there could have been much, or even an adequate, acquaintance with its contents. There were very few in the kingdom capable of following the writer into the question of the fitness of the Scholastic phraseology for the statement and exposition of divine truths. The first look of the text was such that High Church and Low Church would equally recoil from it.

The country members of Convocation, as fast as they came up, implored their resident friends, with pitiable importunity, to tell them all about it, generally in vain, for their resident friends knew as little about the book as themselves. This may seem passing strange to outsiders, but, apart from the special difficulties of this volume, Bampton Lectures, as often as not, are preached and paid for, and duly added to the author's titles of honour, but are not listened to or read. The institution exists chiefly for the simple folks who may naturally think it something that a man has been a Bampton lecturer.

There was once a Bampton lecturer of whom Dr. Hawkins, Provost of Oriel, could justly boast that he was the only man who understood him, or could say what he had preached about. This was Archdeacon Goddard, who delivered the lectures in 1823. Hawkins was *Censor Theologicus* of his college that year, and in that capacity had to attend the university sermons, and comment on the notes sent in by the under-graduates. Goddard's usual plan of composition was to write what he had to say simply enough, and then to expand every word into a sentence, and repeat that process in successive amplifications of the text, till the last cooking had swollen the matter to the required bulk. This is often done to some extent, even by writers wholly unconscious of a plan, but the Archdeacon had carried the license too far. Hawkins perceived at once that the lectures would severely tax his own ever-watchful attention, and probably quite beat the apprehension of the undergraduates. He saw, too, that the strain on his own memory would be considerable, especially as in reading the undergraduates' notes he would find himself in a maze of incorrect renderings. So he took very careful notes himself, and kept them always before him till he had gone through those of the undergraduates. His own notes were a considerable labour. There is no love like that which men have for the work of their own hands, and the Provost in after times would refer to his notes on Goddard's lectures, and show that at least in one matter he had an undisputed superiority, indeed monopoly, at Oxford.

Goddard, whom I once met at the Provost's, was a dignified personage, but as dark as his own sen-tences. His sermon at the consecration of Bishop Howley, copiously quoted in the 'British Critic' of the day, shows him an adept in the art of amplifica-tion ; but in that instance it was done by a free use of the parenthesis.

When Hampden was appointed Regius Professor,

his lectures were almost as unknown a book at
Oxford as Goddard's.   The Provost of Oriel no doubt
had followed and studied them, and had probably
gone some way with them.   Newman also had looked
into them.   Others did the same when Hampden's
name was up for promotion.   Hampden himself, like
most authors, cherished the impression that the friends
or acquaintances to whom he had presented copies,
and who returned their polite acknowledgments, did
this upon some acquaintance with the contents of the
book.   That impression would be probably correct
with regard to some of his friends, for at the delivery
of the lectures he had been a member of Oriel
College twenty-one years—a distinguished member
of it ; and his old friends would be likely to have
some advantage over his newer acquaintances in the
study of the lectures.

But with regard to one of his oldest college
friends, his loved and valued tutor, Davison, there
arose a curious controversy.   Hampden stated on
some occasion that Davison had read the lectures,
that he had agreed with them, and had expressed his
entire approval.   This was thought inconsistent with
Davison's known character and views.   It was even
stated that he had expressed himself unfavourably
of the lectures.   He was a very timid and diffident
theologian, and this grew upon him, insomuch that
when his friends were expecting some fresh outcome
out of his studies, he was found more and more un-
willing to commit himself by publication.   Davison
wrote freely, vigorously, and evet brilliantly on such
matters as education, particularly Lovell Edgeworth's

scheme of professorial education, and the attacks on the University of Oxford in the ' Edinburgh Review,' on civil and judicial institutions, and even on the poor-laws. So, too, in his nearer approach to Christian theology, on the prophecies of the Old Testament, on the origin of sacrifice, and on the evidences ; but even here he always seemed hampered, as if he recoiled from a further advance into sacred ground. When he left college and went into the country, he would certainly be more at large and his own master.

Davison was now regarded as a man who had long been slowly emerging from a school in which he was notoriously and avowedly not quite at home, but for which he felt the bonds of affection, as well as considerable agreement. But the people who were now expecting him to act more like himself, and from the dictates of his own nature, forgot perhaps that he was now past middle age, that he had never had a very youthful mind, that he had always wanted self-assertion, and that the habit of an imperfect development must by this time have become incurable. There was, however, actual information coming again and again that Davison was known to be engaged upon a Commentary on the Scriptures. The hesitations, whatever they were, that had pursued him through life, dictated at last an instruction to his widow to destroy all his MSS. She felt it her duty to execute this order, and no doubt did execute it, though she knew that he had written this Commentary, or parts of it, several times over. Was he likely at once to declare his approval of a work

which it would take much time and close attention
to master?

So the widow was written to. She searched
through the library and found the lectures, only one
leaf cut open, and with no signs of having been read.
This seemed conclusive, and there was much joy at
Oriel in the removal of what seemed a slur on
Davison's memory. Nevertheless Hampden was
able to produce a letter which must be admitted to
have justified him in appealing to Davison's unqualified and intelligent approval. But this opens other
questions ; first Davison himself, and his state of mind,
and then the whole chapter of presentation copies,
presentation letters, and presentation replies.

Davison was now *magni nominis umbra.* The
silence of his house was awful, visitors said, for he
could not bear the footsteps or the voices of his own
children. Going over the same ground over and over
again, he seems to have arrived at hopeless indecision. Why, then, decide so quickly upon such a work
as these lectures ? He had every inducement, and no
doubt every wish, to say something agreeable of the
crowning work of a pupil, indeed a promising and
favourite pupil, whose success in life he had prophe-
sied almost at first sight, and whose only fault in his
eyes was an excess of modesty, interfering with freedom of intercourse. A dip here and there might
afford the materials for a kind acknowledgment, and
save the conscience of the reader. The volume on
his shelves showed that it could only be a dip here
and there. Many people acknowledge presentation
copies at once, in order to save the necessity of

reading them ; but they must say something about the book, and Davison possibly read enough 'to swear by.'

However, he had passed all his days in the *old* Oriel school, in the same rock Hampden himself was hewn from, and possibly the new Oriel school were, after all, mistaken in relying on the permanence of the special convictions which were supposed to have made him an exception to the general character of that school. He had need of something more than convictions to be proof against the fascination of Coplestone, then by far the ablest and most agreeable man in the university. Such a fascination long felt, and endured in the period of rising manhood, would not easily be shaken off in its failing years. It had long been his duty to defer to the judgment of those around him, one of them at least his superior in all that makes personal influence, and so far authority. In the main principles he agreed with Coplestone and others ; and he seemed ever to postpone the inevitable parting. The embarrassment betrayed in his writings was conspicuous in his conversation. It became his habit and his consolation to contemplate with simple awe that mystery which neither mathematics nor logic could reduce to language, and he spoke jealously of the hope expressed by a rising philosopher that he would live to see things now believed inscrutable expressed in mathematical formulas.

There is another consideration bearing on the point. I do not think Davison and Hampden could have seen one another since the latter left Oxford in 1816. Their courses lay wide apart. I resided at Oriel from 1825 to 1832, and I am very sure Davison never appeared in Oriel during that period. Up to the latter date Davison's recollection of Hampden would be that of a very studious and promising youth of twenty-three.

There were old college stories about Davison that might be interpreted one way or another. He was described as like the mysterious old gentleman in the 'Vicar of Wakefield,' who by a single monosyllable would dispose of a long flow of nonsense. He would sometimes cut impertinence very short with an unexpected sally. Driving his own carriage to Gloucester, he put it up at a small inn in the suburbs, and presented himself at one of the principal hotels in the city. He was sharply asked, 'Where did you come from, and how did you come here?' His reply was as sharp. 'From Bristol gaol by the waggon.' Possibly it was some such reply that obtained for him Lord Dudley's 'detestation.'

Other old friends, and other authorities besides Davison, were afterwards appealed to as having read and approved, but at the time they said nothing. They did not make the slightest effort to remove the blackness of darkness which seemed to have closed round the lectures from the day they were delivered.

CHAPTER LIX.

GLADSTONE AND S. WILBERFORCE.

NEWMAN and his friends had been deeply impressed with the necessity of removing this universal ignorance of the matter to be adjudicated on, and of supplying the deficiency. Various writers took it in hand, and no common work has been so extracted, elucidated, analysed, tabulated, and furnished with helps to the eye and the understanding as was this volume, necessarily, in a very few days.

But here again came a new form of the difficulty. Can a book be known by extracts? Illustrations are made for a purpose. Texts are separated from their context. One of the standing jokes of that day were 'textes,' that is the score or two texts which old women would substitute for the whole of the Bible, as containing all they wanted out of it, of course in anything but the true sense of the words. Explanations are constructed, a passage here, a passage there. You may build or carve what you please out of a quarry. It cannot be denied that even if there were as much honesty as there certainly was industry in the presentation of Hampden's book to the assembled members of Convocation, the result would still fall very short of careful study and real knowledge. In fact the work of elucidation, quotation, and comment exceeded the limits of the occasion and the capacities of most of the intended readers. They had neither the time nor the power to do justice to either the book or the commentaries.

Two men, both of whom may be considered great men in their respective ways, and who certainly were not wanting in the power of acquiring knowledge, had many years afterwards to make the humiliating confession that while ready at the time to condemn Hampden's lectures, they in truth knew nothing about them. Eleven years afterwards, when Hampden had been nominated to the see of Hereford, the Church of England protested, it may almost be said *en masse*, against the appointment. The significance of the appointment had now every possible aggravation ; the resistance to it every possible disadvantage. Hampden's chief antagonists had left the field, and in so doing had discredited their old cause, and left it in weaker hands. Samuel Wilberforce, divided, distracted, and beset, after signing a futile episcopal remonstrance against the appointment, allowed himself to be drawn into the difficult path of persuasion pointed with menace, and negotiation concurrent with hostile acts. Acquiescing in legal proceedings, he besought Hampden to give him an easy victory by explaining away his lectures. Hampden had now to fight not only for his opinions, but still more for the Royal Prerogative. The latter was an impregnable position. Hampden did nothing ; said nothing ; and was unassailable. As peace there must be on the Bench, and he would not submit, others must. S. Wilberforce then began to read the lectures seriously ; at least as he had never done before, and the result was an apology to Hampden for all he had himself done, on the plea of ignorance.

The other recantation was still more remarkable. Thirty-four years after the delivery of the lectures, Hampden, to his great surprise, and somewhat qualified pleasure, received a letter from Mr. Gladstone, written in the very abyss of penitence and self-humiliation. He had done his best for a whole generation to understand the lectures, without the slightest success. As it was utterly past his power to understand them, he had been clearly wrong to condemn them on the information of others.

One can imagine Hampden reading the letter backwards and forwards, upwards and downwards, and holding it up to the light, to see what he could make of it. The very curious reason given by Gladstone for his ill-success, viz. that for a good many years past he had found himself ill able to master books of an *abstract* character, must have satisfied Hampden that the case was utterly hopeless. The writer could not possibly have known the meaning of the word ' abstract,' which really is about the last word to be applied to Hampden's lectures, difficult as they are. Hampden wisely put the letter into a drawer and said nothing about it.

His biographer regarded it in the light of a most flattering testimonial from the most competent of judges, and accordingly was proud to publish it. Hampden's extreme modesty and unwillingness to obtrude himself were the only account the biographer could give of its suppression.

What, then, it may be asked, is the difficulty, the

confessed difficulty of these lectures, and why even now is it rare to find any one who can pretend to have read them, and very hard to believe him ? The difficulty lies in the immense quantity of matter that Hampden labours to bring within the compass of eight lectures. The composition suggests the idea of notes made while reading several new authors, in order to reduce to a still smaller compass their over-loaded pages. The taking of ample notes is a process very useful, indeed necessary, in the preparation for a great work to be published without limitations of time or space ; but it is sure to disappoint when all that can be done is just to present the notes themselves in the most grammatical English possible under the circumstances.

Gibbon was not an abstract writer, for he robbed every person and thing of its abstraction. He had a marvellous way of working his materials into continual scenes and pageants, making history an endless drama. Upon the same ground, and with the same materials, Gibbon is a novelist and Hampden a bookworm. Gibbon gave the best part of his life to his work, and Hampden had only a few months for his. Excepting in the Long Vacation of 1831, he had his hands full of work, and his biographer says that he sometimes even ascended the pulpit with his lecture so incomplete that he had to dispense with the MS. before he got to the end.

There comes, then, the question, Ought judgment to have been done, by such a tribunal, and upon such imperfect information ? The only answer is the necessity of the case. There must either be such a

trial of the book, or none at all. Certainly all
England, up to that time, did look to Oxford to protect the orthodox doctrine, and the orthodox exposition of it. The very institution of Regius Professor
of Divinity testifies to that. Unfaithful as the
Evangelical party believed many of the Oxford clergy
to be to their trust, they would have been the first
to accuse them of further unfaithfulness had they let
Hampden's appointment alone. By this time his
opinions were known. He had brought the lectures
to a practical point and a working bearing in a
pamphlet written in plain English and intelligible to
an ordinary reader. There was no choice but to do
what had to be done in the only way possible. Such
has been the common fate of all the most important
and critical acts and facts in history. They have
been done in haste, hurry, slovenliness, with very
mixed agencies and very indifferent tools, and with
much disregard of appearances ; for there was no
other way, and the work had to be done first and
criticised afterwards.

There comes, then, the far more important question,
then hardly entertained, for Hampden's friends advised
him so far to yield to the storm : Was he really in
the right, and was his cause that of truth ? Is it
true that the schoolmen have corrupted Divine truth ?
They who believe it the mission of Aristotle and of
Plato to provide ideas and expressions beforehand
for the Christian revelation will be ready to accept
thankfully and unreservedly the work of their disciples. The old and the new philosophy go together
and cover a large space in the Christian controversy.

Blanco White said that the Athanasian doctrine of the Trinity and Transubstantiation were inseparable, the latter being the necessary outwork of the former. He rejected both; Newman accepted both. Almost every modern disbeliever in the supernatural, whether in the Bible or in Nature, will tell you that it was Plato who corrupted Christian truth and made the Church of history and of the present day.

Hampden, once in the seat of authority, gave up speculation, unless it were speculation to see how far he could satisfy the Evangelical party in the Church without entirely repudiating his own published opinions.

CHAPTER LX.

VOICE, LOOK, AND MANNER.

THERE is one element of the question which has to be stated, as otherwise the story would be imperfect. We may please to regard it as a small matter, but it has much weight in most careers and in all human affairs. The historian, the poet, and the novelist alike do their utmost to bring before the reader the figures and the manners of the principal personages, and we all find these poor externals inseparably associated with their action and speaking.

Dr. Hampden, when he reappeared in Oxford at the age of thirty-six, was one of the most unpre-

possessing of men.   He was not so much repulsive
as utterly unattractive.   There was a certain stolidity
about him that contrasted strongly with the bright,
vivacious, and singularly loveable figures with whom
the eyes of Oriel men were then familiarised.   Even
the less agreeable men had life, candour, and not a
little humour.   Hampden's face was inexpressive,
his head was set deep in his broad shoulders, and
his voice was harsh and unmodulated.   Some one
said of him that he stood before you like a milestone,
and brayed at you like a jackass.

It mattered not what he talked about, it was all
the same, for he made one thing as dull as another.
At one of the Oriel 'gaudies,' or festive anniversaries,
he and Hinds, and one or two others, discussed the
old idea that our first parents were created radiant as
we picture the angels, and even the saints; that this
radiancy was the badge of their heavenly citizenship,
and the chief element of their dominion over the
brutes; that they lost it at the fall, and that the
loss revealed to them that they were naked; that
the Lawgiver reappeared with this radiance from the
Mount, and again with the Prophet at the Mount
of Transfiguration; and that this will be the lost
robe of righteousness to be restored to the saints at
the last day.

Such a topic might be tenderly, reverentially,
and plausibly treated.   Hampden and his friends
brought it down to the level of Rabbinical lumber.
The real question is that on which Dr. Bull has collected the opinions of all the Fathers, and decided in
the affirmative, viz. that our first parents had a

'supernatural habit of grace,' which was in one sense an investiture, inasmuch as they were divested of it at the fall, and were immediately aware of the change.

Hampden's appearance and manner helped to explain the charge of persecution and annoyance he brought against the majority of university men. Both he and they were in a real difficulty. Between all men who had ever met at Oxford there was in those days some recognition, in most cases civil and slight. Hampden, not quite certain whether he was to be cut or recognised, looked for a very marked recognition, which some men doubtless found it not easy to give. Others met the emergency by doing what Hampden evidently looked for, and then he took it rather amiss when they gave their votes in Convocation to incapacitate him from his chief functions. Walking over Magdalene Bridge, I met Hamilton, afterwards Bishop of Salisbury, and found myself, as I thought, the object of a most emphatic and beaming recognition, as if something unusually pleasant had happened. The mystery was immediately solved by my finding that Hampden was just behind me. Yet Hamilton voted to disqualify Hampden.

Henry Wilberforce, as the author of the 'Foundations of the Faith Assailed at Oxford,' and a member of the same college, had his full share of this trouble. He said that Hampden glared at him, and that he recognised in the glare that gentleman's West Indian blood. If, as was possible, the planter glared at the emancipator, it is to be considered that there is much reciprocity in the commerce of eyes, and that it is often hard to say which has begun the friendly, or unfriendly, interchange.

Moreover, it is to be confessed that the English are not such masters of the art of recognition as the French or the Italians. Perhaps they are too honest, as they think it, and would rather be a little rude than seem to dissemble.

In one not unimportant matter Hampden jarred with the Oriel taste, and the taste of the old school as well as the new. They were, with hardly an exception, very simple in their ways, caring nothing for furniture and upholstery. There was not a bit of ornamental work or drapery to be seen in the Fellows' rooms. Newman might never have put a new thing into his rooms since he took them, as the custom was, ready furnished from his predecessor. The only luxury ever seen there was a clean towel always handy, to dust any book that had lain long on its shelf.

The Provost evidently applied to his own house and establishment the same rule of moderation he had afterwards to recommend to me, in vain, in the matter of my church. He must have taken all Coplestone's furniture, and Mrs. Hawkins must have been very unlike other women if it was not a trial to her. When the Duke, after his installation, came on his round of complimentary calls, we were all invited by the Provost to join in the reception. When we were all mustered, and the visit was imminent, there arose an anxious question. There were barely chairs enough, and several of them were in a very untrustworthy condition. The shaky chairs and the lighter weights were relegated to the corners of the room, and a chair that could be entirely depended upon to bear the weight of a hero was disposed opportune for the new Chancellor ; with another selected chair for his guide and prompter on this occasion. Of course the Duke was found well up to Coplestone and other Oriel celebrities.

When Hampden was appointed by the Chancellor Principal of St. Mary Hall, he stepped into a house upon which ' Johnnie Deans ' had spent not only his own fortune, but also all the ' caution money,' to the great disgust of the members of the hall, and to the scandal of the university. As he was a very humorous man, of considerable ability, people were amused perhaps more than grieved at the disclosure. As soon as Hampden stepped in he set about rebuilding and furnishing, Henry Wilberforce said, ' in West Indian fashion, all purple and gold,' to the amount of 4,000*l.*

The result was that when Hampden, only three years after, was made Canon of Christchurch, he could not find it in his heart to resign his hall. The whole university cried out against the plurality. Hampden put in a good man as Vice-Principal, but the university was not satisfied, and there ensued a correspondence with the Duke of Wellington, who stuck to his opinion that Hampden ought to give up the hall. He did not, and the comment he made on the correspondence with the Duke, was that the only thing he was sorry for was that it had disabused him of his old illusion that the Duke was a magnanimous man. The truth is Hampden never could see a bit of good in any human being that thwarted his wishes.

It was said just now that Hampden's voice was not one to invite and enthrall attention, indeed that it was a real impediment in the way of his influence. Oriel College was spoilt for ordinary voices at that time. The richness and melody of Coplestone's voice surpassed any instrument. No one who had only heard him take his part in the Communion Service could ever forget the tone. It penetrated everybody, entered into the soul, and carrying with it much of the man himself, made the least thing he said adhere to the memory and be easily producible. It was no small part of the daily amusement of the undergraduates to repeat what Coplestone had said, and just as he said it, and to vary it from their own boyish imaginations. The gravest men in the college could not resist the contagion of mimicry, and would sometimes go a little farther.

The second of the four Froudes, who died young, made this a special study. Coming out of Tyler's room, after a lecture, he tapped gently at the door, and said in the exact Coplestone tone, 'Mr. Tyler, will you please step out a moment?' Tyler rushed out, exclaiming, 'My dear Mr. Provost!' but only saw the tail of the class descending the staircase. 'You silly boys, you've been playing me a trick,' was all he could say.

A son of Sydney Smith was at Oxford at that time, much amongst Oriel men, and often at the Provost's. 'Mr. Smith,' he said, with much solemnity, 'next Thursday the college will be fifty and I shall be five hundred years old.' 'Indeed, Mr. Provost, I knew you were getting on, but hardly thought you so old as that,' he replied, with paternal readiness.

The most complete instance of unconscious imitation by long and intimate acquaintance was that of Mr. Joseph Parker, the bookseller. He had daily talks with Coplestone, Gaisford, Shuttleworth, and other literary men in his pleasant upper rooms, and though he heard many voices, he was absorbed into Coplestone's. If one turned one's head away, so as not to see the man, one could hardly believe it was not Coplestone speaking—the same sustained note, measured cadence, and careful choice of words.

Tyler had a full, rich utterance, like his genial character. Voice must have had no small part in Hawkins' election to the Provostship. His was a remarkable combination of sweetness with strength, sincerity, seriousness, and decision. Newman's voice has had ten thousand admirers, and needs no description, for it has enthralled half the English world. Whately had a grand roll, sometimes rather overpowering, but such as it is pleasant to recall. Froude's voice combined the gravity and authority of age with all the charms of youth, for he might be at once reasoning with a senate and amusing a circle of children.

The Wilberforces had the sweet voice of their father. A few whispers, a few words of assent, a few scarcely articulate sounds, were all I heard from him, and it was my own fault that I did not hear more, but it was to the last the tone that the House of Commons had known and followed as sheep follow their true shepherd's. S. Wilberforce's voice became by use less natural and more formed. Utility had its cost. The result was that it became the most imitable, that is, the voice most inviting imitation, and most certain to be imitated. The present Bishop of Ely made an absolute acquisition of it. I once heard him preach in a very small country church. Sitting under the pulpit, I could have thought it the then Bishop of Oxford overhead all the time, though I had known the true voice near half a century. The Bishop of Oxford was aware of it, and when asked who was the best preacher in the country, answered, with an expressive smile, 'Oh, of course I think Woodford.' The best he heard was his own echo.

Mannerism of any kind, not the less if it be the mannerism of genius and goodness, perpetuates and propagates itself till it becomes an institution. A very distinguished preacher has carried into the Church of Rome Newman's style and S. Wilberforce's tone, no doubt in spite of himself. A very marked voice will survive long in a household, in a choir, or even in a small congregation, so that its owner will be heard long after he has departed. All this shows the great and mysterious power of that human voice, which is the most perfect of all instruments ; the loss by the want of it, and the mischief done by its imperfections. Pusey's voice might want music and flexibility, but, whatever the cause, it was a powerful engine. A man with a harsh, or rumbling, or husky, or squeaky voice, preaching those sermons, would never have been listened to. Strange it is that when voice is such a power, and has been so in all ages, from the ' falling flakes ' of Ulysses to this day, it should be so little cultivated.

CHAPTER LXI.

NEWMAN, 1836–1837.

THE opposition to Hampden's appointment, bafflea as it seemed, told on the country. The clergy of London and of the great provincial cities realised the existence of a cause and of a work at Oxford. What was its real nature ? What would it tend to ? What good was to be got out of it ? The incumbents of large metropolitan parishes and the secretaries of religious societies came, some by invitation, some on their own motion, to see with their own eyes, to hear with their own ears, and to take a measure of persons and things. Suspicious and jealous to begin with, they did not like the look of things. They were surprised to see so many young men in the affair, young men, too, wholly free from the solemn conventionalisms of old religious partisanship. They had come from town prepared with terms, with a working basis of agreement, and ultimatums to be settled with chiefs ; but they found Newman in companionship with free-spoken men who might wreck a cause in a day. Hume Spry, an old Oriel man, was one of the diplomatic class. The metropolis was to arrange matters with the university, and the larger body was not to be hastily compromised by the impulses or caprices of the smaller. It was necessary to ascertain who were the men doing the work, and whom Newman had about him in a confidential capacity. Who was this, and who was that, and what pretence had they for setting things right, and perhaps thereby putting their feet on the first round of the ladder that leads to promotion ?

Newman called on Hume Spry by appointment, in Beaumont Street I think it was. He asked me to go with him. Hume Spry directed his eyes at us both alternately, as much as to ask who I was, and whether I was a safe person. It seemed to me that he was only wishing to learn the state of things without committing himself. Andrew Brandram came down, an Oriel man, a first class, and a big, heavy fellow. He had his eyes, and what wits he had, always about him. I had a particular interest in him. His father, a London merchant, had been a favourite scholar of my great-grandfather at Gainsbro', who had taken great trouble with him. The father acknowledged it by offering an uncle of mine the choice of a cadetship in the India Civil Service or a berth in an East Indiaman. He chose the latter, not an uncommon preference in those days. Finding Andrew Brandram alone in the common room, I tried to exchange family notes with him. He promptly informed me that he had heard his father was a native of Gainsbro', but that he knew nothing about his education or early acquaintances. While he spoke his eyes were ranging over the room, as if in quest of something strange and significant. He had a great mystery to penetrate. No detective could look more vigilant or more perplexed. It was interesting to speculate on the report he took back to the Bible Society.

The 'Tracts for the Times' of course received a fresh impulse from this movement, however otherwise abortive it might seem to have been.

It was about this time that Newman tried the experiment, for such it must have been, of extempore lectures on ecclesiastical subjects less suitable for the pulpit. They were delivered in Adam de Broome's Chapel, an aisle of St. Mary's Church, but partitioned from it and used for the university robing-room. As the newly-founded lectures on political economy were given in another part of the sacred edifice, there could be no objection to this use of the addition made to the church by the founder of Oriel College. The lectures were well attended, and there were those who could follow them easily, but Newman was not a practised orator. He could only attain fluency by running away from his hearers, unless their attention were as disciplined and as swift-footed as his own intellect. I had to follow him as the toiling hero did the striding Sibyl, always a little behind.

But the changes which this year 1836 saw in the Church, the university, and in the inner circle of friends, were to come even still nearer home. They found Newman deeply impressed with the law of change. It appeared in his letters and conversations. ' Do something ; the time is slipping away from us.' Coming out of St. Mary's with me on Good Friday, he was struck by the sight of very large flakes or feathers of snow, falling into the black swollen gutter and instantly disappearing. ' So,' he said, quoting the quaint language of the Oriel statutes, ' are human affairs tending visibly to not to be.'

The summer of the year saw the breaking up of
the Newman family. About Midsummer his younger
sister was married at Iffley Church to my brother John.
Newman officiated, myself assisting, so there was no one
to give the bride away. Henry Wilberforce kindly
took this part. We had almost to run from Oxford to
be in time, causing some anxiety. Henry had arrived
the evening before up to his knees in thick mud, and
having to appear at a dinner party asked the loan of
my only presentable trousers. After some earnest
reclamations on my part, barely half an hour before
the time fixed for the ceremony, he was engaged
with a table knife cutting and scraping the mud off
his own garment, in order to resume it and restore
what he had on to its owner. A day or two after the
wedding Mrs. Newman fell ill, and in a fortnight she
was gone, when Rosebank had to be given up.

A few weeks later Littlemore church was conse-
crated. Though it was now Long Vacation, many
university men came. Hamilton, afterwards Bishop
of Salisbury, had to stand and kneel, by my side, on the
bare stone. There could not be a church more devoid
of ornament or less fitted to receive it. Newman, on
seeing the design, had doubts about the lancet windows admitting light enough. When I assured him
that they would, though not with painted glass, he
was satisfied. The builder or the glazier was not so
well pleased with the very plain work they had to
execute, and accordingly inserted a single suggestive
quarry of red glass high up in the middle lancet of
the east window. This was gravely described in the
' Record ' as a drop of our Saviour's blood.

They who remember their acquaintance with Newman at this period, and who shared even partially his convictions or his leanings, will naturally search through their own recollections to ascertain what they expected of the movement, which thus far took its name more from Newman than from Pusey. If any of them, as well as Newman himself, proved mistaken as to its probable tendency, it was not for want of being cautioned. But as they had expected this warning, they heeded it not. The common design supposed in their conversation, and no doubt deep in the hearts of the more serious amongst them, was a second Reformation of a reactionary character to bring back the Anglican Church to the faith and practice of that Primitive Church which all had on their lips, and few indeed knew much about. Whatever people may assume to be the Primitive Church, or the Ante-Nicene Church, one point all must agree upon. That Church was not a State Church ; it did not affect to be one with the empire, or to recognise as its actual members all human beings within a certain territory. Such magnificent conceptions were reserved for later, and, as they believed themselves, better periods.

Any reversion to the earlier idea involved at once a question as to the propriety, not to say validity, of infant baptism. The question of propriety, that is the wisdom and the expediency, often returned to Newman's mind. Really, in these days, he said, in towns at least, where there was little security that children would be educated in the true faith, indeed in any faith, or even in common morality, it did seem

a question whether infant baptism was a charitable
act, the ground on which it is justified, or rather excused, in the Baptismal Service. Newman gave not
only much of his mind, but some of his heart also, to
the special pleas of the various dissenting communities. They had a good deal to say for themselves.
The theory of the Church of England had no longer
that basis of facts on which it avowedly rested.

As Newman's friends and admirers credited him
with a much distincter forecast of the work to be
done than they could make themselves, some of them
knew not what to think of the almost indiscriminate
character of his advances in all directions. He invited
and seemingly expected the co-operation of people
whom it was charity to suppose at one with him in
essentials, and who could not have preached a single
sermon without a protest against the views now associated with his name. Like Froude, Newman certainly felt deep respect and warm sympathy with
anybody he believed to be serious, so as he was not
under some utter delusion. What may be called the
hagiology and the traditions of the Low Church
still held their ground in his heart and soul, even
side by side with Saints, Fathers, and Councils. He
lived in a region of faith, and therefore not of exact
calculation.

Men of the world, with defined and practicable objects, easily understand one another, and know both
what they will do and what they will be done by. Their
first instinct is to know the value of instruments and
the efficiency of means. Newman was really not of
the world. Out of the domestic circle, in which he

was invariably kind and affectionate, he could not
freely associate, except for one common object, and
where this was wanting his patience was apt to be
tried, and he was a shy, not to say a reserved man.
He described himself and the movement as *vox
clamans in deserto.* For several later years of his residence in the college he was hardly of it, avoiding
the common room, though having a common breakfast with two or three friends.

The formation of a party which had no regard to
the organisation of the university, and which consisted of younger and still younger men, could not
but be disagreeable at that date to the elders of the
university. Time and growing considerations of convenience had sharply divided Oxford into the elders,
that is the Heads of Houses, Canons of Christchurch,
and one or two of the professors ; and the youngers,
that is the undergraduates, and the Bachelors of Arts,
keeping a term, and still *in statu pupillari.* In the
wide interval between these were the tutors, more or
less, sometimes it is true very little indeed, under the
direction of the Heads. The resident Fellows not
engaged in college tuition were few ; some had private pupils, others came and went; none found much
scope in Oxford. There was only one circle of female
society, and that was the ladies of the Heads and
of the Canons.

It follows that if any one chose to apply to Oxford
the prevalent notions of the outer world, he might
understand by the term ' Oxford society,' the Heads
of Houses, Canons, and their families. It is vain to
say that no man of sense, or intelligence, or high

feeling, or common candour, would do this, for the melancholy truth is that no amount of these qualities will save a man from the grossest mistakes, or from actually grovelling in the dust, where 'society,' social rank, and social recognition are concerned. The philosopher and the saint alike bow to the idols of quality and fashion, even in forms surpassing the stupidity of Buddhist conception.

When Arnold discharged his torrent of abuse at Newman and his friends, the worst thing he had to say of them was that they were nobodies in Oxford ; almost unknown there ; not in society, hardly indeed admissible, so he insinuated. Arnold at that time knew no more of Oxford than he did of Italy, when upon finding himself in Genoa he wrote down, ' I am now in the land of cowards, rogues, charlatans, liars, and impostors,' or words to that effect. He had hardly put his foot in Oxford for many years. He must therefore have derived his estimate of persons and things from his own contemporaries, that is a comparatively small body of elder residents. These latter could not but side with the Provost of Oriel in the quarrel about the tuition, even though most of them left their own tutors to do very much what they pleased, and some were thankful to get a decent tutor on any terms. Nor would they like a religious movement at all of a strength to upheave the surface of the university.

Arnold took their word for it, and tried to crush the movement with social contempt. Unhappily, the most distinguished of his pupils believed themselves justified in saying everything he had said, and they described Newman as an unknown person at Oxford, seen in the pulpit once a week, never at any other time, and having nothing to do with the world, that is 'society.' In a certain sense it may be said that the Apostles, and the Fathers of the first three centuries, were not in society, socially unknown and insignificant. In that sense the studiously contemptuous expressions of Arnold and some of his pupils may be true. The same and even more may be said of John Wesley, whom some of these writers profess to admire. When the Bishop of Exeter asked John Wesley to dinner at the palace, and invited some of the clergy to meet him, the diocese thought his lordship had been much too kind.

The truth is nobody in Oxford was seeing so many people, and such a variety of people, and people of such significance in the matter of religion, as Newman, and, as he had much to do besides, he had to be content with but slight acquaintance in that upper circle of Arnold's imagination, however much, upon Arnold's reckoning, he lost by it.

CHAPTER LXII.

SOME INCIDENTS.

NEWMAN'S well-known rooms, on the first floor near the chapel, communicated with what was no better than a large closet, overlighted with an immense bay

window over the chapel door, balancing that of the
dining-hall. It had usually been made a lumber
room. Newman fitted it up as a prophet's chamber,
and there, night after night, in the Long Vacation of
1835, offered up his prayers for himself and the
Church. Returning to college late one night I found
that, even in the gateway, I could not only hear the
voice of prayer, but could even distinguish words.
The result was, Newman contented himself with a
less poetical oratory. College life, except for strictly
educational purposes, is a fond idea and little more,
and Newman's case is one of many showing how
easily and how soon a man may become a foreigner,
an anomaly, and an anachronism in his own college.

When strangers were daily coming to Oxford and
making it their first business to see the abode of the
man who seemed to be moving the Church of England
to its foundations, they were surprised to find that he
had simply an undergraduate's lodging. Indeed he
shared the same staircase with four undergraduates,
and Charles Marriott who occupied the rooms below.
Marriott's rooms were of exactly the same size as Newman's, but he found himself too straitened to take
all his books out of the boxes they came in, and he
was accordingly obliged to pile the boxes on one
another in lines across his floor for want of wall
space.

In dealing with younger men, whether as tutor
or as a clergyman, Newman kept a sharp look-out
for the hypocrisy of fluent and empty professions,
and put them to some practical test. He exercised
discipline equally on himself and all around, with

more or less success, but he would not be a teacher without acting up to his own words. He and his friends had declared strongly against the new Marriage Act which relieved dissenters of the necessity of coming to church to be married, but did not relieve the clergy of the necessity of marrying them, if they preferred to come to church for that particular occasion. He suddenly found himself called on to perform the marriage service for one of the pretty daughters of a respectable pastrycook in St. Mary's parish. The family were Baptists, and the young lady was not baptised. Newman ascertained this by inquiry, and refused to perform the service, or to allow the marriage in his church. The university was shocked at his inhumanity on such an occasion. Not so the young lady herself. She immediately expressed her wish to be baptised, declaring she was glad of the opportunity. She was baptised and married ; and became an attached member of Newman's congregation, followed in time by the whole family. On another occasion he was not so successful. Braham was advertised to take a part in the annual musical services at St. Mary's for the benefit of the Radcliffe Infirmary. Newman had his objections to Braham, and sent him a note interdicting him the church. Braham opened the note, read it, and made no sign. At the appointed time in the programme he stood up in the organ gallery, and filled the church with his magnificent voice. Newman waited for him at the foot of the organ staircase, to demand an apology for this invasion of his rights. All he got was, ' You did your duty, and I did mine,' saying

which, Braham brushed past him and hurried away.
On one occasion Newman had to forego discipline in
the interest of humanity.   In Bear Lane, the poorer
part of St. Mary's parish, there were houses let in
tenements.   The occupant of one came to Newman
and complained that over her head there were a
number of dogs kept by a woman who could not feed
them ; that they were whining day and night for
food, and must soon be actually dying.   Newman
went to the room, and on entering it found himself
surrounded by a crowd of famished dogs begging for
food.   They had been kept by the undergraduates of
his own college, contrary to strict rule, and these
young gentlemen, upon going down for the Long
Vacation, had left small sums with the dog-keeper,
promising to send her more, but failing to do so.
Newman advanced what was necessary for the main-
tenance of the dogs for the rest of the Vacation.

One little matter of self-imposed duty, arising out
of a painful occasion, will be remembered by all who
ever accompanied Newman in a country walk.   One
morning Dornford asked him whether he was going
to Littlemore that day, and whether on foot or horse-
back.   He had to reply that he was riding there,
when Dornford proposed to accompany him.   This
gentleman, having served two years in the Rifle
Brigade in the Peninsular War, and being proud of
his military character, was in the habit of cantering
on the hard road, and had generally to do it alone.
But Newman was in for it.   In those days the first
milestone between Oxford and Iffley was in a narrow,
winding part of the road, between high banks, where

nothing could be seen fifty yards ahead. Dornford and Newman heard the sound of a cart, and the latter detected its accelerated pace, but the impetuous 'captain,' as he loved to be styled, heeded it not. It was the business of a cart to keep its own side. They arrived within sight of the cart just in time to see the carter jump down, and be caught instantly between the wheel and the milestone, falling dead on the spot. The shock on Dornford was such that he was seriously ill for two months, and hypochondriac for a much longer time. The result in Newman's case was a solemn vow that whenever he met a carter driving without reins, or sitting on the shaft, he would make him get down ; and this he never failed to do.

Several years after this sad affair, I was walking with him on the same road. There came rattling on two newly painted waggons, drawn by splendid teams, that had evidently been taking corn to market, and were now returning home without loads. There were several men in the waggons, but no one on foot. It occurred to me that as the waggoners were probably not quite sober, it was only a choice of evils whether they were on foot or in the waggons. But Newman had no choice ; he was bound by his vow, and he compelled the men to come down. We went on to Littlemore, were there for some time, and then turned our faces homewards. Coming in sight of the public-house at Littlemore, we saw the two show teams, and something of a throng about them ; so we could not but divine evil. It was too true. The waggoners had watched us out of sight, and got into their waggons again. The horses had run away on some alarm, one of the men had jumped out, and had received fatal injuries.

Another resolution constantly observed by Newman would have cost most people even more effort. While at Oxford he never passed a day without writing a Latin sentence—either a translation, or an original composition, before he had done his morning's work. Frequently, when on the point of leaving his room for an afternoon walk, he has asked me to stay a minute or two while he was writing his daily sentence.

One more habit, for such it was, must be mentioned. As well for present satisfaction as for future use, Newman wrote and laid by a complete history of every serious question in which he was concerned, such as that of the college tuition. He had to render account of it, and he prepared himself accordingly. But whatever may be said in favour of such a practice, it may be considered fortunate that to most constitutions it is difficult, not to say repulsive. Few men are, or ought to be, so perfectly satisfied with their own part in a series of transactions as to wish to see a final record ; and it is hardly possible to frame such a record oneself without some excess of self-justification. It must be added that Newman did the same with every book he read and every subject he inquired into. He drew up a summary or an analysis of the matter, or of his own views upon it. As bearing upon his own studies, his pupils will remember that when he set them voluntary tasks, they were not essays on abstract propositions, or moralities, but biographies, and accounts of periods, political constitutions, crises, and changes. He desired me one day to write an account of Cleomenes, the Spartan reformer ; and such were the characters, if I remember rightly, that he generally chose for these exercises. Public opinion has latterly decided very strongly in favour of historical as compared with moral essays. Public opinion may be right, but on the other hand it is to be considered that certainly a majority of young minds can write much more easily on a moral subject than on one mainly and formally historical.

Newman paid visits to my Derby friends, both when I was there and when I was not. He naturally expected to see clergy, and one good man he did see, it was true. But when I took him to the Evangelical vicar, who never entered his parish on a week day, and to the minister of the chapel of ease, who could not either perform the Baptismal Service or take the cure of souls, they were simply surprised to see me, for both regarded me as an unconverted heathen. Newman acquitted himself with his usual tact on these unpromising occasions. He said the few things he could say under the circumstances in a way to make them ' stick,' though it was out of the question to elicit any sympathy.

I cannot be exact as to the year in which I took Newman to a small meeting over a shop in the market-place—the one that suffered in the Reform riot—for a declaration in defence of the Church. It had been got up by my clerical friend, a high churchman, but it had to satisfy his old friend the influential banker, who was quite the other way. The banker of course was in the chair. He insisted on the necessity of Church and State, but was not so sure as to the necessity of retaining everything in the Church that might be found standing in the way of that union. In fact, he thought a good deal of change in the comprehensive direction desirable. Personally and socially this gentleman did not appear to like dissenters much more than we did, but he thought we might give up a good deal, not so much to gratify them as to strengthen our own position. The reader will judge how far this chimed in with the feelings of our Oxford visitor. The result of the meeting was a milk-and-water declaration, which signified nothing, and which nobody would care to read. The chairman had taken the opportunity of laying on the table a petition of a very comprehensive character for the better observance of the Sabbath. I looked at it and signed it, and thereby earned the just rebuke I got from my more conscientious brother John.

On one of these visits my brother James and another brother took Newman to a public meeting for the declaration of dissenters' grievances. It was held in the Independent Chapel. Mr. Gawthorne, a tall, bony man, with a stentorian voice, was the chief speaker. These meetings were frequent, and I had myself attended one of them. Never shall I forget the tremendous energy with which Mr. Gawthorne, after a solemn pause, pronounced the words, ' Awake, arise, or be for ever fallen ! ' or the tremendous acclamation which they elicited. They seemed to go home to every one there On the above occasion, when Newman was there, it was the old story, but I have been told that he expressed to my brothers a good deal of sympathy with the speakers, believing that they had a real grievance. Parliament and public opinion have since concluded that they had, but dissenters don't seem to be so much the better for the removal of their many grievances as they expected. Unhappily the social element preponderates in the great question between the Church and dissenters, and no legislation will eliminate it.

One of my brothers remembers an incident of one of Newman's visits that suggests a curious question. He left by the coach for London, but was warned he would have to change coaches at Leicester. Accordingly at Leicester he was on the look-out, and saw ready horsed the coach that was to take him on. He naturally took the seat corresponding to that he had occupied in the coach from Derby. A Nottingham passenger made his appearance and demanded the seat for his own. He had come in it all the way from Nottingham. Newman stoutly and successfully resisted the claim. This was no longer the Nottingham coach ; it was the Leicester and London coach. To that seat on that coach he had the right of first occupation. He had nothing to do with any previous arrangements that coach had been bound by. This was a new start. He had to fight hard for it, but he carried his point and left the Nottingham gentleman to think over the metaphysical question, Was this the identical coach in which he had come from Nottingham ?

On one occasion, having to pass through the town of Derby, we found our way stopped. There was a so-called funeral procession of two thousand operatives on strike. A young woman had died, they alleged from starvation, a victim to the cruelty of the mill-owners. Wherever we turned we came upon them, for they wound about the town like a huge serpent. Every one carried a sprig to throw into the grave. Each 'lodge,' consisting of about forty men, was headed by the warden and subwarden, both wearing rather short, tight-fitting, white cotton surplices. The operatives generally were pale and thin, but the officials were invariably stout and high coloured. The surplices did not become them. Here was ritualism half a century ago. Little did I think I had before me the surplice of the future. My own surplice of that date, which I still wear, would have cut up into four of them.

One of Newman's topics I ought to have mentioned earlier. Perhaps it was suggested by his almost daily alternation between academic and rural life. It was the moral probation and proper excellence respectively of the rich and of the poor. The former have more to do; the latter more to bear. The former have greater powers and opportunities, which they are to make the best use of; they have also greater temptations to resist and greater difficulties to surmount. The latter have to endure hunger, thirst, cold, heat, sickness, weariness, and dulness. The higher class borders dangerously on the angelic state; the lower on the brutish. The difference is so great that each side can hardly see the possibility of virtue in the other. The rich man sees in the poor man a machine; a creature of instinct, appetite, and habit ; a subject for the natural historian. The poor man sees in his rich neighbour enjoyment, caprice, idleness, selfishness, wastefulness, and a bold attitude alike to God and man. Has he not at least his reward ? How can he expect more ? The answer to the moral question is that each class has to consider its own mission and end. But there is another consideration sometimes forgotten in the contrast. It is that the rich have often to show the virtues of the poor, and the poor the virtues of the rich. The rich have often to endure sickness, loss of appetite, *ennui*, confinement, monotony of place and of persons, quarrels, the cares inseparable from money, house, and land. The poor have often to show the most heroic virtues in the routine of the field, the farmyard, the pit, the manufactory, not to speak of household troubles and vicissitudes. Newman was no morbid philanthropist or indiscriminate alms-giver. Some of us were far too much this way, and perhaps he early detected the dangerous tendency— the first trial of the Church of the Apostles, as should always be borne in mind.

CHAPTER LXIII.

SPREAD OF THE MOVEMENT.

By the end of 1837 the 'movement' had diffused itself all over England. Every month there was a new sensation, and a new controversy. What the 'Tracts' had now grown into appears in the fourth volume, published this year, containing a Letter by Pusey, 42 pages ; Catena Patrum, No. III, 118 pages ; Purgatory, 61 pages ; Reserve, first tract on that subject, 83 pages ; Catena Patrum, No. IV., 424 pages ; total 728 pages of small print. The Catena Patrum supplied the universal want of clerical libraries. Most of the writers quoted were not accessible except by a long journey, or an expensive purchase. This was the first introduction to living eyes, of many works, indeed of many names, famous in their day. These men had lived in controversy. The compiler of the Catena divides the long list into the men who gave to the world the fruits of deep learning, and the simpler sort that handed down what they had received ; but this fails to give an adequate idea of the storm which has raged round these questions in all ages of the Church, so long as it had life in it ; or of the very controversial character of most of these writers. It was, however, a grave and honest appeal to former ages.

The appeal was promptly met on all sides. Fathers of all ages and all churches were collected and published in endless series. As lengthy as any

other series, as unreadable, as foreign to the present
modes of thought and feeling, there came out a series
of the 'English Reformers,' costing many who could
ill afford it a couple of sovereigns a year. They came
out in cherry cloth binding, which soon lost its colour.
At the house of a zealous reformer in Hampshire, I
wished to see what Cranmer said upon baptism.
Mounting on a chair I took out first one volume,
then another, of a long row, and found not a leaf
opened, but thick dust on the upper edges. They
who bought, and they who read, did so to the exclusion of other literature, and many subjects must
have fallen to the rear, while Church controversies
were resuming their old rank in the front of human
action and progress.

The opponents of the movement one and all
pronounced us on our way to Rome. Certainly very
few of us could say where we meant to stop, or what
we had in view as the future of the Church of England. For my own part I never knew where it was
all to end, except somewhere in the first three centuries of the Church, and I have to confess that I
knew very little indeed about them. Happily for us
the case of our opponents was not a bit better than
our own. They did not know where they stood, or
what they would have, or what they tended to.
None of them liked the Prayer Book. As for the
Book of Homilies it was now an offensive missile, a
dead cat, flung first at a Low Church head, then at a
High Church one. Nobody cared to read a line of
it, except to send it flying at his neighbours.

The 'Tracts for the Times' went straight against

the whole course of the Church of England for the last three centuries. That Church had generally given up fasting, daily Common Prayer, Saints' Days and Holy Days, the observance of Ember Days, the study of the Primitive Fathers, even so far as they are quoted in the Homilies, the necessity of the Sacraments and of a right faith, the idea of any actual loss by want of unity, voluntary confession to the clergy, and the desirableness of discipline; all held and transmitted by the Reformers, but since their day gone out of fashion and out of thought. Nor had the disuse been simply that of forgetfulness, for all England had been more than once agitated on these very questions.

The tracts preached what a King and a Primate had lost their heads for; what the monarchy, the Church, the whole constitution, and the greater part of the gentry had been overthrown for; what, afterwards, bishops and clergy had been cast out for, and the Convocation suspended a century for. These doctrines had been all but prohibited in the Church of England, as they probably would have remained to this day, had not the revolutionary aspect of the Reformed Parliament seemed to place the Church of England in the old dilemma between the bear closing up behind and the precipice yawning in front.

The new teaching was accepted as a reactionary protest against the existing state of affairs, and as affording the best basis for the impending general controversy. Some that received it gladly, not all, attempted to put it into practice. The difficulties immediately presented themselves. The clergy had to lead the way. We have only to imagine the not uncommon case of a young clergyman cast in a remote and secluded agricultural parish. He had to invite his parishioners to daily service, when every one of them was all day at work, generally far away from the church. He had to inculcate fasting, when most of them fasted already in the poverty and scantiness of their daily fare. He had to invite to confession those whose practice and antecedents were already well before the eyes of their neighbours. He had to invite to formal unity persons born and bred in schism, when they could not but prefer a good understanding between all opinions and sects, which it was not easy, if desirable, to interrupt. He had to urge the new doctrine in season and out of season, especially to the few educated neighbours who could understand him, and who soon settled the question by reducing their intercourse to occasional and unavoidable civilities. As often as not he found his own household incapable of going along with him. His wife had children to look after, and his servants were no more than the work absolutely required.

Perhaps in spite of every obstacle he persisted. He had the church day after day, year after year, to himself alone, and perhaps two or three school children. His people were then told by authorities they were accustomed to respect that he was making an idol of the church, and that he prayed like the Pharisees in the synagogue instead of his own chamber. He fasted after some fashion, and found himself incapable of work ; not only weak but light-headed. He found his elder clerical neighbours generally dead against him, and the squires only too glad of the excuse to have nothing to do with him. If he tried weekly communion, it was with results too sad to tell.

It seems to be forgotten that there were two movements—two restorations, Oxford the centre of one, London of the other. Blomfield and his advisers had their compromise, or middle course ; they took their stand on it, and fought it out. It consisted of such requirements as the offertory and Prayer for the Church Militant after the sermon, the use of the surplice in the pulpit, baptism in the course of the afternoon service, and a more rigid inquiry into the character of sponsors. These restorations were quite as unpalatable to the people generally as anything proposed in the ' Tracts for the Times ; ' but the ' Tractarians ' felt themselves bound to contend for them, coming as they did from high episcopal authority, and with several centuries of antiquity in their favour. There was a period, and a long one, when the London ordinances were raising far more dissatisfaction and actual rebellion than the Oxford ones, but Oxford got all the credit of these consequences.

The authors of the movement lived in a university, in the midst of cheerful and educated, if not always congenial society, libraries, magnificent buildings, frequent services, and it must be added, all the comforts and elegances of life. Something amounting to an appreciable sacrifice could be taken out of this superabundance, and yet leave a large and solid remainder. Even a saint, not to say a confessor, might enjoy life at a university.

But it was quite impossible that these saints and confessors could enter into the case of men banished far away from all these things, and amid the very opposites. The position of a country clergyman is the least understood thing in the whole sphere of British intelligence. Nobody understands it. Statesmen and Prelates are alike at fault. Metropolitan Societies, managed by the race that looks upwards and flocks to the centre, only regard the country clergy as sheep to be fleeced or butts to be laughed at.

Then country people, and country clergymen, soon become countryfied, and are apt to be simple and literal in their apprehensions. By fasting they understand doing without pleasant food, or very nutritious food, and by consequence doing without cheerful society. Early in the movement I heard that one of the Oxford leaders fasted on boiled mutton, because he did not like it. It is one of the luxuries of a tithe dinner, and I have been accustomed to look forward to it. I now think he was a sensible man ; but at the time I was puzzled to see how it could be fasting.

In after years I had to go to Oxford from the country on the affairs of the ' British Critic,' and my principal apprehension on going there was that my incurable worldliness would clash with the serious and saintly tone I imagined to be inspired by the movement. I felt guilty of irreverence by intruding on one of the contributors, the largest contributor I may say, one Wednesday in Lent. He was observing the fast no doubt honestly and in a true sense, but he was still in bed at 11 A.M., and a large dish of mutton chops was keeping hot for him at the fire. The scout informed me this was his custom. I have not a word to say against this mode of fasting, though I do remember some of my Oxford friends making rather merry at the expense of Coplestone, a martyr to dyspepsia, asking one of the tutors how he got through the morning, and adding, with his usual gravity, 'About twelve o'clock I feel a sinking in the stomach, and must have a mutton chop.'

Such free and enlightened understandings of fasting are simply impossible in the country. If a clergyman were to begin Lent by proclaiming a fast, in any sense intelligible to his simple flock, and were next day to lie in bed till noon, and then rise to a good *déjeuner à la fourchette,* he might speedily find himself gibbeted or burning in effigy.

The men at Oxford worked indeed, and that was their enjoyment, and so they might be held indifferent to the ordinary attractions of the place ; but the very fact that the clergy scattered far and wide over meadows, marshes, and downs, are seldom men of a high intellectual quality or of unusual energy, was an aggravation of their difficulties. They had to fight against odds without and within. Many persevered in a dogged way. In the true lines of the Church they could not be wrong. But they made mistakes ; they were inconsistent ; they had no friendly advisers ; they lost their temper ; and they found themselves confronted with men wise in their generation, over full of common sense, and able to command their tempers even when their own cause was bad and their conduct indefensible. There is too much reason to fear that from the beginning, and still more in after years, many disciples of the new school, especially those of the weaker sex, lost their health and strength by too much working, fasting, and praying, and shortened their lives.

But while the central agitation was telling on the whole of the country, it became itself the object of reciprocal influences. Everybody who had a want, everybody who had a difficulty, everybody who had a quarrel, everybody who could not do what he wanted to do, wrote to Newman, or to one of his friends, or to an editor, or an author, or simply to a man at Oxford. What was he to do ? His parishioners were dead against him. They took in such a newspaper. His preaching had been grossly misrepresented. He had tried more perfect services, but could get nobody to come. He must restore his church, which had been pewed up to the altar. Then how was he to understand such a text, or such a passage in the tracts, or in Newman's sermons, or in the 'Christian Year'? He thought it meant so and so, but he had been criticised, perhaps lampooned for saying it. Ought he to read the Homilies ? Should he insist on the parents not being sponsors ? Must he allow any stranger to communicate ? What books would his friend recommend, what hymns, what prayers ? Nobody knows, till he has turned agitator, the immense preponderance of what may be called the feminine, or dependent, element in society. The greater part of the world cries out—' Lead us. Put your stamp on us. Fix your bit in our mouths, and have a good hold of the reins. Save us from the trouble of thinking.

Spare us that terrible responsibility. We incline to do this or that. Tell us that we ought and must, so that, like a beast of burden, we may do our duty without thinking of it.'

Of course all this reacts on the leader, deciding him, intensifying him, hardening him, allowing him no retreat, not even time to think about what he is doing. Had it been his nature to give his whole life to anxious questions, and pass them on undecided to the next generation, he is not allowed a day. The applicants have put off writing to the last moment, and now want answers by return of post. Are they to exercise godly discipline the very next day, and pronounce the sentence of excommunication? Are they to tell the Bishop he is another Balaam, or the Primate that he is no better than Caiaphas, the very next morning—the latest hour at which the solemn duty can now be done?

Many such questions appear in newspapers, and in that case it is the public that is invited to answer them. The public is not backward in doing so, but there is a certain gaiety, not to say levity in its tone, that hardly betokens a painful sense of responsibility. A religious agitator, on the contrary, becomes a father confessor and director. Thousands pour their scruples or their troubles into his ear, and ask private direction. If he complies, he finds himself directed in return; or rather swayed by the surging movements of the mass of which he has now constituted himself the organ.

In the year 1836 Newman had entered into an engagement to supply a quarter of the contents of the ' British Critic,' which, from being a monthly of

some standing, had lately assumed the form of a
quarterly, and was now edited by Boone, with Le Bas
for his chief contributor. The latter gentleman was
a pleasant and even a brilliant writer, as well as a
man of large general acquirements. Some approach-
ment of views seems indicated by the fact that the
writer of the Lives of Wiclif and of Cranmer was
now engaged on a Life of Laud. Still there is
something almost ludicrous in the partnership, which
did not last long. Two years after this, in 1838,
Newman became sole editor, and the review, always
' High Church,' in the old sense, became the organ
of what had now come to be called the Oxford party.
In 1837 Newman published a work that had cost
him years of labour, and frequent changes of shape
and plan, the 'Prophetical Office of the Church
viewed relatively to Romanism and Popular Protestantism.' The title was meant to indicate an
Anglican theology based on Anglican authorities,
and, as it challenged both sides, was not likely to
please many. Whatever its success, it appears to
have been what may be called a ' pet ' of the author,
not always the best judge. The ' Library of the
Fathers of the Holy Catholic Church anterior to the
division of the East and the West,' the original text
and translations, had now been announced a year,
placed in many hands, and worked at with an expe-
dition hardly compatible with even that moderate
grace of style which is all a translation admits of.
Perhaps it is impossible to translate a Christian
Father so as to make him pleasant reading, or
even to satisfy the requirements of common sense.
Every attempt at a translation only brought out the

immense superiority of that Book, which is the unfailing delight of the rich and the poor, the learned and the unlearned, in all places and times. The first volume of the ' Library of the Fathers ' came out the following year, containing a translation of the Confessions of St. Augustine revised from a former translation by Dr. Pusey. It is the first book of patristic theology put by the French Seminarists into the hands of their pupils.

The Oxford party was not wanting in enterprise or even in aggressiveness this year. As the ' Tracts for the Times ' had been now four years coming out with increased energy, it may be asked why the movement was allowed to take its course with so little serious challenge. We must bear in mind that other topics divided attention. The Church and the universities were menaced with radical and violent change. The Conservatives of the Church did not like to quarrel with its foremost and ablest champions, however rash and self-willed they might seem to be, and perhaps were waiting, like wise Gamaliel, to see by the result whence this new doctrine had come.

The Oriel tutors from 1837 to 1840 inclusive were Clement Greswell, Charles Marriott, Charles P. Eden, Church the present Dean of St. Paul's, Pritchard, Fraser, now Bishop of Manchester, and W. J. Coplestone. Rogers, now Lord Blachford, was also residing. Newman had no college office or work, and was seldom seen in hall ; but he gave receptions every Tuesday evening in the common room, largely attended by both the college and out-college men.

CHAPTER LXIV.

BISHOP BURGESS.

BISHOP BURGESS one used to hear of as an Apostolic Bishop. He was reputed to be a man of very simple habits, and, if I mistake not, the expression 'gig bishop' arose from some one having met him making the round of the diocese of St. David's in a vehicle of that sort. At Salisbury he did as his predecessors had done. In 1831 I passed some days at old Mr. Stevens', the Rector of Bradfield, with whom Bishop Burgess had been staying over a Sunday not long before. The Bishop kindly preached. The church is barely half a mile from the parsonage, and the road to it then lay across private grounds. The Bishop went in his carriage, with two apparitors bearing wands walking before the horses all the way, making it, as the old Rector said, very like 'a black job.' The year after this I conducted a respectable detachment of Buckland parish to be confirmed by his lordship at Abingdon.

It was four years later, in 1836, when, immediately after my actual resignation of Moreton Pinckney, I went to Salisbury to be instituted to the rectory of Cholderton. My Oxford friends had warned me that the Bishop would probably try to make me promise to study Hebrew, so that I must make up my mind beforehand on that point. I had to wait some time in the drawing-room, in the company of a pleasant young fellow who was there on a similar errand. He confided to me that he did not expect to find the Bishop in the best of humours, and accordingly, when I had finished my business and had returned to the drawing-room, he asked me rather anxiously what mood I had found his lordship in. He was to be instituted to the rectory of Fuggleston, comprising Bemerton, George Herbert's church and parsonage, and he knew the Bishop did not like the appointment. What made matters worse was that in a fortnight he would have to come to the Bishop again to be instituted to the equally important and valuable rectory of Fovant, to hold with the other. It would be too great a trial to the Bishop's equanimity to tell him of both the appointments at once, so Fovant was to be mercifully reserved till the Bishop had recovered from the first shock.

This young gentleman has now held these livings, I believe with credit, for forty-six years. The parsonage, when I saw it three years ago, had been much enlarged, but it retained as much as possible of George Herbert's edifice, evidently thought ample in his days. A new church has been built some years, and the old church, a small barn-like structure standing before the parsonage, not ten yards from the front door, has been entirely cleared of internal fittings, but otherwise put into good order, and left open all day for all Christians to enter and pray their own prayers where George Herbert prayed

But I must return to my new Bishop. He asked many questions about Oriel, naming Charles Marriott as a great scholar. He very soon began upon

Hebrew. At Cholderton I was likely to find my time hang heavy on my hands. Could I not take the opportunity to learn the sacred language ? If I once began I was sure to go on, and find it an unfailing resource. He would always be glad to see me and hear how I was getting on. I could only hold out the barest possibility of my following his lordship's advice. Indeed I am ashamed to say I shared the common opinion of those days about Hebrew, derived probably from the old prejudice against Jews. Latin and Greek were then everything ; and that not to master the great classical authors, but to make feeble and useless attempts to write in their style. Not far from Bath, in 1827, I met a Mr. Longmire, a laborious Hebrew and Oriental scholar. All he got for it was that his neighbours played on his name and called him Mr. Talmud.

The only convert to Hebrew that I ever heard of the Bishop making was his own nephew, that I had known from his boyhood. Poor little Burgess, the only son of the well-known manufacturer of sauces and pickles in the Strand, came to Charterhouse in a skeleton suit at the age of ten or eleven, the same day that I did. Ours was a new house, and for a whole term there were only seven in it. The poor child was very shy, very silent, very helpless, and perfectly inoffensive. How he was shut up ! What had he not to endure ! How case-hardened did he become against insult ! Chow Chow was the least offensive name by which he was familiarly called. The day after his arrival there came two honourables, who could only express their disgust at finding themselves in the same room with the son of a fish-sauce maker. For five years was I in the same room with him, and I could almost say that I had never once seen him open his mouth, except that I do seem to remember the convulsive and mechanical action of the jaws when suddenly and peremptorily called into exercise.

Burgess followed me to Oriel, which he must have found a pleasanter place. There he studied Hebrew, and I believe won a newly founded Hebrew scholarship. Thus qualified, he received from his uncle the living of Streetley. His father, passing through Oxford, asked me to dine with him and his son at the Angel. He was a pleasant, conversible man, with a good deal to say for himself, and, as it appeared to me, quite competent to find out for himself the motto commonly said to be found for him by his brother the Bishop, *Gravi jam dudum saucia cura.*

The Apostolical Bishop left 70,000*l.*, appointing his widow, with a life interest, Archdeacon Clarke, and Mr. Fawcett, a young cousin of his wife's, executors. A year or so before his death the third executor was crippled for life by an injury of the spine, and at the Bishop's death must have been confined to his bed, and forbidden to exert either body or mind. The Bishop, however, did not name another executor. The Archdeacon died first ; after some years Mrs. Burgess. Mr. Fawcett, still an invalid, received one day a copy of the will, with an intimation that he must immediately see to its administration. On looking into it he found that all was left to be divided amongst nephews and nieces, several of whom were dead. His lawyer told him at once that he must let the will alone, as it would raise questions, and might involve litigation. So he wisely renounced his executorship, and the will was administered by the next of kin. As it happened, the nephews and nieces recognised the claim of the great-nephews and great-nieces, and all ended well.

CHAPTER LXV.

CONVOCATION.

FROM early in the movement Convocation was a frequent topic at Oriel. There was an increasing sense of indignity at the suppression of the Church's only legislative organ, continued from one Parliament to another, even when every class, every community, and every interest had its regular opportunity and form of discussion. The whole of the Church system was under attack, and on all sides were popular writers and orators urging Parliament to step in and make a clean sweep, in order to a new Church of some kind or other. Yet the existing Church was not to be allowed to stand on its defence and speak for itself. I cannot recall that Newman ever went beyond the initial fact of its being an insult, a wrong, an incapacity, and a point to be insisted on in any discussions for the reformation of the Anglican Church.

The Church had a Convocation, and it ought to be a real, living, and active one, instead of a piece of lumber dragged out one day and dragged back into its closet the next. For the existing form of the Convocation Newman could not be an enthusiast, for it was, and indeed is, a close corporation, very similar to the worst of the old municipal corporations then condemned. It had far less of a representative character than the old unreformed House of Commons. Convocation was and is nothing more than a Royal Commission, and for that character fairly well constituted, at least in the opinion of its Royal and Parliamentary conveners.

But while Newman himself said little or nothing, others, such as Henry Wilberforce, Wilson, and perhaps generally the country clergy, took up the subject of Convocation warmly, reopened the discussions of the last century, and even tried to persuade themselves that in Convocation they saw the assembled Church of England, only waiting for leave to think and speak. A new reign seemed to present a new opportunity. The two Houses of Convocation would have to address the Crown, and the form of address would have to be proposed and put to the vote. That would be an opening for an amendment, asking leave to meet and confer upon the affairs of the Church, as in old times.

It fell upon me, I know not how, to put about such a form of amendment, and indeed to act upon it. Perhaps it was simply because I was now rector of Cholderton, not more than eleven miles from Salisbury, where I had at least one friend in Daniel Eyre, an Oriel man. Like the rest of the clergy I received a regular summons to a meeting somewhere about the cathedral, not in the Chapter House, if I remember right, to elect two Proctors for the diocese.

I presented myself in my gown, rather to the surprise of the two or three officials. There certainly could not have been half a dozen heads altogether, counting my own. I stated that as the names must be formally proposed, I should propose other names, and have hands counted, unless some one could undertake for the names first proposed that they would move Convocation to ask for freedom of debate. I wholly forget the name of the official that took me in hand, unless it were Grove. Surprised as he was, he did it well, according to the rules of high ecclesiastical art. Everybody there present, he said, was as desirous as I could be to see Convocation free ; but no such amendment as I proposed could be moved in Convocation without previous conversation and concert with other members, and it must rest with every member to decide whether it would be worth his while to take any action. After some civil words, I folded up my gown and came home, not quite knowing whether I had received a pat or a blow.

Among others to whom I sent the proposed amendment was Manning, who had lately become a widower, and was said to be entering warmly into the coming struggle for the independence of the Church. I had known him, as a friend of the Wilberforces, from his first coming to Oxford, and had frequently heard him at the Union. It is not easy for me to identify the Manning of my early recollections with the Father of the Council whom I heard preach at the church of S. Isidore on S. Patrick's Day, and whom I saw lately in company with his brother Cardinal at the Oratory. He must have grown taller, and his head larger, since he was a very nice-looking, rather boyish freshman. When S. Wilberforce left Oxford, Manning seemed to drop quietly into his place at the Union. He spoke at every meeting, on all subjects, at length, with unfailing fluency and propriety of expression.

It is a thing elders don't sufficiently bear in mind that there is nothing young people like better than talk. There is no music sweeter to them than a musical voice that never flags. They can bear any amount of it, so as it does not offend the taste. Indifferent speakers and disappointed speakers may sneer at it, but they have to admit that all the world, except themselves, run after it and cleave to it.

There are occasions that seem to defy eloquence, but Manning was more than equal to them. Some one came in to me one evening, and observed that Manning had just made a very good speech an hour long. On what subject? I asked. It had to be explained, and then I fully recognised the occasion. The Union took in an immense quantity of newspapers, about half of which were never read. Among the latter were two American papers—one the 'Baltimore Democrat,' and the other a Republican paper, I think of Philadelphia. My impression is that nobody ever looked at either. It had become necessary to economise, and the committee proposed to discontinue one of the American papers. The ' question ' of the evening happened to have been disposed of quickly. So time was no consideration. Manning arose, and began by deprecating any retrograde step in the progress of political knowledge and international sympathy. Did we know too much about the United States ? Did we care too much for them ? It was the order of Providence that we should all be as one. If we could not be under the same Government, yet we had a common blood, common faith, and common institutions. America was running a race with us in literature, in science, and in art, and if we ceased to learn from her what she could teach us, we might find ourselves one day much behindhand. So Manning had gone on, til his bewitched hearers had quite forgotten the original proposal to save a few pounds, and only felt themselves going along with Manning, whatever he might be driving at.

When Manning left Oxford he passed rapidly and completely from politics to a high ecclesiastical part. He was heard of as a great speaker at religious meetings, and as a rigorous disciplinarian in his church and parish. Among other rules, he insisted that none had a right to join in the service unless they had joined in the confession and received the absolution. To mark his displeasure at the late ones, he made a rule of stopping till they were seated, and had presumably done penance for their remissness. The church door opened one day. Manning stopped. An old lady was heard slowly tottering to her pew.

There was a terrible fall. It was Manning's own mother, who had vainly endeavoured to hurry her pace during the reader's awful pause.

Manning was soon appreciated by his Bishop, who made him Archdeacon. He became prematurely bald, venerable, and wise. Henry Wilberforce used to affect, in his own amusing way, a continual sense of injustice in the comparison made by the world between him and the Archdeacon. As a fact, he was several months the elder of the two, but people would persist in regarding the Archdeacon as ten years older. Repeatedly in company he was desired to hold his tongue, for the Archdeacon was speaking, when poor Henry declared he was quite sure that what he was saying was much better worth listening to.

But I have wandered far from my own mark, which is Convocation. It must have been in the summer of 1837 that I sent Manning the proposed amendment. I take the liberty, which I am sure His Eminence will excuse, to give his answer in full :—

MY DEAR MOZLEY,—I have been many times at the point of writing to you to thank you for your letter, and the draft of the amendment, and also to ask you to consider whether a somewhat different line would not more surely attain our purpose ; and that is to move your amendment, substituting for the prayer for license to debate in Convocation, either a petition that no measure of the Ecclesiastical Commission should be laid before Parliament until it shall have received the assent of the Church in a Council of the Province, or offering both this, and your proposal as an alternative, of which without doubt, if either, the Provincial Council would be most favourably received. Perhaps the *expressed* alternative of Convocation might have a very good effect in that way.

The reasons for suggesting this are—1. That Convocation probably contains three parties. One (z) against all change ; the second (x) hot for Convocation ; the third against Convocation, but anxious for some active measure. The two last, if combined, will be a majority ; if disunited, altogether defeated. I cannot say decidedly that I could vote for your amendment as it stands. For the alternative I could ; and so would the Convocation men.

2. The Bishops would to a man resist your proposal, but a large number would vote for a Provincial Council ; probably all who are now so opposed to the Commission, and in this way the amendment would probably pass both Houses, and for once unite them.

3. I believe many laymen in and out of Parliament are ready to support a measure to obtain the consent of the Church, and to restore some canonical Council, but not Convocation. These are some of the reasons why I believe the amendment as it stands would be both defeated in Convocation, and unpalatable out of it. I write in great haste ; pray let me hear how it strikes you, and what is doing in your Diocese. In our Archdeaconry the address is going on very successfully—forty-five replies, and only five

refusals, and that in about a fortnight. It is also in circulation through the Proctor in the other Archdeaconry (Lewes), and I know of some approvals.

Believe me, my dear Mozley, yours very sincerely,

H. E. MANNING.

Festival of All Saints.

Do you know Mr. Strutt, who married the Bishop of Chichester's daughter? Tell me if you know anything of his religious opinions.

The answer to this is that there was a Convocation, whereas there was no such thing as a Provincial Council. Parliament at that time would not have listened to any project for reviving an obsolete institution in order to give independence and power to the Church of England ; whereas it might come to see the injustice of not allowing an existing assembly of the Church to exchange opinions, or even freely exercise the constitutional right of petition. The practical differences between a Convocation and a Provincial Synod are very nice questions, and could not be stated in any accurate or probable form without much inquiry into ecclesiastical law, historical fact, and the tendencies of human nature under various circumstances.

It is quite certain that Provincial Synods have not always conducted themselves with judgment, or even common sense. ' In the year 1281,' we read in Collier, ' in the reign of Edward I., Archbishop Pecham convened a Provincial Synod at Lambeth. In his mandate to Richard Gravesend, Bishop of

London, after having mentioned the convening of
the suffragans, he gives him to understand that he
designed to summon all the inferior prelates ; those
dignitaries, according to the canon, being obliged
to appear in council. Now, by inferior prelates we
are to understand abbots, priors, deans, and arch-
deacons. But of any other representation of the
inferior clergy the mandate takes no notice ; which
is an argument the state of the Convocation was
different from what it is at present. . . . By the
second canon (passed in this Provincial Synod), the
parish priests, when they administer the Holy Communion, are enjoined to acquaint the more ignorant
sort of the laity (*simplices*), that the body and blood
of our Saviour, in the integrity of the Sacrament, is
contained under the single species of bread. They
are likewise to teach them that what they receive in
the chalice is unconsecrated wine, and given them
only that they may swallow the other species with
more conveniency.' In the year 1287, in the same
primacy, a Diocesan Synod, convened by Peter Quivil,
Bishop of Exeter, made a solemn protest against
this explanation, and enjoined 'that the priest tell
the people what they eat is the body of Christ, and
what they drink His blood.'

The debates of the Lower House of Convocation
some years since on the subject of the Athanasian
Creed may suggest a comparison with the above most
extraordinary rubrical interpretation ; yet it would be
unfair to describe them as more blasphemous and
ridiculous.

CHAPTER LXVI.

THE confidence and strength of the movement, now
about at high tide, could not be more illustrated than
in some remarkable numbers of the 'Tracts for the
Times,' on reserve in communicating religious knowledge.   There never was a more extraordinary combination of privacy and publicity, shyness and
audacity, and, it may be added, wisdom and rashness,
than in these treatises.   That which people do in-
stinctively and even unconsciously, by methods and
rules of their own, was here built up into a grand
argument, swollen to the bulk of a volume, and
dinned into the ears of the whole world.

Isaac Williams was the simplest of men.   He
had the happiness to live among friends with whom
he entirely agreed ; whom he loved and admired ;
whose sympathy almost excluded the outer world,
and whose loyalty and power made him indifferent
to vulgar opinions.   Whatever he had said, or his
friends had said, wisely and truly enough, he proclaimed from the house-top.   In some respects this
was the common temptation and the common fault
of all the writers.   Moving in a phalanx, with a
certainty of support, they all said with tenfold freedom
and fulness what they would have thought a good

deal more about had they been called on to do it
singly on their own separate account.

But what was it that was done in this instance
by a man retiring and modest even to a fault, who
could never have seen a dozen people together without a wish to hide himself? He first looks out for
the word that shall bear the most terrible significance, raise the most alarms, and give the greatest
offence. Common enough as the word 'reserve'
may be in its application to manners and morals, it
is an entirely new word as applied to education and
religious instruction. Having thus put on the most
questionable of guises, and grasped the most dangerous of weapons, Isaac Williams blows the trumpet
and convokes the whole Church—indeed the whole
world. 'Listen to me,' he proclaims, 'I've a great
deal to tell you. But I shall keep back from you the
most important things that I have to say till you are
quite fit for them. I shall wait to see whether you
are ever fit for them. You would reject them now,
for you would not care for them or understand them.
You would probably hate them. So I must educate
you for them. I must be clever and crafty, reserved
and economical. I must ensnare you, hook you,
hoodwink you, decoy you into my net, commit you
to my ulterior designs before you know what you are
about. I must exercise upon you artifices, frauds,
stratagems, plots, and conspiracies.'

Nobody would say this in so many words; nobody would intend this in fact; but anybody who
announces that he means to practise reserve is at
once understood to mean all this. He will say that

he means no more than all teachers do, all fathers, mothers—all who are older, wiser, or better than those they have to deal with, as a matter of fact, and by sheer necessity. That may be quite true, but the difference is they don't proclaim it and he does. All the world practises all kinds of reserve, but never mentions the word. The world does not write in large letters over this spot 'secret'; over that 'strictly private'; over another, 'a deep mystery'; over another, 'a dark corner'; and over the darkest corner of all, 'this is what you are to come to at last.' If, as it is said, there is a skeleton in every household, it is kept in a closet, and the closet door is not labelled 'a skeleton here.'

Secrets of State there must be, else there need be no Secretaries of State, or 'Cabinets,' except what anybody might walk into. No statesman can help having a policy which stretches into the future. He must have something behind; that is, yet to come. His opponents do their best to draw this out of him, or to create the impression that it is something very objectionable; but it is not he that invites attention to it, or avows that the most important part of his policy is that which he will not at present reveal, so odious would it be thought.

In the whole matter of preaching the Gospel and of Christian education there will be the question what part shall take precedence, that is what doctrine ought to be presented first and foremost. Some will put one part first, some another. This inevitably implies that some part will be left a little back, for of two things, if one be before, the other must

be behind. But this question of priorities and preferences must not be carried too far, for neither nature nor
circumstances admit of such regular succession. Dr.
Johnson said on the matter of education that if you
thought too much and too long which of two things
to teach first, you would find that your quicker
neighbour had taught his pupil both before you had
taught yours one.

Isaac Williams in truth only made a pretty theory
of what all the world does in one way or another.
It was his application of it that provoked a general
attack on the policy of reserve. Now for a long
time it has been the way of the religious world
whether Roman Catholic or Protestant, to put the
Atonement foremost. A large part of the Christian
world, in this country at least, preach the Atonement,
and nothing more, on the simple reckoning that
without the acceptance of the Atonement everything
is worthless ; with it everything else is unnecessary.
The Roman Catholics cannot be accused of deficiency
in their teaching, but the Incarnation and the Passion
are what they put foremost, and proclaim in the
streets and highways. If out of twenty dissenting
communities in a town, one were to avow an unwillingness to place the Atonement before mere
children or hardened sinners, it would be scouted by
all the rest.

The Church of England is supposed to show her
highest wisdom and her most maternal tenderness in
the Catechism, meat for very babes and sucklings.
In this Catechism, immediately after the infant
catechumen has lisped out the Apostles' Creed, it

is asked what it chiefly learns from the Creed. Three short answers are put into its little mouth. The second of these is, 'I learn to believe in God the Son, who hath redeemed me and all mankind.' Those words are universally explained in the sense of the Atonement—yes, in the popular sense of the Atonement; as salvation by the death of Christ offered to all who will accept that doctrine. Nor can it be said that after bringing this doctrine to the very front, and emblazoning it over the very portals of the Church, the Catechism throws any reserve over the doctrine in its exposition of the Sacraments. What then can be the use of inculcating reserve, unless one is prepared to quarrel with the very groundwork of the Church of England's doctrinal method ?

But this quarrel with the Catechism and the Church of England will not stop there. There is no knowing how far it will widen. Isaac Williams insists very much on the teaching of our Lord and of the Apostles as being always adapted to the occasion, to the state of knowledge, and to the character. But in two or three generations all these teachings were collected and read all over the world, to all ages, and to all the varieties of faith, education, and character. The facts, too, which covered the doctrines were everywhere known. Whatever the tongue or the pen of man then failed to do the press has since done, and the Bible is now the most universal book in the world. Where it goes there can be no reserve.

No doubt the result of the actual universal usage has been the very wide acceptance of doctrine in place of a consistent life. For many centuries practice has lagged in the rear of faith. Isaac Williams hoped to bring duty more to the front; but it was scant wisdom to tell the world he proposed to cheat it out of its easy confidence and reduce it to hard service. Could the man himself have been exhibited at Exeter Hall, interviewed in *soirées* at Willis's Rooms, or even invited to show the almost sacred lineaments of his face in a fashionable London pulpit, people would have seen what a simple rogue the poor child was, what an imitation Guy Fawkes what an innocent Inquisitor.

As it was, and in total ignorance of the man, the world fell or affected to fall into a paroxysm of terror at the infernal machinations preparing against it. The front line of the advancing foe it could venture to cope with in open fight and measure swords with. It was the awful indefinite reserve and the dark ambuscade that made ten thousand pulpits tremble to the very foot of the steps. For many years after, whenever the preacher had exhausted his memory or his imagination, and run out his circle of texts and ideas, he could easily fall back on the dark doings of Oxford. Congregations of London shopkeepers were told that Newman and Pusey inculcated and practised systematic fraud, concealment, and downright lying in a good cause—that is, in their own. When one looked round to see the impression made by the dreadful charge, the congregation either were so fast asleep or they were taking it so easy that they must have heard it often before, or perhaps after all did not think habitual lying so serious a matter. It could only have been under the protection of numbers, loyalty, and talent that anyone would ever have promulgated such a policy as reserve. Not even when so protected would anyone have done that, had he not lived in great seclusion from the common sense and common feeling of the world.

The Bishop of Gloucester denounced the tract very heavily, upon the title alone, without any acquaintance with the tract itself. Thomas Keble, a singularly quiet man, was moved to remonstrate with his Bishop, and to point out that the tract itself did not justify his lordship's remarks. The Bishop made so lame and reluctant an apology and so little retractation, that T. Keble resigned his rural deanery, and elected to remain for the future on cool terms with the Bishop. Yet it is hard to see what the Bishop could do but protest against the thesis contained in the title of the tract, even though his many occupations might prevent him from ever opening it. A Bishop has to defend his Church from ill surmises, and to disavow complicity in ill teachings ; especially when some of the writers are in his own diocese.

Suppose, for example, some clergyman with more learning than discretion, under Bishop Wilberforce, had published a thick closely-printed octavo, entitled ' Doubt the School of Faith.' If the Bishop had been true to his rule of stamping out doubt instantly, lest it spread further, he would certainly have condemned the book, and preached against it, without reading it, probably without seeing more than a picked sentence or two. Since the man chose to affix such a title, proposing evidently to do half his work by his title, he must stand the consequences.

In the course of the movement there befell to many of the writers, indeed to all of them, that which themselves had done—some very lightly, indeed—in the Hampden business. They had not read the famous lectures, and could only know of them second hand. They came up to Oxford to condemn him, and did condemn him there and then. By the same rule they found themselves condemned without being read. It may be said, that within a certain circle of intelligence, there is more writing than reading. People will write big volumes, and people will not read big volumes. Nobody in his senses will read several hundred closely-printed pages in favour of a practice which he knows he cannot observe, and does not intend to observe, and has no intention of trying to make others observe.

Most books, those of great interest and importance, are known only by their titles, and an author may be considered fortunate if his title has been read right, and right through. The majority of those who talk about Butler's Analogy have taken upon hearsay half the title, quoting it as the 'Analogy of Natural and Revealed Religion.' Butler, they proceed to argue, must have been a very bad logician, and the victim of a ridiculous fallacy, if he could suppose Christianity the more likely to be true because it had a strong family resemblance to Paganism. The title really is, 'The Analogy of Religion, Natural and Revealed, to the Constitution and Course of Nature ;' a thesis which requires careful argument, but is very different from that in most instances substituted for it.

Till the ' Tracts for the Times ' finally exploded with No. 90, Isaac Williams must have been working night and day to retrieve the error of an ill-selected thesis and an offensive title. In the year 1840 he brought out No. 87 of the series, Part IV., on Reserve, 143 closely-printed pages. Had the tracts gone on, and had he lived long enough, he would have published a library on the duty of not telling people all we believe and know, be it ever so neces- sary to be believed or known.

A man so sensitive to the least touch of irreve- rence received many a wound, which he survived to tell. Finding himself one Sunday at Southampton, and not being acquainted with the churches there, he walked up the High Street to enter the first that promised well. He found himself before a church of the best architecture, went in, and was placed in a pew which looked old-fashioned enough. The con- gregation was respectable, better dressed indeed than his own poor rustics. One or two things produced a queer sensation rather than a positive misgiving. A hymn was sung, not very unusual in country churches. As the last note of the organ died on his ear, the minister sprung up—' Last Sunday, if you remember, I was telling you about Matthew the publican.' Isaac Williams quickly disappeared.

CHAPTER LXVII.

ATTACKS ON THE MOVEMENT.

THE next year, 1838, saw the burst of the storm
which may be said to have raged round the devoted
band, till by the loss of its chiefs, and to a large
extent of its original character, it settled by degrees
into the somewhat less heroic form and consistency
of the 'Ritualistic' party.

Newman was now sole editor of the 'British
Critic.' The only other religious periodical admitting
essays, or reviews, of any length, was the 'Christian
Observer,' which had but little circulation in Oxford.
The most urgent appeals were made to the clergy to
read and to circulate the 'Observer,' but the importunity itself betrayed weakness. It might be twenty
years after this date I was passing through a by
street from Blackfriars to the Temple, when I saw
two immense waggons, which had just received from
a warehouse huge loads of waste paper. I never see
a bit of printed paper without a certain curiosity, and
on examining the loads closely I found they consisted entirely of unsold 'Christian Observers' for
many years back.

At this time, or about 1838, they that were of the
movement had full swing, they that were not of it
had to content themselves with publishing sermons
and pamphlets, that cost money and were not read.
Thus reduced to an extremity, they could not be ex-

pected to be particular in their choice of a champion.
Dr. Faussett, the Margaret Professor of Divinity, had
approved himself as a *matador* of great courage and
some skill in an attack on Milman's ' History of the
Jews,' preached at St. Mary's in 1830. The sermon
nearly threw poor Blanco White into convulsions. He
could only speak of Faussett as 'that butcher.' The
sermon was so far in unison with the general sentiment
at Oriel College, that the Provost, when Milman
came to be his guest, could scarcely get a single
Fellow of the college to meet him. But Dr. Faussett
was now charging in another direction. He was not
a man of great learning. When Henry Wilberforce,
as successful candidate for the Theological prize, had
to confer with him, he found him wholly unacquainted
with that portion of Dr. Bull's 'Defence of the
Nicene Creed,' on the 'Subordination of the Son,'
which brought that divine into much controversy
and some disfavour. Dr. Faussett was however a
scholar, a clever writer, and a telling preacher—that
is, capable of striking hard blows. He had also to
fight for dear life. The Margaret Professor is elected
by the graduates in Divinity for two years only, though
always re-elected. Divinity was now becoming a
study, and there was no knowing how many graduates in Divinity, or with what bias, there might be in
a few years. So he preached and published on May
20, 1838, a sermon on the 'Revival of Popery.'

His style, if not his tactics, was the same as that
which had proved so effectual to give pain on the
former occasion. He had carefully culled from Newman's writings, from the 'Tracts for the Times,' but

most of all from Froude's 'Remains,' all the expressions used by writers more anxious to speak to the full extent of their feelings and convictions than to regard the perplexity or the pain they might inflict on some readers.

Froude, for instance, was brimful of irony, and always ready to surprise and even shock men of a slower temperament, when he could by a smile soothe or disarm them. As he talked, so he wrote in his letters. The editors of his 'Remains' were under a temptation, which they construed into a necessity, to reproduce him as he really had been, to the very words and the life, and let his words take their chance. Upon the whole they were right; for no one ever charged, or could now charge, on Froude that his expressions had brought anyone to Rome, or could doubt that Froude himself was Anglican to the last.

Dr. Faussett avoided all personal allusion to Newman, probably in compliance with the university etiquette that the preachers occupying the same pulpit shall steer clear of one another. Newman, however, could not but reply, which he did at great length, giving the Professor a hundred pages for his fifty. Dr. Faussett published a second edition, with notes, in which he complained bitterly of the length, and, as he would have it, the irrelevance of the matter he was expected to read. It must be admitted that Newman did not always take into account the patience of his adversaries, or their physical capacity for enduring a protracted castigation. On the other hand, no one has a right to complain who can release himself from the triangle by simply shutting the book or throwing the pamphlet aside.

The weak point in Dr. Faussett's case was that while, eight years before this, he had solemnly protested against the corruption of the faith by the new German philosophy, and had now testified to the immense increase of Papists and Popish chapels in this century, previous to the Oxford movement, he had done nothing to stay these evils. All that he had done during the ten years he had held the chair was to deliver two sermons, neither of them quite fit for a Christian pulpit, and both calculated to give pain and do nothing more.

Shortly after this passage of arms the Bishop of Oxford (Bagot) delivered the Charge which gave the note to the more vehement and less unreserved utterances of all his brethren. It illustrates the crisis and the terror which then possessed even wise and moderate men, that in this Charge the Bishop protested against the Board of Ecclesiastical Commissioners, as 'a power as irresponsible as it is gigantic, an *imperium in imperio*, which before long must supersede all other authority in the Church, and whose decrees are issued in such a manner as to render expostulation and remonstrance unavailing.' Newman respectfully thanked the Bishop for the attention he was giving to the new Oxford publications, assuming apparently that where there was so much 'vigilance,' what was not condemned was approved.

In July this year Newman had to take what he no doubt felt the very painful step of telling Samuel Wilberforce that it was evidently impossible that the

'British Critic' could continue to insert articles plainly at variance with the tenor of the periodical —indeed, positively antagonistic to the other writers. Of course the same difficulty had occurred when Boone was the editor and Newman the contributor, and it was then settled by Newman acquiring the undivided editorship. In the present case the only possible solution was S. Wilberforce's retirement. This was small denial to a man who had the university pulpit, some hundreds of other important pulpits, and as many more platforms, competing for the aid of his charming and persuasive oratory; and who had only to put his name to a publication to secure for it as many readers as the 'British Critic' could help him to.

Dr. Shuttleworth, Warden of New College, and in times past a guest at Holland House, now presented himself as a controversialist in a pamphlet, which, when he had finished it, he did not know whether to call 'Not Tradition, but Scripture,' or 'Not Tradition, but Revelation,' and left that question, as well as his meaning generally, a riddle to his readers. Dr. Shuttleworth shared with others of his school a combination of intellectual facility and practical indecision. He became, not unworthily, Bishop of Chichester, but would have been Bishop of that see several years earlier had he not felt as the Bishop of Oxford did on the new Church Acts.

CHAPTER LXVIII.

DEAN HOOK, DEAN CHURCH, AND CHARLES MARRIOTT.

In June 1838 Hook preached on 'Hear the Church' before the Queen and her Court at the Chapel Royal. The sermon had a prodigious circulation, and raised a corresponding amount of discussion. The Queen was only just nineteen, and barely a year on the throne. She was unmarried. Was it right to attempt to infuse into her mind what most people would be ready to call a one-sided view of the great question? Hook himself had evidently felt the difficulty of bringing the question home to her in a sermon written for the purpose. He had gone to the heap, and had there found an old sermon that would do. It had acquired prescription, for he had preached it at Coventry, Leeds, and elsewhere. Even if it had been too uncompromising, would it not have been cowardice to soften it down to royal ears?

It had been preached to the units of a great multitude, perfectly free to choose their own religion, and to apply the principles of that religion as they pleased. It was now preached to the Sovereign of three discordant realms, professing as many, and indeed many more, religions, herself bound to respect all. But with the preacher, so Hook appears to have thought, there must be no respect of persons.

Its being an old sermon was no defence, for it is

almost invariable that offensive sermons are old ones,
and, if you are to be run through the body, an old
sword is as bad as a new one. A sermon preached
up and down the provinces was likely enough to put
things in that absolute form which does not much
signify to those who have no special concern in them.
You may safely tell village and even town congregations that Saul was bound to obey Samuel, and
David to accept the rebuke of Nathan and the
judgment of Gad. It is another matter when you
are addressing a Queen, and when the question of
the day is, Who is Samuel, who is Nathan, and who
is Gad ?

In further extenuation of the sermon it is stated
to have been one of a series ; but a series is a
machine, a mere process of mathematical evolution.
It goes its own way, unswerving, pitiless, and reckless
of consequences. The truth is a sermon must justify
itself, if it is to be justified at all. It won't do to say,
' I hit you at random,' or ' You had the ill-luck to
come in the way of my machine.'

To prove the absence of premeditation and design,
Hook pleaded the slovenly composition of the sermon,
which he purposely published without correction.
But the truth is he was always too full of matter and
of feeling to express himself accurately.

The Queen is said to have been much pleased
with the sermon. She might well be, for everybody
listened to Hook with admiration, and even with
pleasure, whether agreeing with him or not. But if
she were pleased, and could not help being pleased,
that might be all the more reason why the sermon

should not have been preached to her. The Queen's advisers were not pleased. They had to square matters with the Church of England, the Church of Scotland, the Irish Catholics, and the English dissenters, and they did not feel themselves assisted by a peremptory command from the pulpit of the Chapel Royal to hear the only true Church, viz. the Church of England.

However, the sermon set all the reading world talking, thinking, and feeling too. It announced to many for the first time the doctrine of Church authority, and the claim to be the Church possessed of that authority. The political bearings of the sermon were both for it and against it, for Hook was one of the most eloquent exponents of Conservatism in those days. The Conservatives generally liked the sermon : the Liberals of course did not.

Manning, long known as an eloquent and agreeable speaker at Oxford, became now more widely known as the preacher of a learned sermon at Chichester on the Rule of Faith. This year came out a translation of Cyril's Catechetical Lectures, almost wholly by Church, Fellow of Oriel, and nephew of General Church, who fought with the Greeks in their struggle for independence.

Within five years of the beginning of the movement, which cannot be put earlier than Newman's return home from the Mediterranean, July 9, 1833, it had acquired numbers, energy, and momentum sometimes the work of generations, or only won to be lost as easily. There had never been seen at Oxford, indeed seldom anywhere, so large and noble a sacrifice of the most precious gifts and powers to a sacred cause. The men who were devoting themselves to it were not bred for the work, or from one school. They were not literary toilers or adventurers glad of a chance, or veterans ready to take to one task as lightly as to another, equally zealous to do their duty, and equally indifferent to the form. They were not men of the common rank casting a die for promotion. They were not levies or conscripts, but in every sense volunteers.

Pusey, Keble, and Newman had each an individuality capable of a development, and a part, beyond that of any former scholar, poet, or theologian in the Church of England. Each lost quite as much as he gained by the joint action of the three. It is hard to say what Froude might have been, or might not have been, had he lived but a few more years, and been content to cast in his lot with common mortals bound by conditions of place and time.

Charles Marriott threw in his scholarship and something more, for he might have been a philosopher, and he had poetry in his veins, being the son of the well-known author of the 'Devonshire Lane.' No one sacrificed himself so entirely to the cause, giving to it all he had and all he was, as Charles Marriott. He did not gather large congregations ; he did not write works of genius to spread his name over the land and to all time ; he had few of the pleasures or even of the comforts that spontaneously offer themselves in any field of enterprise. He laboured night and day in the search and defence of Divine Truth. His admirers were not the thousands, but the scholars who could really appreciate. I confess to have been a little ashamed of myself when Bishop Burgess, as I have mentioned above, asked me about Charles Marriott, as one of the most eminent scholars of the day. Through sheer ignorance I had failed in adequate appreciation.

I remember he could address himself at once to any difficulty, but he must not be disturbed in the work. While so engaged, or absorbed, he felt an interruption of any kind as he would the stroke of a bludgeon or the shock of a railway collision. It was agony, and with upraised hands he closed eyes and ears. Nothing could exceed his singular tenacity of purpose, of which he once gave an amusing illustration. He had to go to town one day and return the next. This gave him an evening, and he resolved to spend it with his twin fellow, now Lord Blachford, at Eliot Place, the other end of Blackheath. His first idea was to be in time for dinner, failing that for tea ; but business, accidental delays, trains not suiting, the distance of the station from the house he was seeking, and his finally losing his way, as he might do easily, several times, ended in his ringing the bell some time after the family had retired to rest. However, he was there. Rogers was waked up, and was very glad to see him. They had a pleasant talk, but whether Marriott could even then be persuaded to stay the night I do not remember. Marriott had but a poor constitution, and, working his head continually, was frequently ailing. An Oxford doctor told him he must reduce his wine, which Marriott promised to do. It occurred to him, however, to ascertain the exact reduction to be made. Restrict yourself to four glasses a day, the doctor said. Marriott replied that he never drank more than half that in a day. I have often found the most extraordinary misapprehensions arising from the use of general terms.

Charles Marriott was for some years the very diligent, and, I believe, the very successful Principal of Chichester Theological College. Before entering upon his work he had to see the Bishop, who happened to be at Derby, with his son-in-law, William Strutt, afterwards Lord Belper. My eldest brother met him at dinner there, and thought him a great curiosity. Several kinds of light wine were passing round the table. 'Which wine are you taking, Mr. Marriott?' the host inquired. Which you please,' the guest replied. This was ridiculous, but Marriott was hardly to blame for it. Was he to affect a preference or to avow indifference? In fact he was only submitting to necessity, for he probably did not know the difference between the wines, and did not want any at all. Was the host right in assuming him to be choice in his wines? Marriott was not in his element that day. How he managed to get on with Bishop Otter, 'neither fish, nor flesh, nor fowl' as he used to be called, I can hardly understand.